'Dearest Squirrel...'

'Dearest Squirrel…'

The Intimate Letters of
John Osborne and Pamela Lane

Edited by Peter Whitebrook

OBERON BOOKS
LONDON

WWW.OBERONBOOKS.COM

First published in 2018 by Oberon Books Ltd
521 Caledonian Road, London N7 9RH
Tel: +44 (0) 20 7607 3637 / Fax: +44 (0) 20 7607 3629
e-mail: info@oberonbooks.com
www.oberonbooks.com

HB ISBN: 9781786823922
E ISBN: 9781786823939

Cover design by James Illman

Author photograph by Eva Whitebrook

Pamela Lane
Photograph by John Vere Brown
Credit: Mander and Mitchenson / University of Bristol / ArenaPAL

John Osborne
Credit: Joe Bangay / ArenaPAL

Printed and bound by CPI Group (UK) Ltd, Croydon, CR0 4YY
eBook conversion by Lapiz Digital Services, India.

For Eva

and for William

always

Acknowledgements

As with my biography of John Osborne, my primary debt is to Gordon Dickerson, John Osborne's literary agent, who with such tenacity and flair administers his Estate on behalf of The Arvon Foundation. Gordon has supported this book from its inception, and his advice and insight have been both generous and invaluable.

Once again, I am grateful for the encouragement, vigilance and patience of George Spender, Senior Editor at Oberon, and to publisher James Hogan. I am indebted to the kindness of Richard Digby Day, a distinguished director with whom Pamela Lane frequently worked and who became a close friend, and to the director Angie Langfield and the actress Julia Lockwood, all of whom have answered many questions. Professor Jonathan Powers in Derby has painstakingly recovered as much of the Playhouse archives that survived the disastrous fire in 1956 and kindly compiled and provided a full listing of the productions in which Osborne and Pamela appeared.

I am grateful to Pat Fox, and the staff of the Harry Ransom Humanities Research Center at the University of Texas at Austin, and to Helen Melody, Curator of Contemporary Literature at the British Library. Jamie Andrews, Head of Culture and Learning at the British Library and who has himself written on Osborne, has been as helpful as always, as has the staff of the Manuscripts Reading Room. I appreciate the goodwill of The Arvon Foundation.

I am also indebted to Lottie Alexander, Academic Support Librarian at the Historic Collections, York St John University; Karen Archer, Maria Bewers, Alan Bryce, Beryl Bunn, Roger Davenport, Mike Dewey, Bucks Free Press; Susan Dowell, Peter Egan, Jessie Faulkner, Bromley Historic Collections; Jeremy Howe, Simon Jervis, Angela John, Helen Jones, Pauline Marshall, Saul Reichlin, Gaynor Richards, Malcolm Sinclair, Paul Venables, David Weston, Angus Wark, National Library of Scotland, the staff at Somerset Archives and Local Studies, and the special collections staff at the National Library of Australia and the National Library of Wales.

And once again, I thank Eva, my wife, for all her encouragement, belief, and critical perception along the way.

A Note on the Editing

The surviving letters between John Osborne and Pamela Lane now form part of two collections: those to Osborne are part of the Osborne Archive at the Harry Ransom Humanities Research Center at the University of Texas at Austin, while those from Osborne are at The British Library, London.

The writer, recipient, the nature of the item, whether manuscript or typescript letter, postcard and occasionally telegram, and its current location is noted in bold face in the text. The following abbreviations have been used.

JO: John Osborne

PL: Pamela Lane

ms: handwritten

ts: typewritten

pc: postcard

n/a: no address given

n/d: no date given

BL: The British Library, London

Texas: The Harry Ransom Humanities Research Center at the University of Texas at Austin.

When no address or date is given by the writer, I have suggested one where possible, deduced from internal evidence. These are indicated within square parentheses: [ ]. Text within square parentheses within an item of correspondence indicates my own additions, while square parentheses around ellipses [...] indicate my deletion of unnecessary repetition. All semi-circular parentheses ( ), capital letters and underlinings are those used by the correspondents. While the correspondence is reproduced as originally written, I have sometimes silently amended punctuation to make easier reading.

Where most appropriate, I have indicated the equivalent value of sums of money at the time of going to press.

Contents

Introduction

■ ■ ■

'I was glad you'd kept some of the old letters,' reflected Pamela Lane, writing to John Osborne, her former husband, on 28 August 1983; '—as I have some of yours—they seem to have survived burglaries, fires and floods, as well as the ravages of time and transport—as much moved as moving. Well, they are, oddly, the latter, don't you think?'

By this time, they were both approaching their mid-fifties and had known each other for thirty-two years. An actress working mostly in the regions, highly regarded within the profession but barely known outside it, Pamela was writing from her home, a rented basement flat in a Victorian terrace in Kilburn, north London. Her letter landed on the mat at Christmas Place, Osborne's secluded and impressive Edwardian house set in extensive grounds at Marsh Green, a village deep in leafy Kent, and bought a few years earlier with the substantial earnings from his astonishingly successful stage and screenwriting career. Pamela was Osborne's first wife, and since their divorce in 1957 when they were twenty-six, she had had other relationships but had never remarried and now lived alone. By contrast, when Osborne picked up her letter that summer morning, he was sharing his breakfast table with Helen, his fifth and, as it turned out, last wife.

For thirty years, Osborne had been a public figure. Critics and cultural journalists provided a commentary on his plays and assessed the standing of his professional reputation while gossip columnists fielded by an increasingly intrusive popular press filleted his private life, speculating on his relationships and recording his register office marriages and his appearances in the divorce court. Nevertheless, Osborne had successfully retained a secret for almost three decades: that of his enduring, protective, deeply loyal, exasperating, frequently blustery and sometimes sexually intimate relationship with his first wife.

Over the years, from *Look Back in Anger* onwards, Osborne had attempted to write plays in a language in which, he declared, it was 'possible only to tell the truth.'[1] Language was his great gift, his supreme weapon, its invective, its lyricism and its intensity reinvigorating the English theatre. He was also a man who made friends easily but discarded them equally effortlessly, who found it almost impossible to dissemble and seldom managed to temper his passions and prejudices with caution. It was all the more remarkable, then, given that he was forever under journalistic surveillance and he was temperamentally unsuited to subterfuge, that he succeeded in keeping his continuing relationship with Pamela hidden from many of his friends and the kind of journalists given to rooting about in dustbins. She too, for various reasons, volunteered little of her association with her former husband either to friends or the actors with whom she worked, to whom she appeared thoroughly professional, sociable yet intensely private. 'She was incredibly difficult to read, and gave little away,' acknowledged the distinguished director Richard Digby Day, with whom she often collaborated and who became a close friend for over forty years.[2] Yet as Osborne read Pamela's letter that morning in August 1983, they had become closer and more trusting than they had been since their earliest years together. It was an 'astonishing reunion,' Pamela told him, and one that felt 'more than ever firm and enduring… which, since it's taken some thirty years, is as it should be.'[3] 'It is odd surely,' agreed Osborne, 'to be in love for thirty years.'[4]

■ ■ ■

They had met in her home town of Bridgwater, a market town in Somerset, in March 1951, as twenty-one-year-old actors in the local Roc Players. Three months later, they were married. Three years later, after an interlude in which work often kept them apart, they spent six domestically catastrophic months at Derby Playhouse, working together in weekly repertory. In the summer of 1954, when the Derby season ended, and having appeared in twenty-four plays together, husband and wife went their separate ways. Osborne wrote *Look Back in Anger* in London the following year. Although unknown to audiences at the time, it is now well established that both the atmosphere of the play and many of the incidents in it are based upon his experiences in Derby, and that Jimmy and Alison Porter, the central characters, are largely modelled upon himself and Pamela.

On 8 May 1956, while she was appearing in repertory in York, *Look Back in Anger* opened at the Royal Court Theatre and became an immediate and unexpected talking point in London's cultural circles. Pamela went down to see it in July, when she had the unnerving experience of watching a lightly-fictionalised account of her own marriage, in which Alison, the character modelled upon herself was being played by Mary Ure, the woman whom Pamela knew had become her estranged husband's current lover. A year later, she and Osborne were divorced. She was then appearing in a contrived Naval comedy in the backwater of High Wycombe, thirty miles to the west of London, while he joined the audience for the first night of *The Entertainer,* his second play for the Royal Court, starring Laurence Olivier as Archie Rice, undisputed theatrical royalty playing a down-at-heel music hall comedian.

Osborne's career flourished spectacularly. The newspapers loved him. He was an Angry Young Man and his views on this and that suddenly of huge interest, while he and Mary Ure, the daughter of a Glasgow civil engineer and a rising star, became a 'Golden Couple.' They were glimpsed in the company of the famous: Richard Burton; Arthur Miller and Marilyn Monroe, his then wife; Laurence Olivier and Vivien Leigh. They were photographed and interviewed. Already a half-eclipsed presence, Pamela Lane quickly slid from view as being of no interest at all. Dropping out of Osborne's story, she never established one of her own, at least not one that set the fingers of metropolitan gossip journalists twitching over the keys of revealing typewriters, and for this much she was grateful. Instead, she fought on with building her own career, mostly in the regions, while ensuring her personal life was shielded from public view. She was bright, talented, creative and hard-working, her work earning the plaudits of local critics. But this was not a time when national newspapers published regular reviews from the regions and nor was it usual for London-based critics to monitor theatre beyond the capital. Her work went largely unnoticed by the national press.

Yet as I indicated in my 2015 biography of Osborne, and as their letters further reveal, while pursuing their own vastly different careers in the theatre and often many miles apart, John Osborne and Pamela Lane remained a vital part of each other's lives. Not long after the ink was dry on their divorce papers they resumed a tentative correspondence that led quickly to their spending time together again:

a weekend here, a few days there whenever opportunities could be found in their increasingly busy schedules.

By this time, Osborne was married to Mary Ure. He and Pamela continued to write and meet after Osborne and Mary divorced and while he was married to Penelope Gilliatt, a socially well-connected journalist and film critic of the *Observer*. In 1968 and having divorced Penelope, Osborne married the actress Jill Bennett, who appeared in several of her husband's plays until their acrimonious divorce in 1976. A substantial gap in the correspondence between Osborne and Pamela accompanies a lengthy hiatus in their relationship during the Jill Bennett years, but in 1981, three years after Osborne married Helen Dawson, an arts journalist, they began writing and meeting again. 'My feelings—no, passion, always passion—are unchanged,' Osborne assured her two years later. 'I feel so… <u>vindicated</u> by my love for you,' he added. 'It hasn't changed, it hasn't been disrupted by events or distorted in the memory.'[5]

'I <u>am</u> in love with you still,' Pamela replied, '…you have… my abiding passion for as long as you want.' [6]

In 1986, Osborne and Helen left Kent and moved north to The Hurst, a large and isolated grey stone house set in its own grounds outside the village of Clun in Shropshire, and surrounded by Housman's 'blue remembered hills.' It was the furthest he had ever lived from London and made all the more remote by the complexity of its access by public transport. The relationship between Osborne and Pamela had undergone a shift, almost a geological realignment and the surviving correspondence between the self-styled country gentleman and his first wife apparently ceases, seemingly in mid-flow, in 1988. From now on, there was little opportunity for them to meet. Although he still visited London, by the 1990s his increasing frailty and his perilous finances made such excursions hazardous to contemplate, and while Pamela had visited Christmas Place, mingling with the crowds at Osborne's fabled summer garden parties, she never visited the more exposed fortress of The Hurst. One further, rather forlorn letter survives, adrift on a sea of surrounding silence, written by Osborne in 1991, informing Pamela that he would be at the Cadogan Hotel in London 'for 24 hours… on my own, for what it's worth.'[7] If Pamela replied by letter or note, that too is lost.

It was at Clun that Osborne wrote *Déjàvu*, his final play. Thirty-six years after *Look Back in Anger*, Jimmy Porter reappears, holding court in very much the kind of Aga-dominated kitchen in which Osborne negotiated the nutritiously robust meals his doctors advised. Produced in 1992, the play was a critical disappointment, a financial failure, and quickly closed, leaving its author chastened and angry. Two years later, on 24 December 1994, a few days after his sixty-fifth birthday, Osborne died of liver failure, a result of years of heavy drinking, in hospital in Shrewsbury. Sixteen years later, on 26 October 2010, Pamela died in hospital in London. She was eighty, and had outlived Osborne's four subsequent wives and many of the people whom they had known in earlier times.

Almost a hundred letters, many more postcards and a few telegrams between Osborne and Pamela seem to have survived 'the ravages of time' and now form part of Osborne's archives in London and Texas. Sometimes the correspondence runs consecutively, sometimes intervening items are missing and letters and postcards appear suspended in space, detached from those around them. Certainly, many letters were either lost or destroyed. Yet those that remain chart the course of a restless, perplexing relationship in which rancour was over time replaced with frivolity, a relationship between two people each with their own emotional and professional struggles to resolve, who failed to live with each other and yet who remained mutually dependent. It is the story of two parallel but very different careers in the English theatre during the latter half of the twentieth century, one unique, at times astonishing, the other perhaps representative of the untold stories of many repertory actors who played the spectrum of drama and many leading roles with flair and distinction, but never had the luck of national recognition. Their letters give added insight into *Look Back in Anger*, raise intriguing questions about the play *Déjàvu*, its 1992 'sequel,' might have been, disclose an otherwise unknown aspect of the nature and affections of one of the most influential of twentieth century English playwrights, and reveal the forbearing, resilient woman so long in his shadow.

■ ■ ■

From the beginning, in Bridgwater, Osborne identified in Pamela a powerful determination that he had not previously discerned in anyone else and that he found immensely attractive. Yet he quickly detected there was also something hidden, something mysterious about her that puzzled and eluded him. It was, he wrote later, 'as if she had once known a secret divinity that in time would reveal itself and her.'[8] Patience, he thought, might be rewarded by the revelation of this holy grail. Her apparent supreme strength of purpose on the one hand and equivocation on the other bewildered the young, temperamentally volatile, emotionally needy Osborne, who, reassured by the former and confounded by the latter, failed to see how the two could co-exist within the same person. It was an unsettling, intangible quality he recreated in Alison Porter, whose 'silence and obdurate withdrawal were impregnable,' in his view thereby making her and not her raging husband 'the most deadly bully.'[9]

For her part, Pamela immediately recognized in the twenty-one-year-old Osborne the buccaneering spirit of rebellion and readiness to act upon it that she wished she possessed herself. The daughter of local tradespeople, she still lived at home. Osborne, that vivid young man, became an instant part of the armoury she was assembling to overcome her parents' opposition to the acting career upon which she was determined but which they insisted was far too risky to contemplate. Into the deeply conservative middle-class world of post-war Bridgwater, Osborne brought an exhilarating zest of London sensibility, a refreshing gust of 'the dashing life,' that Pamela had recently glimpsed as a student at the Royal Academy of Dramatic Art and to which she was longing to return.[10] Astonishingly well-read, he overflowed with opinions about most things both within their orbit and beyond, and was already enviably accomplished, having run his own theatre company and seen *The Devil Inside Him*, his first play, produced. 'We were absolutely mad about each other,' she recalled.[11] She was swept up in the slipstream of his passions. It was emotionally intoxicating. Each confirmed the other's ambition, he to write, she to act, both to establish themselves and change a little bit of the world.

When Alison in *Look Back in Anger* recalls her first meeting with Jimmy, she probably encapsulates something of the romance Pamela had identified in Osborne, as well as her own pragmatism:

'It had been such a lovely day, and he had been in the sun. Everything about him seemed to burn, his face, the edges of his hair glistened and seemed to spring off his head, and his eyes were so blue and full of the sun. He looked so young and frail, in spite of the tired line of his mouth. I knew I was taking on more than I was ever likely to be capable of bearing, but there never seemed to be any choice.'[12]

The precise nature of the affinity between two people is often impenetrable to outsiders and frequently to those involved as well. Yet the empathy between John Osborne and Pamela Lane endured despite Osborne reflecting in 1970 that: 'I can see all my personal relationships as an unbroken series of defeats, every one of them bitter and bloody.'[13] From the outset, they believed implicitly in each other. He saw her as a natural rebel, a scintillating talent imprisoned by middle-class conformism. She agreed; that was precisely what she was. By rescuing her, he reasoned, they would strike a joint blow against the enemy and together they would be invincible. For added dramatic weight, he cast Pamela's mother in much the same role he had assigned to his own. He had long professed a loathing of Nellie Beatrice, his barmaid mother, whom he perceived as having been indifferent to the plight of Tom Godfrey, his beloved father, who died of tuberculosis when his son was ten. Ethel Lane, he claimed, was her exact counterpart: 'joyless, calculating, blackmailing, completely without scruple or integrity, a veritable monster of a woman,' he informed his friend, the actor Anthony Creighton.[14] Liberate Pamela, therefore, and he would snatch a victory against both his mother and hers. For her part, Pamela felt constricted both personally and professionally by Bridgwater. It was agonizing, and she desperately sought escape. Osborne offered the reassurance, the inspiration and the means. She was prepared for a great adventure and grasped the opportunity. It was: 'The old story of the knight in shining armour,' reflects Alison in *Look Back in Anger*, '—except that his armour didn't really shine very much.'[15]

From the outset, Pamela encouraged Osborne's writing, proving a perceptive and sometimes a harsh critic. Yet along with Anthony Creighton, with whom Osborne was to write two plays, *Personal Enemy* and *Epitaph for George Dillon*, she was enormously supportive, insisting that he abandon the cloying romanticism of his earliest efforts and jettison the bizarre idea that he could write verse. Instead, he should concentrate on finding a language appropriate for saying something about the ideas and the fears of their immediate post-war world. She encouraged his admiration of Shakespeare and the Jacobeans and of such playwrights as Tennessee

Williams, whose language would inspire him in developing his own theatrical voice. Later, although Pamela did not appear in any of Osborne's plays, she saw the first productions of most of them, particularly admiring *Luther* and *Inadmissible Evidence*, while he sent her copies of his plays as they were published. His great achievement, she told him, was to bring the range and the relish of the English language back into the theatre. He was, she declared, 'a lone revivalist, a one-man restoration act.'[16]

To some extent, though, Osborne and Pamela were always Jimmy and Alison. Some of Osborne's letters read as though written by an older Jimmy Porter, still as prickly as ever. 'You owe me nothing but good manners are <u>always</u> welcome,' he informed her in December 1983, after she had failed to communicate a change of plans about an arranged meeting. 'In this respect, I <u>do</u> have some reason for complaint. At the least, your behaviour is churlish and, at the worst, unkind. Gratuitously so. But there it is, and no doubt ever will be… Happy New Year.'[17] An apparent slip of the pen when Pamela signed herself 'yours Squirrel' instead of her customary and more intimate 'your Squirrel', produced by return of post what Pamela described as 'scourge' of a letter—unfortunately now lost—the ferocity of which took her several days to assimilate. 'I am mortified that you could see my last letter in the way that you did,' she cried, 'and the "friendly chat" surrounding my thanks [for a gift of money] as DISSEMBLANCE, FEIGNED AFFECTION rooted in self-interest.' There is more than a suggestion of an older, more resigned Alison in her weary acceptance of 'your continuing jurisdiction and my long-standing trial…I'm <u>always</u> answering charges, that will never change, I know.'[18]

And yet: 'I am so struck by my <u>good fortune</u>,' he signalled late one sleepless night from Cornwall. 'My fortune to have loved someone for a lifetime, someone who always stuns and enlivens me…'[19] 'I do love you, my savage, benign bear,' she responded, 'wherever we are in our separate necks of the forest, and to re-encounter you suddenly, briefly, is as literally breathtaking as ever.'[20]

'Bears' and 'Squirrel,' familiar to audiences of *Look Back in Anger*, were the endearments they used for each other during the 1950s, and again when they were at their closest thirty years later,. 'Darling Bears'… 'Ever your S,' wrote Pamela during the 1980s. 'Squirrel darling…', replied Osborne, 'Take care, B.' During their earliest years together, they used the even more whimsical diminutives of

'Teddy' and 'Nutty', and both in earlier and later years they talked of their health and their disposition as the condition of his 'fur' and of her 'bushy tail.' A rapid retreat from this into the more formal: 'My dear John…,' 'My love as ever, Pamela,' is a certain sign of something amiss.

During the 1960s, Osborne's accumulating royalties and the success of *Tom Jones*, a film for which he had written the screenplay, made him a millionaire. Pamela, by contrast struggled to find work, often facing several weeks of unemployment. In 1962, five years after their divorce and in debt, she appealed for his help. He answered her call and although there was no legal requirement for him to do, he continued to support her financially whenever she needed assistance. Two years later, he instructed his accountants to send her a share of the royalties from *Inadmissible Evidence*. After twenty years of responding to her appeals, he formalized matters as a 'monthly allowance,' paid through his accountants. There is no suggestion in the letters that he gave her money from a sense of either obligation or guilt. After all, it had been Pamela who had initiated their separation in Derby. A generous man in many ways—and not, in many others—his money seems to be freely given, even during the 1980s when he could ill-afford it.

Osborne valued the quality of friendship above almost everything else. Friendship meant loyalty and kindness, although some might have said he was more successful at receiving than giving. They were qualities equally valued by Pamela, as were reticence and an acceptance of what life offered. According to many who encountered him, Osborne was a congenial companion, interesting in himself and interested in others, an entertaining conversationalist and generous with both his time and hospitality. Yet he was also alarmingly quixotic, a man who conceded as early as the mid-fifties that the characteristic an enemy would most readily identify in him was that of 'cruelty.'[21] His two volumes of autobiography, while garnering admiring reviews and substantially reviving a wilting professional reputation, incensed many critics and readers by his caricature of his mother—who was still alive—in the first and his bitter denunciation of Jill Bennett—who had recently died—in the second.

Yet Osborne and Pamela seldom spoke of each other and rarely disparagingly. 'If he thinks I'm going to dish the dirt on my former husband,' Pamela once said about the notoriously indiscreet actor Robert Stephens, who knew them both and had asked her a leading question, 'then he doesn't know who I am.'[22] Osborne, on the other hand, rarely refrained from dirt-dishing. Acutely sensitive, he was feverishly attuned to the slightest signals of what he interpreted as disloyalty and betrayal, and several of those who knew him, both socially and professionally, found themselves having fallen foul of him and peremptorily cast from favour. Some, such as Tony Richardson, the director of several of his early plays, Jill Bennett, and Nolan, his daughter by Penelope Gilliatt, were the recipients of what Oscar Beuselinck, his lawyer of forty years, called 'torrents of outrage,' letters in which extravagantly expressed invective becomes a stylistic form, the voice clearly recognizable from his plays.[23] Others were dismissed with a pithily expressed postcard. After Peter Hall, the director of the National Theatre, told Osborne in 1976 that *Watch It Come Down* would close early as ticket sales were falling, he received a terse card from Osborne declaring that he was giving up writing and taking up weaving instead. Still others, such as Anthony Creighton, were simply flung aside.

But of all those with whom Osborne remained on speaking terms, even though it was touch and go at times, it was Pamela Lane who lasted the longest. In their earliest years together, as they embarked upon their great adventure, she withheld much from him, masking the inner confusion with which she struggled, yet in later years she discovered in him a well of tolerance and goodwill that might have surprised many. They colluded in the great art of discretion. While she remained an enigma to him in many ways, and each at times found the other tormenting, they recognised the strength of a loyalty and trust forged over many years. Perhaps this is what they most deeply appreciated in each other. 'There was something so deep, so important between them,' remembered the actress Julia Lockwood, one of Pamela's oldest friends, 'that they just couldn't let go.'[24] In the end, and almost until the end, they were the oldest, and the closest of allies.

■ ■ ■

It is worth remembering that Osborne and Pamela met at a time of post-war austerity. Basic foods including eggs, meat, cheese, sugar and tea were still subject to rationing and in some cases would remain so until 1954. Occasional references to the general privations crop up in the early letters. Travel between different parts of Britain was primarily by steam train, while travel abroad remained the preserve of the wealthy and a perk of the privileged. There were plenty of signs, if one cared to read them, of the social changes that would soon transform the country but little indication in what Osborne called that post-war 'climate of fatigue' of the enormous technological changes that would follow.[25] The main avenues of entertainment remained the radio, the dancehall and the local repertory theatre. But these simple pleasures were already being threatened by the expansion of the cinema and audiences once happy to go along to the local theatre were increasingly being lured away by the glamorous American dramas and British comedies flickering across the screen at the Picture Palace over the road. Soon audiences would be seduced again by the bright new medium of television, the box in the corner bringing the world into the nation's living rooms and so saving anyone the trouble of leaving an armchair, going out in the rain and buying a ticket.

Both Osborne and Pamela began their careers in the final days of weekly repertory. This was a movement that had begun in the early years of the century and had reached its height in the years immediately preceding the war, providing entertainment to millions. The arduous system of weekly rep, when a play was performed for six nights plus a Saturday matinée, while the same actors rehearsed the following week's production during the day, was a mainstay of regional theatre. London's West End, both before and for several years after the war was controlled by a small number of commercial managements of which the most powerful was Hugh 'Binkie' Beaumont's H. M. Tennent organization. From his office at the Globe Theatre, Binkie supplied the theatres of Shaftesbury Avenue and the Strand with a relentless succession of long-running mild comedies and opulently decorated country house dramas, vehicles for the stars of the day. In the regions, the beleaguered managers of weekly repertory theatres, similarly reliant on box-office takings, gamely fought the threat of the cinema and television by fostering a family atmosphere between their actors and 'their friends in front,' audiences who returned week after week to see much the same thing.[25] There was an unofficial contract under which the actors played a benevolent part in the local community in return for audience loyalty. Actors opened fetes, bought jam, judged cake contests and were photographed alongside the winners, spoke at Rotary Club meetings and met the town's football team. The local rep was duly rewarded in ticket sales, many people booking weeks in advance, and presenting the actors with small gifts at Christmas. Home-made cakes, made with precious rations, were favourites; otherwise the men inevitably came away with a stack of socks, and the women with an assortment of headscarves.

The repertoire was largely determined by which plays could be banged together in a week's rehearsal, would recoup the financial outlay and had parts suitable for actors in the company still loosely specializing in 'character', 'leading' and 'juvenile' roles. If an actor was 'known' locally for a specific kind of performance, an eccentric aristocrat, for example, a domineering matriarch or a likeable rogue, then this was considered a safe bet and something to be repeated as often as possible in plays chosen to suit. For reasons of time and expense, a large cast was out of the question, which ruled out Shakespeare and his contemporaries and quite a few more besides. Considering the war was still very much in living memory, too much seriousness was best avoided and this limited the choice of play—and of dramatist—even further. Bernard Shaw was alright, depending on the play, as he was mischievous, otherwise plays dealing with 'social problems', unless set in the nineteenth century, needed to be approached a bit warily. Pinero was acceptable, and Oscar Wilde was always reliable because his seriousness could easily be glossed over by his wit and the actors behaving in an appropriately superficial manner. Rattigan was acceptable, especially *Flare Path*, and, slightly more daringly, *The Deep Blue Sea*. Agatha Christie guaranteed full houses, while Daphne du Maurier's dependable *Rebecca* offered good roles and an enticing opportunity for glamorous costumes, which was always an advantage. There was also the previous year's West End thriller and comedy hits to be plundered, and York, where Pamela appeared at the end of the fifties, went in for this almost exclusively.

Otherwise, there was a huge cargo of pre-war domestic dramas, inoffensive farces and light comedies long thrown overboard or even avoided by West End managements, that existed only in the murky depths scavenged by regional reps. *The Shop at Sly Corner*, *Mrs Gibbons' Boys*, *Life Begins at Fifty* and countless more could be found here, still salvageable and raised again and again. During the fifties, though, repertory theatres in several of the larger cities were moving into more ambitious territory and Kidderminster, where Osborne appeared, and Derby, both advanced with *Hedda Gabler*, and *A Streetcar Named Desire*. At the end of the decade many reps took on *Look Back in Anger*. But once the weekly and then the fortnightly repertory system eventually faded during the 1960s, a great many plays, and a certain style of actor, largely disappeared. The actress known locally for her benevolent aristocrats or her scheming supporting roles, and the 'character' actor, his countenance obscured by make-up and employing one of his carefully contrived walks and accents, became figures of the past.

Repertory survived in places and still does. The Bournemouth Summer Theatre, where Pamela appeared in 1968, is now defunct, but its counterpart at Frinton still survives at the time of writing, while several regional theatres continue to employ actors on a seasonal basis. But otherwise, theatres were changing rapidly. Local and state subsidy meant that regional theatres were no longer wholly reliant on the box office for survival and could afford longer production schedules. More complex productions could be attempted, and by the 1980s, regional theatre managers who also acted and directed, such as Leslie Twelvetrees at Derby, were quickly being succeeded by a new breed of artistic directors, usually university educated, who directed but did not act. Anxious to develop their own careers, they planned seasons encompassing a far greater range of plays, classical, contemporary, and, increasingly, from other parts of the world. In offices just down the corridor, financial directors scrutinised the books and publicity officers planned promotional campaigns.

Longer rehearsal and running schedules meant that productions were being cast on a play-by-play basis, and therefore the relationship between the actor and the audience changed. It was no longer part of the actor's job to be photographed for the local paper, as Pamela once was, munching a sandwich in support of the town's Bacon Week, radiate genial optimism with the local Scouts or Guides or judge a seaside beauty contest. Actors and their audiences were no longer 'friends' or an extended family. These days, actors contracted for one or two plays were thinking of the following weeks and months, telephoning their agents, hopeful of a leading part at another theatre, or a television or film role. Audiences, no longer needing to knit socks for Christmas, were left instead to 'education officers' who cajoled the public into the more serious, or what Osborne would have derided as the more joyless, realm of post-show discussions.

Much had changed for the better: the average regional theatre-goer could see a greater range of world drama, at its best more appropriately cast, produced to a high standard and with innovative sets. Young people, especially, could take part in the life of the theatre much more so than in the past. But for Pamela, and for many actors of the time negotiating the transition from the reliability of weekly repertory to a more ruthless freelance world, making a successful long-term career was more than ever a matter of careful judgement and luck.

■ ■ ■

It is worth remembering too that the social and moral climate of the late-1940s and the 1950s differed vastly from that of today. Although many people, including Osborne and Pamela—and Jimmy Porter—were very aware of social class and talked about the 'class struggle' and the need for greater social equality, they still generally lived their lives according to prevailing convention. Very few male and female partners, for example, lived together before marriage in the 1950s, although the figure would increase rapidly. A child born out of wedlock was considered by many in all social classes as an all too visible moral and social shame. As abortion was illegal, a woman who 'got into trouble' had the option either to have the child and struggle against possible social ignominy, or take the chance of an illegal 'backstreet abortion,' practiced sometimes by individuals who were well-meaning but lacked any medical qualifications. In 1950, those convicted of murder might be sentenced to death by hanging, and male homosexuality was considered a crime punishable by social ostracism and a prison sentence. The theatre was still bound by the Theatres Act of 1737, under which all new plays and new additions to those already written were required to be submitted for scrutiny to the Lord Chamberlain's office, where they would be perused for any morally or politically seditious content. Although both Osborne and Pamela became of age during an era that would now be regarded as morally and socially repressive, they would see extraordinary and liberating changes during their late-twenties and thirties: capital punishment was abolished in 1965, homosexuality was decriminalized and the Abortion Act legalized terminations in 1967, and the Theatres Act was abolished a year later.

Communication during the immediate post-war years was conducted mainly, if not exclusively, by letter. Accustomed therefore to writing and to using the postal service, Osborne and Pamela continued to rely on it throughout their lives. During the 1950s, they used inexpensive writing paper commonly available from high street stationers, Pamela for several years favouring a shade advertised as 'azure' before changing to a utilitarian white. During the 1960s, she ordered paper with her name printed at the top in small black capitals. Osborne did the same. Headed notepaper looked authoritative, implying the correspondent had attained some status in the world. Later, Pamela abandoned this, cutting down on the expense, although she continued to write with a fountain pen and blue ink, only occasionally and in later years using a ball-point. For a couple of years during the late fifties, Osborne went through a phase of typing his letters, often on English Stage Company notepaper, which perhaps appealed to his vanity. He was very conscious, according to his lawyer, of being seen to have 'made it' professionally and socially. His business correspondence continued to be typewritten by the secretary who typed the final draft of his plays and to whom he would dictate. More personal correspondence, however, including his letters and cards to Pamela, was mostly hand-written with a pen loaded with either black or blue ink, and later sometimes by a red or green felt-tip, the colours signifying nothing. He used whatever came to hand.

For short messages or speed, they often used postcards, quickly thrust into an envelope for privacy. Osborne had postcards printed with his name, and, once he had moved to the country, also with his address but omitting the postcode, an innovation he regarded as superfluous and a symbol of a creeping bureaucracy that should be resisted. Pamela bought 'art cards' of the kind for sale at museums, showing classical paintings or sculpture, reproductions of cartoons or decorative prints. Very occasionally she sent him sentimental pictures of teddy bears, once with a printed greeting: 'Someone somewhere thinks you're rather cuddly.'[27] Osborne preferred 'vintage' theatrical illustrations, sepia photographs of chorus girls, and humorous cards of the sort bought at the seaside and especially those illustrated by Donald McGill, the so-called 'king of the saucy postcard.' Many of these he obtained from specialist dealers. He liked them for what they were, but they were also an emblem of his taste for things he thought thoroughly English, the simple pleasures of the music hall and the rakish, kiss-me-quick vulgarity of the seaside.

However much they relied on letters and postcards, though, they were not averse to the landline telephone. However, during the early-1950s, only about ten per cent of households possessed one. This would be a bulky black Bakelite model, the receiver cradled on the top of a square body with a rotary dial on the front equipped with ten finger holes corresponding to the numbers 0-9, which one used to dial the number one wanted. Making a long distance, or 'trunk' call, though, say from Derby to London, which Pamela and Osborne did often, tended to be a complicated and precarious process, involving an unseen operator at an exchange 'putting you through' by plugging various cables into a system of sockets.

As it was widely assumed that the operator eavesdropped upon your conversation, and telephone users were anyway vividly aware of their part of the proceedings being easily overheard by others nearby, there was an apprehension that the telephone was not entirely confidential. This was a particular anxiety in rented accommodation, where landlords or landladies eager to keep a track of their lodgers' comings and goings might have large ears. As a lodger in Derby in 1954, Pamela explains her reticence in a letter to Osborne: 'Miss Maltby [her landlady] was in the kitchen just off the room where I was phoning you and it always cramps my style when there's someone around.'[28] A street corner telephone box might be more private, provided nobody appeared outside in a hurry, banging on the door and demanding you finish your call.

Extremely urgent communications would be made by telegram, the message sent from a Post Office by telegraph, the strips of thin newsprint on which it was tapped out in capital letters glued to a khaki-coloured slip of paper and inserted into an envelope of the same distinctive shade. 'It was such a useful SOS for begging money or dashing off impulsive declarations of passion,' reflected Osborne, lamenting the ending of the service in 1982. It was also beloved by repertory playwrights, the arrival of a telegram being an invaluable device for advancing the plot. The telephone, thought Osborne, was by contrast 'a clumsy, unsubtle instrument. I dread its peremptory intrusiveness. It distorts and over-simplifies.'[29]

Even in the 1960s, a busy professional or social life made communication by the telephone, still a housebound apparatus, only randomly efficient. 'I've been ringing you but no answer,' complained Osborne on 26 April 1966, the day after Pamela's thirty-sixth birthday. 'Perhaps you're away or working.' The introduction of the answer machine enabled incoming landline calls to be recorded and played back later, but as this was an instrument plugged into the telephone, it needed to be brought separately, something a disorganized person might easily put off. 'I was afraid I might have been missing a call during [the] daytime,' apologised Pamela in 1983, 'never got round to an answering machine.'[30] As often as not, a postcard was a quick, efficient way of arranging, confirming, or rearranging meetings: 'My darling—will drop in on Monday about 11am unless I hear otherwise, longing to see you,' was a typical Osborne message. 'If you're free December 4th afternoon, will try to pop over with champagne for an hour or two....'[31]

Suddenly, and within a few years, the bulky apparatus of communication diminished to the size of a microchip. Yet the personal computer armed with an email facility and the mobile telephone with its text messaging devices arrived just too late for Pamela Lane and John Osborne, set in their habits, suspicious of the long arm of technology and among the last generation of consistent letter and postcard-writers.

■ ■ ■

Pamela Lane's parents were the descendants of large families who for several generations had lived in and around Bristol, moving to the more rural areas as their prosperity, and their professional and social prominence became more established. When William Ivor Lane married Ethel Winifred Ecclestone Ford at St John the Baptist Church in Keynsham, a small town between Bristol and Bath, on 1 August 1923, it was therefore an occasion to merit a splash in the local newspaper. 'The contracting parties are well-known in the area,' asserted the *Bath Chronicle and Weekly Gazette,* their wedding attracting 'a great crowd.' The reporter enthused about the subtle intricacies of the bridal dress and the abundant floral arrangements, and approvingly noted that the groom had presented his bride with a diamond ring to which she had reciprocated with a gold watch. The reception was similarly impressive. Over a hundred guests bearing 'numerous, and very handsome' presents, arrived at Hemleaze, the ample Georgian home belonging to the bride's family, where food and drinks were served before the newly-weds decorously withdrew for a honeymoon at Bournemouth, a sedate, well-to-do resort on the south coast.[32]

William Ivor's father, William Joseph Lane, a Bristol draper, and Florence, his wife, were both married for the second time. Each had brought a child to their marriage in 1906: William Ivor, born in 1899, and Olive, Florence's daughter, born two years earlier. Ethel Ford, William Ivor's bride and two years his younger, was the youngest daughter of Alfred Ford, a market gardener renowned particularly for the quality of his roses, and his wife, Emily. Both William Joseph Lane and Alfred Ford had inherited their businesses from their fathers, and while he had no sons himself, Alfred guaranteed the succession by bringing his wife's nephew into the family home and training him in the business instead. Once William Ivor returned with his new wife from their honeymoon, he followed the family tradition by opening a draper's shop in Bridgwater, no doubt with the help of a generous parental subsidy.

In stark contrast, Thomas Godfrey Osborne's marriage to Nellie Beatrice Grove over 150 miles away at Hammersmith Register Office two years later, on 4 June 1925, warranted no local newspaper coverage at all. The Osbornes and the Groves were unknown to each other and had nothing in common other than a long association with public houses, both as managers and as regular paying customers. There was no honeymoon for the newly-wedded couple, but instead a swift, almost undignified withdrawal to rented rooms. Unlike the Lanes and the Fords, the Osbornes were a family in retreat. Failure hung over them like a mist, shrouding them from view. Thomas Godfrey was the twenty-five-year-old son of James Osborne, a Newport jeweller. Having absent-mindedly allowed the business to collapse, he and his wife, Annie, with Thomas Godfrey in tow, had left Wales and arrived in London in the hope of a new beginning. It was not a success. They remained the poor relations, their family exchequer being embarrassingly subsidized by Jim's more affluent publican brothers.

Standing in his Bridgwater shop, situated prominently on the corner of Eastover and Monmouth Road, surrounded by his fabrics and with his tape measure and scissors at the ready, William Lane could look to the future with confidence. But in London, Thomas Godfrey neither had the luck of a family business behind him and nor had he the advantage of vigorous health. He had some talent as an illustrator and copywriter and found work for advertising agencies in Shoe Lane, near the Strand, but his tuberculosis prevented him from working as consistently as he would have liked. He had met Nellie Beatrice in a nearby pub, where she was employed as a barmaid. She was the daughter of William Crawford Grove, a lifelong publican, and his wife, Ada. He had finished up as the manager of a pub near Trafalgar Square, strategically situated to cater for his liking for the theatres and the chorus girls of the Strand, before retiring to a small terraced house in Fulham. Tom Godfrey and Nellie Beatrice set up home in rented rooms a few streets away. They had two children, Faith, born in 1928 but who died, twenty-two months later, of tuberculosis and meningitis, and John James, who arrived on 12 December 1929. In Bridgwater, meanwhile, where they lived above the shop, the Lanes produced three children, two sons and, lastly, Pamela Elizabeth, born on 25 April 1930.

Considering this was a time of economic depression followed by six years of war, Pamela lived a charmed life, navigating smoothly into the secure waters of the Bridgwater Grammar School for Girls and soon afterwards seeing news of her triumphs cropping up in the *Taunton Courier*. She excelled in a cake competition, gave public recitals of poetry and at seventeen, two years after the war ended, won the Bess Fowler Trophy at the Bristol Eisteddfod for having 'attained the highest standard of efficiency in the senior poetry and drama classes.'[33] At the same time, she was appearing in plays staged by the local Amateur Dramatic Club, their productions, whatever the standard of acting, 'always enjoyable,' pronounced the *Taunton Courier*, 'for the playing of Mr. V. Tout's orchestra.'[34]

In London, meanwhile, Osborne's youth had passed entirely anonymously. His father's death in 1940 had left mother and son largely dependent upon a charity for incapacitated advertising industry personnel and their dependents, to which Tom Godfrey had wisely subscribed. Osborne's childhood became a dispiriting trail with Nellie Beatrice through south London suburbs from one rented room to another. Several months spent bedbound with rheumatic fever further disrupted his already random formal education, and deepened his sense of isolation and his profound antagonism towards his mother. 'There is little of my childhood I can look back on with any pleasure,' he told an interviewer in 1962. 'Most of it I regret.'[35]

When Osborne was seventeen, he found a job as a journalist on a trade paper serving the gas industry. At the same time, he took a course of evening classes in elocution and ballroom dancing in preparation for life as an actor, recalibrating his south London accent into a passable middle-class drawl and polishing up his foxtrot before launching himself upon a series of auditions. Eventually he was rewarded. In January 1948, he joined a touring company presenting *No Room at the Inn*, a wartime melodrama written by Joan Temple, and spent a year trundling about the country as an assistant stage manager. Two years later, on 29 May 1950, in the unlikely setting of Huddersfield, he was watching the first night of his first play at the town's Theatre Royal. *The Devil Inside Him* was written in collaboration with Stella Linden, who had played Mrs. Voray in *No Room at the Inn* and had quickly became the eighteen-year-old Osborne's lover. *The Devil Inside Him* was directed by Patrick Desmond, Stella's husband, a rumoured homosexual and in any case a man too intent upon his own ambitions of becoming a theatrical impresario to bother about his wife's affair with a nascent dramatist. The play, advised the critic for *The Stage*, was 'a study in morbid psychology,' surely a disconcerting trend in modern drama, but rescued by 'humour [that] springs naturally out of situation and character.'[36] Having run for its allotted week, the play promptly disappeared, unredeemed even by the weekly repertory circuit before it resurfaced twelve years later in Croydon, under a new title and by a purportedly different author.

Meanwhile, Pamela had effortlessly advanced from the amateur to the professional, graduating from the Royal Academy of Dramatic Art in London in 1949. Like Osborne's, her voice had been tailored to her aspirations. Any trace of West Country burr had been streamlined by RADA into the required Received Pronunciation of the Home Counties. She was, though, proud of her voice and the range of accents she could assume and worked hard on sounding authentic. She appeared briefly in repertory at Salisbury and Tunbridge Wells. Such resolute independence disconcerted her parents, who considered her youthful Eisteddfod success and amateur dramatics as enhancements to her marital prospects rather than a precursor to an almost certainly insecure career that might eventually take her far away. In the spring of 1950, therefore, she reassuringly returned home, appearing again with the Dramatic Club as June Farrell, Viscount Pym's American fiancée in *The Chiltern Hundreds*, a political comedy by William Douglas Home. Her 'dramatic training was clearly evident in her spirited interpretation,' proclaimed the *Taunton Courier*, 'accent included.'[37]

Within a few months, she joined the local Roc Players, a newly-established company managed by Michael Goodwin and Rae Allen. 'Sweethearts in real life as well as on stage,' they had appeared in repertory throughout southern England before marrying after the war and descending upon Somerset, where they inaugurated the Players at Bridgwater Town Hall, a three-story Georgian-styled building in the High Street. 'We feel that the world is a bit drab,' announced Goodwin, 'and that the public need a laugh, so the accent will be on comedy.'[38] 'We don't profess to be "arty and crafty" in any way', he added, 'and if by any chance we are cultural, it is purely by accident.'[39] Accordingly, the company of eleven proceeded to serve an aggressive diet of domestic light comedies and farces.

While the Roc Players considered Pamela a prized asset, elsewhere in England Osborne's employers were discovering that his acting, adequate at best, negligent at worst, was determined simply by whether or not he liked the play in which he was appearing. When the Saxon Players in Leicester gave him the sack soon after his arrival, he was scooped up by the Saga Repertory Group, a chaotic and impecunious company touring the seaside towns of the north Devon coast, coincidentally not too far from Bridgwater. It was there that Osborne encountered Anthony Creighton, an actor seven years his elder, an aspiring writer and the company's director who would become a close friend and collaborator. At Christmas 1950, while Pamela was earning plaudits for her turn as the Good Fairy in the Roc Players' production of *Sleeping Beauty*, Osborne was hamming his way through both Abanaza and the Dame in *Aladdin*, a hastily-assembled pantomime that lasted only one performance at the Saga's new home at Hayling Island before advancing creditors resulted in the company hurriedly disbanding and Osborne and Creighton catching the night train to London.

They arrived at Creighton's flat at 53 Caithness Road in Hammersmith. While Creighton submitted to expediency and quickly found work serving tea and pastries in a branch of the Lyon's restaurant and café chain, Osborne scoured the advertising columns of *The Stage*, the weekly show business newspaper. At last, he struck lucky, and in the spring of 1951, he boarded a steam train from Paddington to join the Roc Players in Bridgwater.

The 1950s

■ ■ ■

■ ■ ■

They first met in a close embrace on Monday, 19 March 1951.

The posture was a fiction. Both were rehearsing, Osborne as Willie and Pamela as Sally, in *My Wife's Family*, a farce widely advertised as 'the funniest play in the world,' and written in 1931 by Fred Duprez, an American film actor and vaudeville artist, who also had a successful career in Britain.[1] A confusion of assumed identities, explosions in the summer house, a piano and a missing baby, it opened at Bridgwater Town Hall the following week, another salvo in the Goodwins' mission of delivering jollity to their audiences. To the sound of *Yes, Sir, That's My Baby*, the curtain rises to reveal the library of a substantial country house where Willie Nagg, according to the stage directions a 'well set up' young man in his early twenties, is clasping Sally, an 'ingénue type' in his arms. Having disengaged themselves, the besotted couple's first few lines of dialogue meticulously explain to the audience what Willie and Sally already know, that they have been secretly married for a year but are in such woeful financial straits that she is obliged to work as a parlour-maid while he hopes to win £200 by fighting a professional boxer for six rounds without being eliminated.

From the outset, Pamela mesmerised Osborne. 'She startled and confused me,' he recalled in his memoirs thirty years later, and their embraces onstage quickly became more fervent in the wings. 'I knew that I was in love... I waited for the curtain to go up, holding in my arms this powerful, drawn-up creature dressed in a green maid's uniform of all things. Life was unimaginable without her matching green eyes.'[2] She had undoubtedly dazzled him, for in fact, Pamela's eyes were blue. She was equally enthralled by him, identifying Osborne as a bracingly unconventional young man, already burnished by achievement as a playwright and overflowing with ambition. He represented the future she wanted for herself.

While the details of the 'dashing life,' Pamela had lived while a RADA student in London appear irrecoverable, it would be highly unlikely that a woman of her intelligence, good-looks, talent and ambition, had not been involved in previous relationships. According to Osborne's memoirs, while he was living with his mother in the London suburbs and working as a trade journalist, he had been briefly and seemingly indolently engaged to a girl who worked at a building society. On tour with *No Room at the Inn*, he had been swept up by the worldlier Stella Linden, with whom he had had written *The Devil Inside Him* while living with her in a flat in Brighton, flamboyant evidence of his readiness to defy social convention. Nevertheless, Osborne and Pamela proceeded with some decorum, she living at home, he at his digs, and during the following three months appearing in a succession of creaking comedies and frenzied farces, each rewarded in the local newspaper by an approving paragraph, the productions particularly noted for their 'increasingly decorative' set design. [3]

Meanwhile, the Lanes, and especially Pamela's mother, horrified by their daughter's romance with a young man they thought highly unsuitable son-in-law material, began a concerted crusade to derail it. Both incensed and buoyantly invigorated, Osborne relayed the details of the Lanes' offensive and his belligerent counter-attacks in a volley of reports to Anthony Creighton, still working at Lyon's in London. Both Osborne and Pamela were tall, whereas Creighton was a much shorter and more compact figure, hence his nickname of 'Mouse.'

JO to Anthony Creighton ms letter n/d Texas

Repertory Theatre
Bridgwater
Wednesday
[April-July 1951]

My dear old boy—

When troubles come they come not in single spies but in battalions... Inevitably, you know very little of Pam. I have told you little enough, except that we are so utterly, incredibly, insanely and yet so rationally in love. Believe me please, old friend, and understand me when I say that I love and want her in every kind of way: my mind wants her, my bowels, my soul, my body, my peace and quietness, my terrible passions. Every part of my life and most certainly my theatrical life would be incomplete without her. My love for Pam is quietly paramount in the way that if ever I felt the need for children (God forbid for many years), I could never consider anyone else to mother them; whatever happened—come love, poverty, war, the lot.

We are mad, impulsive, stupid in some ways, maybe, but talking 'all in all' we are both very intelligent, adult people with the same kind of approach to things.

All her life, Pam has had to contend with almost exactly the same home-life as I have. Her mother seems—if it is possible—to be an even worse tigress than my own mother—and you know what that means! She is selfish, indulgent to the point of every kind of mental horror, dishonest to a degree, joyless, calculating, blackmailing, completely without scruple or integrity, a veritable monster of a woman, a beast trying to devour her daughter every day of the year.

You marvelled at my patience over the years with my mother. Well, I marvel at Pam's incredible strength—and it is not the kind that comes from coldness—she has all the world's passion.

For years, all the time, good, striving things about her have been threatened by this black hole of her home life. What with her wasting away with the Roc Buns, and all this as well, I determined many, many weeks ago to get her out of it.

Well, now something has happened that looks like precipitating almost immediate action.

Pam's mother has discovered that Pam and I are in love. The hurricane that followed was inevitable, vulgar, sordid and unpleasant. She hates me—and always has. (She hates the theatre and everything about it.) Her big gun that she brings out against me is that I am QUEER (Yes!) Or as she puts it: a NANCY BOY. She points to my long hair, the dying Keats face and body, my complete oddity, my affectedness, effeminacy—even Vicky [a small dog owned by his landlady]. The rest you can imagine: that a daughter of hers should be seen with anyone as low as that, etc. And so on and so on—I'll confess it all made me feel a little sick and ill.

Pam was horrified, virulent and firm. The family says: you must get away out of Bridgwater; we'll give you the money. But you must go.

Pam of course said she was going to make up her own mind. Pam and I have talked rationally about it. <u>We have made plans accordingly</u>:—

We are waiting 24 hours to see what will come out of the family storm (they'll probably come after me with a shotgun! Actually, I think they'll probably try and get me the sack.)

What will happen, I don't know. But if we don't get one or both sacked for being in a local scandal, we shall most likely one or both be obliged to give in our notice.

In the event of this happening—and everything at the moment points to it most strongly—we shall join Mouse in London in a fortnight. It probably sounds mad to you, old son, <u>but I am in deadly earnest.</u> I won't see her threatened and bullied. And even though God knows I can't afford it I'll risk everything to stay with her. We'll come to town, and if we starve it will be in dignity.

I'll wire you if the balloon goes up. In which case… Firstly, can you put out some feelers for a job for me, perhaps at Jo Lyons with you? Also, when I send you the details, you could fix us up with a room somewhere? Oh, Mouse, in a way I hope this does happen. Perhaps the three of us together will have better luck.

Pam is expecting a cheque for some interest she gets on capital. It should be, all being well, within the next week. This would be for at least £80 or £90, [equivalent to £2300 and £2600 in 2018] which would stop us starving if we were careful for months—and give us time. Also, she is going to have a big legal battle for her legacy which she inherits when she is 25—another four years. It is all very complicated, but there is a chance. (It's about £2000 [£59,000].) <u>Anyway, we shall work something out.</u>

My love, always forever,

Johnny

Osborne was under the impression that in appearance he somewhat resembled Keats, a romantic delusion that was short-lived. Pamela's parents, people of thrift and foresight, had invested money in shares on her behalf, on which she received dividend payments, while at twenty-five, she was also due to inherit a 'legacy'.

No sooner had Creighton read this, than another Bridgwater bulletin was thrust through his letter box. In the hope of neutralizing Osborne with incriminating evidence of his homosexuality, Mrs Lane had hired a private detective to shadow him. When the investigation proved fruitless, she prevailed upon Lynne Reid Banks, one of Pamela's friends from RADA and later a prominent novelist and author of *The L-Shaped Room*, to come to Bridgwater in a last-ditch hope that Banks might persuade her daughter to think again. By chance, Banks and Osborne also knew each other, both having been members of the Saga Repertory Group. They had not got on well and Osborne was intensely suspicious of her.

JO to Anthony Creighton ms letter n/d Texas

Rep Theatre
Bridgwater
Tuesday
[April—July 1951]

My dear old boy,

And now—to tell you of the terrible nightmare of the last few days. Horror has heaped upon horror. Rage, tears, disgust and utter horror have been mine.

Last Thursday it began. I was summoned down to Pam's house in the afternoon. I went down determined to be completely ruthless and uncompromising. And I was. The family tried to attack me with everything of course, but they had never met anything like me before, and I scattered all before me. They tried abuse, remorse, tears, appeals to my better nature: the lot. I knew just how to deal with it. I stamped on it. I told them firmly that I knew they hated me and everything I stood for (they even tried to timidly deny it) and that I hated them. I said that I loved Pam, admired her and believed in her and would take her away. They were horrified and taken aback by the first taste of honesty in their lives.

On Friday I gave in my notice. It was accepted with obvious regret but without much ado. Then Pam gave in hers. Saturday arrived. In the evening, to my HORROR, who should arrive at the theatre but LYNNE. We looked at each other with open loathing, as you can imagine. She stopped, ironically enough, with Pam who was with her at RADA, who had no choice but to put her up.

After the show on Saturday night, I gave in written confirmation of my notice. I knew Pam was going to do the same; to add to my apprehension, her parents arrived at the theatre just as I gave mine in. I waited the following day in an agony of not knowing, phoning Pam constantly but not getting through. I got through. Her voice nearly sent me frantic. She sounded like some ghost. She had been up all night with Michael [Goodwin] and her people, and then her mother.

Pam has enormous strength. I love her for her guts. But those bastards had given her particularly a third degree, abused me and insulted me as a person, as an actor—everything. Every kind of bullying, blackmail. I put down the phone. I thought I would go mad.

On Monday evening I phoned again. She seemed to be locked up in the house with her mother standing guard. I managed somehow to smuggle a note into Pam's house through the ASM [assistant stage manager]. I discerned to my amazement that everyone (at the theatre) believed that for one thing I was getting hold of Pam because she has a legacy (a paltry £2000—useful, God knows, but I wouldn't suspect my worst enemy of those motives.) Immediately wrote to Pam telling her to sign over the money to her parents forever. The next day I discovered they'd already forced her to do this. The bloody oafs, natural born fascists, blind, intolerant and stupid. Quite without scruple. That vampire mother of hers!!

We have thought the whole situation out very, very carefully. And we have reached one decision. It sounds quite, quite mad, I know. But I know—oh God I do know—that it's RIGHT. We are going to get married as soon as we possibly can. Nothing can stand in our way then.

Put out that red carpet for this mad, crazy but confident stallion with fourpence in his pocket.

With you always,

My love

Johnny

PS: Aren't we extraordinary people?

PL to JO ms letter Texas

73 Eastover
Bridgwater
18 June 1951

My dear,

God, it's desperately difficult to get any kind of coherence into this when I have to keep putting it away every time my father or brother or Lynne comes into the room, and it's so important that I advise you what to do in your dealings with the rest of the company. I must hurry in case Rita comes, and in any case I have to be at the Bank with my father in a quarter of an hour and I'm not even dressed yet. Darling, it's not that I don't trust your instinctive knowledge of how to behave in any situation which might arise... I'll try to tell you all about it when they let me see you again. Until then, just trust me enough to know that you must follow the small points of advice I'm going to give you—they're the only things that can save us— at least, not 'us', as nothing can destroy that, but the chance of any future for us. A repeat of what I said over the phone this morning—please, please don't antagonize anyone in the company, especially Rae and Michael, by a ruthless and defiant attitude. Don't try to defend me in anything they may say about me. He'll (Michael) probably say that I couldn't love you as much as I say I do.

Just know that whatever happens, I love you more and more through all this and always shall. Pray God that gives you the courage and strength to deal with whatever comes along. I'm with you and closer to you than ever. I don't know what the future will be like. Let's tackle the present first.

My everlasting and enduring love.

Pam

Rita Street was an assistant stage manager and actress with the Roc Players, acting as go-between carrying letters between Osborne and Pamela. Many years later, recalling her 'unwarranted attempt to dissuade Pam from marrying,' Banks remembered that: 'She certainly loved him and wasn't going to be put off by anybody.'[4]

Five days later, at 9.30 in the morning of Saturday 23 June, Osborne and Pamela were married at St Mary's Parish Church. They had chosen the time partly because they were required for the matinee performance later that day and partly to evade the Lanes, whom they had not told of the arrangement and whom they hoped would be occupied in the shop. Nor had Osborne informed his mother, and Nellie Beatrice would remain in ignorance of Pamela for another six years, her son only revealing her existence on the eve of his divorce in 1957. Their only confidante, apart from the Rev E. H. Hughes-Davies, was Frank Middlemass, a fellow Roc Players member and later a distinguished character actor, who had a room at Osborne's digs and acted as his best man. In the event, though, a member of the parish council discovered the arrangements and informed the Lanes who attempted to dissuade the vicar from holding the ceremony. In this they failed and instead they arrived at the church to despairingly watch their daughter marry a man they ardently wished had never arrived in Bridgwater.

Immediately afterwards, the bride and groom departed for a rehearsal at the theatre. 'Our marriage,' Osborne noticed, 'seemed to have settled the cast's lines and moves wonderfully.' William Lane, 'more weary than angry,' turned up at lunchtime and took the newly-weds to a hotel and a melancholy meal of 'pilchard salad and light ale' eaten in 'almost complete silence.'[5] After the evening performance, Pamela returned home and Osborne wandered back to his lodgings. The following week, they appeared in *Grumpy*, a tired comedy-melodrama by Horace Hodges and T. Wigney Percival. Originally produced in 1913, it was generally thought of as a cosy, heart-warming piece, the eponymous leading role of a bumbling lawyer making the play a strong candidate as a 'vehicle' for a leading actor who liked to be thought of as well-loved. Naturally, Michael Goodwin took the part. Pamela appeared as the irreproachable young Virginia who allows herself to be seduced by the villainous, diamond-thieving Chamberlain Jarvis, thereby temporarily forfeiting the love of Osborne's Ernest Heron, her virtuous fiancé, who does the decent thing and generously forgives her in the end.

Before leaving Bridgwater for London on the Sunday, Osborne himself did the decent thing by writing a letter to Pamela's father. The envelope survives; as it inscribed only to 'Mr Lane', and lacks both a further address and stamp, the letter was perhaps either delivered by Osborne himself, or handed to Pamela's father as husband and wife boarded the Paddington train:

JO to William Lane ms letter n/a BL

July 1ˢᵗ 1951

Dear Mr Lane,

Try not to worry too much about Pam. It may not seem so to you now, but I know she is doing the right thing. One day, you will know what I mean. She will be looked after and cared for always. I give you my word.

—John Osborne

■ ■ ■

'Pam is so kind and generous in all things,' Osborne assured Creighton. 'I know you will get on well.'[6] But as Creighton had rented his spare room at Caithness Road to a lodger who still had a few weeks of his tenancy remaining, Osborne and Pamela, with '£20 (equivalent to £590 in 2018) between us,' spent their first night together at a small private hotel in the Cromwell Road 'patronised by polite impoverished Indian students.'[7] A few days later, they moved to a room in Richmond where the elderly landlady asked only a minimum rent on the condition they played mahjong with her in the evenings. Once Creighton's lodger left and having played enough mahjong to last a lifetime, they moved into the newly vacated room in Hammersmith, paying Creighton thirty shillings (£1.30) a week rent from their unemployment benefit. Having equipped themselves with an agent, they set about finding acting work. Meanwhile: 'I was unable to take my eyes off her,' Osborne remembered. 'I watched her eating, walking, bathing, making-up, dressing, undressing, my curiosity was insatiable... There was little doubt in my otherwise apprehensive spirit that I had carried off a unique prize.'[8]

As Osborne had hoped, Pamela and Creighton liked one another and the trio quickly adopted a three-musketeers approach to both life and employment. All were vegetarians. It was cheaper, and far easier in those days of continued rationing, and husband and wife were keen advocates of the health benefits of a meat-free diet. They also agreed that whoever was offered work should accept it, no matter where it might be, and subsidise the others if necessary. After a few weeks, Osborne found work with Harry Hanson's Court Players at the Camberwell Palace on the corner of Denmark Hill, a run-down former Victorian variety theatre nearing the end of its days. Hanson was a former dancer, 'pink and plump and amiable, [a] quite overt homosexual who wore a succession of improbable silver-haired toupees,' according to one of his actors.[9] Despite the implausible toupees, Hanson's audiences were loyal and appreciative and many actors might have been delighted to join one of his several companies dotted across England. Osborne was not one of them. Hanson, he declared, was 'a byword for tatty, ill-paid, tyrannical, joyless work,' and after only a few weeks of travelling across London to Camberwell, war damage still clearly visible from the bus, he succeeded once again in getting himself sacked.[10] It was during these weeks, he noted in his memoirs, that 'Pamela declared herself pregnant. No, she didn't declare it, she mentioned it like a passing comment.' Creighton's mother, he added, supplied 'a packet of something called Penny Royal pills' which Pamela apparently swallowed to induce a termination. 'If she was relieved, she never expressed it, nor I my disappointment.'[11]

While he had earlier told Creighton he did not want children 'for many years to come,' the inference here is that little was said about Pamela's pregnancy and its termination, the latter an event that Osborne mutely accepted. As he was writing almost thirty years after the event, his recollection may not be entirely accurate, yet he and Pamela would undoubtedly have recognised that the birth of a baby would irrevocably transform their lives. Pamela would initially, and possibly in the long term, be obliged to give up her career, while it would have been incumbent upon Osborne to choose an occupation more stable than acting—or, more accurately, looking for acting work—in order to support them. As abortion was illegal, many women apprehensive about the potentially dangerous manipulations of the 'backstreet abortionist' resorted to remedies recommended by folklore: moving heavy furniture, taking a succession of especially hot baths while drinking gin, or swallowing pennyroyal. If this is indeed what she did, then she took a calculated risk, as in certain dosages pennyroyal is a highly toxic herb having potentially unpleasant and sometimes dangerous side-effects.

She recovered, however, to make a quick dash to Folkestone for a couple of days' film work, appearing uncredited as a competitor in a seaside beauty contest in *Lady Godiva Rides Again*. Despite the implied raunchiness of the title, this was an innocuous comedy starring Stanley Holloway, a popular comic actor, and Diana Dors, an actress touted as Britain's answer to Marilyn Monroe. Creighton, meanwhile, failed to find any acting work and instead relied on a series of casual jobs, first at the café, and then at a debt collectors and a telephone exchange.

With no other employment forthcoming, husband and wife spent the Christmas weeks delivering the seasonal mail from the Blythe Road Post Office, just around the corner from Caithness Road. Osborne would do this each Christmas for the next three years, delivering his last greetings card in 1955, after which he was liberated by the success of *Look Back in Anger*. In early 1952, though, things took a turn for the better. Osborne appeared as Wingate, a prefect, in two episodes of the *Billy Bunter of Greyfriars School* television series, before leaving for Kidderminster, where he had secured a season's work with the Repertory Players. To the great approval of local critics, he appeared in several leading roles in plays he admired, including Maxim de Winter in *Rebecca*, Malvolio in *Twelfth Night* and Stanley Kowalski in *A Streetcar Named Desire*. Pamela, meanwhile, had also found work and was touring as both actress and assistant stage manager with a company run by the actor-manger Phillip Barrett, taking an adaptation of *Jane Eyre* and Noël Coward's *Present Laughter* around the southern counties before descending upon the theatre-goers of south Wales with *The Maid of Cfen Ydfa*, a Welsh romance by Rhys Davies. Osborne dispatched a succession of good luck telegrams to speed her on her way:

JO to PL telegram Kidderminster to Bridgend, Glamorgan BL

11 August 1952

THINKING OF YOU DARLING BE GOOD LOVE TEDDY

JO to PL telegram London to Neath BL

13 October 1952

THINKING OF YOU DARLING BE BRILLIANT LOVE TEDDY

Meanwhile, he was busily completing the writing of two verse plays *The Great Bear, or Minette*, and *The King Is Dead*, the former a Celtic fantasy, the latter a historical tragedy. Verse was a dramatic form popularized by such writers as T.S. Eliot and Christopher Fry and Osborne was under the impression that he might be good at it, although both Pamela and Creighton vehemently disagreed, urging him to write prose instead. *The Great Bear* seems to have been left incomplete, but he had high hopes of *The King is Dead*, the script of which now appears to be lost. It was probably something in the style of John Webster, one of the Jacobean authors Osborne was reading avidly and whose language he very much admired. However, when he asked Pamela to read it, her response, 'characteristically bland, and possibly affectionate,' was that it was 'dull and boring.'[12] This casual dismissal of his efforts—as he saw it—was a crushing blow, yet the expression, 'dull and boring,' or 'd and b,' remained a lifelong shorthand between them to be applied to anything they considered to be not worth their while.

On 23 January 1953, Pamela appeared as Miss Limbird in a live BBC television broadcast of Pinero's *The Gay Lord Quex*, and at the end of June secured the small role of Elsie in *Nadia*, a new play by C. W. Blanchard at the Gateway Theatre Club in Notting Hill. A comedy set in the aftermath of war in which the eponymous character, assumed to be one of Europe's displaced people, turns out to be an international spy, it failed to impress a critic from *The Stage*, who nevertheless conceded that Pamela had 'one emotional scene.'[13] Her husband, meanwhile, appeared briefly in a minor part in an episode of the *Robin Hood* television series.

A month later, though, Pamela struck lucky, and signed a contract for a year's season as leading lady at Derby Playhouse at £10 a week (equivalent to £260 in 2018). Although this was the average salary for the time, for a young repertory actor it was well-paid and represented considerable security. She had secured the job by the usual procedure at the time of dispatching a written application accompanied by a head-and-shoulders studio portrait photograph. As it was then conventional for young people to look like second editions of their parents, Pamela's photograph, taken in profile with her head tilted towards the camera, makes her appear to contemporary eyes much older that her actual age of twenty-two. Her hair is swept up above a heart-shaped face and an off-the-shoulders evening dress. Her make-up emphasizes carefully-shaped eyebrows and prominent cheekbones, while her demurely bland expression and the three-band pearl choker at her neck make her look as if she might easily blend in among the guests in the country house drama prevalent in the West End, which is probably exactly the effect she intended. Here was an actress aiming for the upstairs, rather than the downstairs roles. In his own audition pictures, Osborne also looked slightly older than his years, his corduroy jackets, shirt and tie making him appear an enquiring, thoughtful young man, perhaps well-cast as a curate or a young schoolmaster at a private school. Only their awkward, assumed maturity, the freshness of their faces and the innocent alertness in their eyes proclaim the youth of a couple not yet twenty-five.

Having waved Pamela off at St Pancras, Osborne left for Frinton, a genteel resort on the Essex coast, to join the Summer Theatre company in a season of detective thrillers and comedies, competition for the local golf course and the often-windswept beach. Arriving in Derby, Pamela moved into a room on the top floor of 32 Ashbourne Road, a two-story house near the city centre owned by Dorothy Maltby, a single woman in her sixties who let rooms to actors. Her largest initial expenditure would not have been the rent but a complete set of evening wear, as actors were expected to provide their own. Women incurred additional expense as it was hoped they would not wear the same dress too many times in a season.

The Playhouse turned out to be a converted Baptist Church Hall on the corner of Sacheverel Street. 'It has a splendid stage and comfortable auditorium,' enthused a reporter for a local paper at its opening a year earlier, 'freedom to smoke, and to stroll and chat at intervals, and the blessed privilege of a licensed bar – luxury to the patient enthusiasts who had awaited them so long.'[14] The acting company included Charles Workman, an 'admirable master of character parts' and the son of Charles H. Workman, once a long-standing member of the D'Oyly Carte Opera Company and famed for having played the principal baritone roles in Gilbert and Sullivan.[15] Leslie Twelvetrees, the tall, bespectacled, forty-four-year-old director, also had a musical father and additionally imposing social credentials. Clyde Twelvetrees was for many years' principal cellist of the Hallé Orchestra, while his his wife, Leslie's mother, had the distinction of her name being recorded in James Joyce's *Ulysses*. Having accompanied her husband on tour with the orchestra to Ireland, Joyce had noticed her name in a newspaper and appropriated it for one of the guests at a fictional Dublin wedding. Leslie's wife was the former Hon. Catherine Simonne du Parocq, the daughter of a recently ennobled law lord and a former member of the Permanent Court of Arbitration at The Hague. Since her marriage, Pamela's relationship with her parents was icy, if not entirely Arctic, but if they learned of Leslie's connections then their apprehensions over her career might, for the moment, have been allayed by a touch of class. Immediately upon her arrival, Pamela began rehearsals as Paula, 'a woman with a past' and the leading part in Pinero's *The Second Mrs. Tanqueray*, one of the most perennial of the late nineteenth century 'social problem' plays. By the following Monday, according to the *Derby Evening Telegraph* critic, she had whipped up 'a performance of consummate artistry.'[16]

During the 1953-54 season, Pamela was scheduled to appear in forty-five back-to-back weekly productions. Once finished with *The Second Mrs. Tanqueray*, therefore, she sped through *Master of Arts*, a public school comedy by William Douglas Home in which she tried 'very hard to look like Matron.'[17] This was followed by *The Shop at Sly Corner*, a preposterous crime drama by Edward Percy, a Conservative politician turned dramatist, in which 'given nothing to do by the author except stand around waiting to give a hand in the general disentangling at the end', she was merely 'decoratively unemployed.'[18] While being decorative in the evenings, by day she was rehearsing the following week's offering, *French for Love*, a supposedly *risqué* comedy by Marguerite Steen, an immensely prolific historical novelist, and Derek Patmore, a Balkan war correspondent and advisor on interior décor, in which a young man learns the arts of love from his prospective father-in-law's mistress. This at least gave her a run at her French accent. Then it was on to *Duet for Two Hands*.

The Frinton summer season over, Osborne settled down at Caithness Road to collaborate with Creighton on *Personal Enemy*, the play that Creighton had begun during the summer. That it was set in the United States and dealt with one family's experience of the Korean War, which had ended in July, and roped in the continuing threat of Senator McCarthy's anti-Communist witch-hunts, Creighton explained, meant that it was both topical and daringly radical, exactly the kind of play Osborne should be writing. In September, he notified his wife of their progress, while at the same time sending her a precious loaf of rationed bread:

JO to PL ms letter n/a n/d BL

[53 Caithness Road, 23 or 30 September 1953]
Wednesday

Nutty beautiful,

Putting the last touches to the play today and trying desperately to get the ms off to the typist tomorrow, so can't write as much as I should like today. However, will do better tomorrow.

Saw this one and only loaf in the health shop today, so thought I'd send it to you. It's not much to send, I know, but I thought it might help out. It is an ALLINSON loaf. I don't know what it's like. I'll try and get some more to supplement Mouse's baking.

Hope 'French for Love' went off well, and 'Duet' isn't too much hell. Don't let the guest producer drive you too hard. Remember, he's got fuck all to do all the evening. You've got a performance and a lot of lines to learn.

Wish I could come and see you—now, today. Everything is so utterly different and alien without you. Must go to the post with this.

Love you

B

This letter is undated, although alternative Wednesday dates might be judged depending upon whether Pamela was appearing in *Duet for Love* and rehearsing *Duet for Two Hands,* or whether the former play had closed and she was appearing in the latter. Allinson bakery was founded by Thomas Allinson, a London doctor who promoted the health-giving properties of wholemeal bread. *Duet for Two Hands* by Mary Hayley Bell, a Jekyll-and-Hyde drama in which a young poet whose hands are amputated following an accident and who, through a surgical error, gains those of a deceased murderer, had been a huge West End success. 'The fact that a play is nonsense does not prevent it from being good theatre,' observed the critic James Agate when it opened in 1945.[19] This was evidently true, as it became a repertory fixture for both professionals and amateurs for many years. Osborne knew it well, having played the leading role of Stephen Cass for the Saga Repertory Group in Devon. The guest producer was Neil Gibson, an actor and director with whom Pamela would later work at High Wycombe.

At the beginning of November, she appeared as Lydia Languish, the wealthy young heiress in *The Rivals,* Sheridan's sharp comedy of love and money in eighteenth century Bath. The *Derby Evening Telegraph* critic, however, was startled to discover that she had inexplicably transformed Lydia's 'girlish whims' into 'the mature tantrums of a Coward heroine after an evening at the bottle.'[20] Perhaps in recompense, Pamela would play a 'particularly restrained' Mrs Malaprop in the same play at Colchester thirty-seven years later.[21] Immediately after *The Rivals,* she took on her first demanding leading role, that of Hester Collyer in *The Deep Blue Sea*, Terence Rattigan's powerful 1952 portrait of a post-war nation adapting itself uncertainly to the peace. One of the great leading roles of the decade, Hester is a judge's wife trapped in a loveless marriage, driven to defying the social taboos of the time in a final attempt at finding the emotional fulfilment she craves. Abandoning the security and comfort of her home, she moves in with Freddie Page, a young fighter pilot both unable to adapt to the peace and, it transpires, give her the love and support she thought within her grasp. Midlands critics celebrated Pamela's performance as 'brilliant,' and a 'tour de force.'[22] Osborne, who visited his wife when he could, travelled up from London to see it and agreed. Distant echoes of the play would later be heard in his own *Look Back in Anger*.

Pamela was exhausted but invigorated. She was popular, appreciated by critics and audiences, valued as an asset by Twelvetrees and the management, and in *The Deep Blue Sea* had set out her credentials as a potentially outstanding actress. She had also encountered one of the Playhouse's more flamboyant, invigorating and abrasive characters. This was John Dexter, an occasional actor and gossipy homosexual who would later become a director at the Royal Court Theatre and subsequently in the West End, at the National Theatre and in New York. Both

Osborne and Pamela would come to know him well and work with him regularly in the future.

PL to JO ms letter n/d Texas

The flat
Tuesday
[8 December 1953]

Darling much-missed one—

Must scribble these few lines to you before I get too sleepy and 'drop off.' It's the middle of the afternoon, but God, I'm tired almost to hysteria, silly isn't it? It seems to have crept up on me over the last two weeks, I think I must have got terribly tired during 'The Deep Blue Sea' and haven't quite got over it yet. And now, of course, you're not here and that makes things worse. We've had an awful read-through of that play 'The Gift' which I think is a shocker, though most of the people in it seem to think it's quite good. B. Dodd was more than usually insufferable this morning. I'm going to say something to Leslie about him.

'The Ghost Train' was a RIOT last night—the [audience] screamed with laughter and fell about, biggest laughs we've had all season. We nearly all corpsed, and miracle of miracles, I was the only one who got through it without a prompt! The set was perfect and the train effect got terrific rounds—it's the most utterly convincing and realistic effect of any kind that I've ever heard, smoke hissing through the set windows, pistons going, the LOT!

All of which helped to take my mind off the morning and that other train that chugged you out of my ken and back to London. It must not be long before we see each other again. Being apart for Christmas is bad enough. We're having Esmé for Christmas, she'd be very lonely on her own in her room, and besides she can contribute some food—will see what I can rake up to send you and Mouse, darling, wish I could send you lots of wonderful things and that we had a bonus for Christmas. Heigh-ho.

Dexter dropped into the theatre yesterday with 'Such Darling Dodos' which I yearn to start, but I've so much in the first act of 'The Gift' I must get down to that first—which I will do forthwith before I decline into a doze.

Darling, could you send me back my keys of this flat, pliss [sic]? I keep on bringing Miss Matlby to the front door to let me in when I'm not with the others.

Don't think I can get over to Nottingham for the Wanamaker play tomorrow afternoon at all—the matinée starts at 2.30 and we shall surely not finish rehearsal till 1.30, so I couldn't make it in time, it takes nearly an hour on the bus.

I expect I shall hear from you tomorrow, <u>must</u> get up early and catch the early bus to rehearsal.

Ooooh – I <u>was</u> cold in bed last night, aggers and mizzers. However, I think I'm 'preggers' again, so I've got at least a <u>baby</u> bear to keep me warm. Lovings and blessings, sweetheart—

Nutty

Brian Dodd was leading man and Esmé Easterbrook an actress in the Playhouse company. *The Ghost Train,* a repertory perennial by the actor and writer Arnold Ridley, is a 1923 comedy of suspense involving a group of passengers stranded overnight at a remote railway station. It demands special effects unusual at the time to create a sufficiently impressive illusion of the spectral train thundering past. *The Gift,* by Mary Lumsden, a success in 1952, is a now-forgotten family melodrama in which a woman bestows the 'gift' of a corneal transplant upon her ailing sister. *Such Darling Dodos* is a collection of short stories of post-war life by the then much-talked about Angus Wilson. Osborne, who read it on Pamela's recommendation, also admired it. Sam Wanamaker was a leading American actor and director and briefly a member of the Communist Party, who had moved to England in order to elude the attentions of the House Un-American Activities Committee. The play referred to is *The Big Knife* by Clifford Odets, then touring to the Theatre Royal, Nottingham, before opening at the Duke of York's Theatre in London early in 1954. Wanamaker both directed and played the leading role of Charlie Castle, a disillusioned movie star who exchanges idealism for material success. Osborne and Creighton were preparing to send Wanamaker a copy of *Personal Enemy* in the hope that he might be able to secure a production.

'Aggers and mizzers' is Pamela's private slang for 'agonies and miseries'. The letter above may be the one Osborne recalls in *A Better Class of Person,* in which in reference to Pamela's assertion that she might be pregnant again, he writes: 'Her letter, as always, was hard to interpret. She might have been displeased or dismayed.

The Penny Royal pills may have been put to work again but the crisis stole away as it had come'.[23] Once again, the inference is that little was said at the time.

As well as appearing in *The Gift* ('Pamela Lane, as we have learned to expect, makes us sit up and take notice',) she was rehearsing for the Christmas show, the rather unseasonal *It's a Boy*, a 1931 farce by Austin Melford, in which a man who is about to be married is confronted by a younger man claiming to be his long-lost illegitimate son and threatening blackmail.[24] Osborne, meanwhile was back at the Blythe Road Post Office.

PL to JO ms letter n/d Texas

Playhouse

Monday morning

[shortly before Christmas 1953]

Darling, darling one—

I was just leaving the flat to make an excursion to the Health Store to get you a few Christmas buns when there was a 'phone call from the ASM to say an extra rehearsal has been called for this morning and now there's no time to go on my bun-hunt after all. So instead—herewith £1 for you both to buy a few things: I only wish it could be more, but I just haven't got it to send you, otherwise I would with all my heart. Darling, I'm afraid presents are out unless someone sends me money for Christmas, but I'll send you something after Christmas, even if it's only an ounce of tobacco.

I do hope the Post Office work isn't taking it out of you—I know you haven't been able to afford much to eat lately, and I'm worried in case you're finding the hours too long and the work too heavy. I only hope it isn't as cold in London as it is here—there's a freezing wind blowing from the fells and it's agonizingly cold. Whatever happens, we must do something so that the fucking Post Office thing doesn't come up again next Christmas. I know we say this each year, but I feel something's <u>bound</u> to turn up this year—we've reached rock bottom already and can't go any further, so it must be UP from now on.

Now enough of this depression and gloom and dread—I shall be thinking of you both all over Christmas: put present worries aside for the time being and have a good break while Christmas lasts—and <u>use this present on things for yourselves</u> and don't put it towards any fucking debts.

Now I must scramble off to rehearsal.

I don't suppose another letter will reach you before Christmas even if I write it—mail is taking 3 or 4 days to reach us from London at the moment.

Bless you, bless you, my darling. Christmas is not going to be anything like the same without you.

I love you,

Nutty

JO to PL telegram BL

23 December 1953

ECSTATIC THANKS FOR CASH BLESS YOU SO BLEAK WITHOUT YOU LOVE TEDDY

There appears to have been a difficulty with the Caithness Road telephone; possibly an unpaid, or late-paid bill, or perhaps bad weather affecting overhead cables had resulted in the telephone being 'off.' However, Osborne was able to report that by Christmas Day, all was well and telephone was 'on' again:

PL to JO ms letter n/d Texas

Playhouse
Sunday
[2 January 1954]

Darling one—

So wonderful to know that the telephone's back, and that I could speak to you on Christmas night. The only thing was that Miss Maltby was in the kitchen just off the room where I was phoning and it always rather cramps my style when there's someone else around while I'm ringing you. Wanted to say all sorts of idiotic things and couldn't really.

We've only just cleaned up the last bit of the Christmas debris and will soon be inundated with more, we're having about six people in tonight for cider and mince pies, and as they're the kind of people that usually stick around till 5 the next morning, I daresay all today's clearing up will have been in vain. However…

Esmé came in for Christmas Day and we had a rather nice candlelight dinner in the evening with a bottle of wine. The others had turkey and I had a rather luscious [vegetable] roast with all the trimmings (kept wondering what you and Mouse were having). The success of the meal turned out to be a massive trifle which I'd made which was really very good.

Darling, it's sweet of you to offer to send me a Christmas present, but please don't, 'cos Nutty hasn't sent you or Mouse anything, and I shall feel just <u>AWFUL</u>. Mouse's box of soap was a lovely surprise, bless him, and his mother sent a lovely striped scarf.

Two very good houses yesterday for 'It's a Boy' and we were all rather tight through both performances so the ad libbing that went on was nobody's business.

Thank God the Post Office is over for you now. I hated the thought of your having to do it. Although we've worked over Christmas up here, it wasn't anything like the reluctant drudgery of getting up at dawn and delivering smelly parcels to revolting Poles. The past two days have gone terribly quickly and soon back to work again, and 'Prunella'—we're working all day every day next week on it, and it's so unexciting. Donald has a Stratford audition in London on Wednesday, and will have to feign gastric 'flu to get away for the day. If he gets it, he'll leave here, of course, or rather I should think so, as he doesn't seem quite sure whether to take the Stratford walk-ons or not. Well if he does, there'll be a job going here, and I'll snap in straight away and try to get you up here, which would be wonderful.

Reading at the moment in the few bits of spare time—Angus Wilson's 'Such Darling Dodos' and a delightful book by T. H. White called 'The Sword in the Stone'. What are you reading?

Isn't the New Zealand train disaster horrifying? Biggest thing since the Tay Bridge.

God, the post will be going out in ten minutes, so I must scramble out to the box and then back to make a few mince pies and sausage rolls for the carnivores tonight.

Oh, darling, I *did* miss you more than ever over Christmas, such a <u>cold</u> end to the festivities climbing into an empty bearless bed—I've got your beautiful Christmas Bear Card on my mantelpiece, and, my beautiful furry lover, it <u>shall</u> be the last Christmas apart if I can help it.

Now to the post—expect I shall hear from you tomorrow with the Salisbury accounts.

Please go on missing me and loving me, darling,

Yours, Nutty.

Prunella is a whimsical turn-of-the-century love story by Laurence Housman and Harley Granville-Barker, the latter an actor, playwright and director of productions at the Royal Court Theatre between 1904 and 1907, where he premiered several plays by Shaw. Donald Pickering was a twenty-year-old Playhouse actor who also rented a room at 32 Ashbourne Road, and who later became a familiar television actor, often playing suave figures of authority. He was about to audition at the Shakespeare Memorial Theatre at Stratford-upon-Avon, then directed by the actor Anthony Quayle. *The Sword in the Stone*, a novel by T. H. White, tells the story of the boyhood of King Arthur. The 'New Zealand train disaster' refers to the tragedy of the Wellington-Auckland night express that crossed the Tangiwai Bridge over the Whangaehu River just after 10 pm on 24 December 1953. Severely weakened by storms and battered by flooding, the bridge collapsed, resulting in the train plunging into the water, where over 150 of the 285 passengers lost their lives. Such was the scale of the disaster, and that most passengers were returning to their homes for Christmas, that the story became international news. Pamela compares this to a similar incident over seventy years earlier, on 28 December 1879, when the Tay Bridge in Scotland, destabilized by furious winds, collapsed beneath the weight of a Wormit—Dundee train. On that occasion, over seventy passengers were drowned in the River Tay.

The Salisbury accounts refers to money—perhaps her share dividend payments—that she had agreed to invest in Claridge's, a hotel in Salisbury managed by Jack Grove, Osborne's uncle and the younger brother of Nellie Beatrice. According to relatives, Jack was 'a bit woman mad' and had fallen out with the rest of the family.[25]

'The trouble arose when he sent his mother some caste [sic] off clothing belonging to some actress,' explained a relative[26]. Jack had been involved in several business schemes, all of which had spectacularly failed. As a precaution against a similar fate, Osborne and Pamela retained the right to inspect the six-monthly accounts from Claridge's, which, when they eventually surfaced, made for dispiriting reading. And yet: 'I never heard him complain,' wrote Osborne, 'about any of his unsupportive wives and mistresses or his failing circumstances.'[27] Jack was due to go into hospital in January for an operation.

Although Pamela may not have bought her husband a present, he sent her a pair of evening gloves, vital accessories for her stage wardrobe. Equally importantly for her, though, was the opportunity created by Donald Pickering's successful audition at Stratford for Osborne to join her in Derby.

PL to JO ms letter n/a n/d Texas

Sunday evening
[3 January 1954]

Darling Treasure-bear—

The evening gloves are <u>perfect</u>, darling, what a lovely present, and bless you for being so extravagant—I was badly in need of a pair. I've been borrowing them up till now. Thank you, thank you, and for your lovely note with them. I wanted to get this letter off to you today, but had to go out to lunch and have only just got back, so it won't get to you till Tuesday.

I rang Salisbury yesterday as I hadn't heard anything for some time and was anxious about it. Jack wasn't out of hospital when I rang, but Chips told me he's expected back today. Apparently, it was more serious than I thought— he's had an operation for phlebitis, and there was a chance that he might never be able to use his hand again, which with him of course, would have been disastrous, but the operation turned out to be a success. I should think that Chips would be a hindrance to anyone's convalescence—she regaled me with a full account of her tribulations on the 'phone yesterday, and told me very little about Jack, do drop him a line, darling, if you haven't already done so. I know he'd like to hear from you.

Now, as there really is nothing else new to tell you, I'll get on to the important thing—you remember I told you Donald had a Stratford audition in town on Wednesday? He must have made a very good impression because Kaye Flangan has 'phoned him to offer him a season at Stratford to play Paris in 'Romeo and Juliet' and to play as cast in the other plays. He had a charming letter of confirmation from Quayle yesterday. Anyway, this means that they'll want a juvenile to rehearse on February 1st (Don starts rehearsing at Stratford then). I can't say anything to Leslie about you yet, because nobody knows about Don till he gives in his notice on Friday (so please, if you see Penrose before then, don't say anything about the Stratford job—in fact, don't tell anyone. We don't want all the juveniles on John P's books putting themselves up for the job). After Friday, of course, it doesn't matter if Penrose knows. Darling, I'm rather taking it for granted that you want to come here—I wish it could be as leading man, but as Dodd's beginning very slightly to decline in Leslie's estimation, there's always the chance that you might take over some of his parts later on, especially as you're not a juvenile type anyway. Here I am talking about the thing as a fait accompli and I don't know whether you feel free to come here, not even if Leslie and the management will agree to a joint engagement, though I should think they would. Anyway, let me know bear's thought and feelings, and perhaps it wouldn't do any harm to look up Her Majesty in Rupert Street in the meantime.

It would be so wonderful if you could come up here, darling, at the moment the season seems to stretch ahead interminably, 'specially as it's just been extended to July 17th, but with you here, everything would be different: at least you know that you wouldn't be coming into squalid digs up here, and we really could put by a bit of money with the two of us working. Wish there was a job here for Mouse, too, but at least if he feels lonely in town (if you do come here) he can come and stay here whenever he likes.

This is the first Bright Event of the New Year. I think it's an omen of more to come—Christ knows, we deserve them. Keep wondering what you're sick with, and how you're feeling—poor, poor fur mustn't be without her when he's off his buns. [sic]

Fuck it, I've run out of paper now and can't find any more. 'Prunella' tomorrow—it's going to be abysmal, I should think, about half the cast are fucking amateurs. I shall start invoking clauses in the contract soon—Esmé and I have the smallest parts while some amateurs go right through the play. However, I'm getting a name for awkward mutiny anyway by now. I love you so, my dear

NUTTY

The reason why it would have been 'disastrous' for the accident-prone Jack to lose the use of a hand was that some years previously he had lost part of an arm after being run over by an ice-cream van in Southend. 'Chips' was the latest in a line of girlfriends. Kaye Flanagan was a long-standing and influential member of staff at the Stratford Memorial Theatre.

In spite of Pamela's scorn for some of the Derby repertoire and her fellow actors, the Playhouse had the reputation of having an acting company 'of considerable strength' presenting 'plays of content and quality,' and any opportunity of joining would have attracted considerable interest, while the city's proximity to Stratford, Birmingham and London significantly increased the possibility of an actor being noticed by producers and agents.[28] John Penrose was an actor turned actors' and playwrights' agent, operating from 40 Rupert Street in Soho, London. He was one of several to whom Osborne had applied for work and to whom he and Creighton sent copies of *Personal Enemy*. Others included Robert Allen, a theatre manager employed by the Harry Hanson Company, and Robert Birch, an impresario who ran several provincial theatres. They also tried Jimmy Wax, who later became Harold Pinter's agent. They had no luck, but Sam Wanamaker, also a recipient, was sufficiently intrigued to invite Osborne and Creighton to meet him in London.

Meanwhile, in snow-bound Derby, Pamela had begun to fret over her lack of money.

PL to JO ms letter n/d Texas

Playhouse
Derby
Thursday
[7 January 1954]

My darling—

So sorry not to have written for a few days—I've been rather low with money-depression and there's been quite a bit of study for this fucking

Armitage Owen play next week—there is nothing to do but send it up all the time. I haven't been sending you any crits [newspaper critical reviews] lately, darling, because I'm being what is called 'rested' with 'also ran' parts which don't even warrant criticism. My last good part was 'The Deep Blue Sea' and I'm seething with frustration—if the Heather Stannard part in 'The Bad Samaritan' isn't up to much, I shall go to Leslie and demand a good lead.

Anyway, darling—thanks ever so for your letter yesterday—yes, I did get the letter from the Bank, darling, sorry I forgot to tell you. It was only to remind me of an overdraft of [£]11/10[s], [equivalent to £290 in 2018] but as it's been existing for about nine months now, I don't suppose they're really hoping to get it.

I spoke to Leslie about your coming here last night. Unfortunately, the news had got back to him (about Donald's leaving, I mean) from someone outside, we think it must have been a certain Derby actress called Jean Morley, who is going to Stratford too, and as people had apparently been ringing up the Box Office to know if it was true, he knew a few days before we intended. I didn't know he knew until last night, but went straight to him then and boosted old Bears to high heaven. He's worked very quickly, because he's already got five men down on his list for the job, but he agreed that it would be nice (understatement!) for me if you could come here. The only thing is that he doesn't know anything about you, so he asked me if you would write him and tell him about yourself and what you've done. An awful bore, I know, but apparently necessary, as the applications go before the committee. Yes, of course, you're quite right, it would be to rehearse on the 26th January.

(Forgive this writing, darling, it's so bloody cold I can hardly hold a pen. The snow's quite thick up here).

So glad, so very glad to know that you're being so active, darling, and seeing so many people (I do hope you're not sick any more). Is the Robert Allen of Ralph Birch Prods the Camberwell Robert Allen? Bastard.

Bully for Bears, going to see Wanamaker—I can just imagine the interview! If nothing else happened to the play, it's good to know that he'll read it in 6 weeks' time. Meanwhile, I'm keeping my fingers crossed for you with Wax. Do let me know as soon as anything happens. The phone call you had sounded hopeful from what you said but I understand why you don't want to say anymore at the moment.

 Much as I want you to come here, I shall kick myself if you come up here or go to any rep job just as things start happening to 'Personal Enemy' though of course it would only take a fortnight to get out of the job, and Mouse at least would be in town. But I have a vague feeling that irony will out and everything will start happening at once.

 I shall do my level best to put away some money for 'Spotlight', though at the moment I can barely scrape through each week. This may sound absurd to you, as I'm earning £10 [equivalent to £260 in 2018] a week, but the gas and electricity bills for this flat will be in soon and I haven't put anything by for them yet. Rent and food come to £3.10 a week, commission 10/-, I send you £3, sometimes £4 a week, laundry averages 5/- and I have a £1 a week debt to pay off and hardly a week goes by without some small item of clothes having to be bought. The £1 a week debt I started paying off last week—I didn't tell you about it before, darling, as there didn't seem any point in mentioning it, but I had to get an evening dress a couple of months back for one of the shows, as I'd already worn my purple one in another show, and couldn't produce another dress as well. I had to borrow £10 from Joe Selby to get it, which I agreed to begin paying back on January 1st.

 Oh, I didn't mean to make such a dirge out of the money business, darling. I'm terribly sorry: while I'm still on the subject of money, though—I'm a wee bit worried about my zircon ring, which I pawned with 'Horns' in Hammersmith Road last July. The pledge expires on the 17th of this month, and as it's fairly valuable and I don't want it to slip out of possession, I thought I'd ask you if there's any way in which I can renew the pledge or anything. I couldn't possibly raise £4 to redeem it before the 17th of course. Sorry to worry you with it, but I don't know what I can do to keep it safe.

 God, it's 6.30 and I must drop a line to Jack before I go down to the theatre.

I love you, my darling, and don't be put out by my 'aggers and mizzers'.

All my love, Nutty.

Love to Mouse.

The Armitage Owen play was *Life Begins at Fifty*, a 1952 domestic comedy brazenly guaranteed to be 'a winner all the way.'[29] Owen was the lessee of the Grand Theatre in Llandudno, from where he launched his winners not at London but straight at the regional repertory circuit. It was followed by William Douglas Home's cumbersome moral drama, *The Bad Samaritan*, first produced in London in 1953. Perhaps Pamela 'went to Leslie' as instead of playing June, the role originated by Heather Stannard, she appeared as Veronica, first played by Virginia McKenna. Not that it sounds particularly rewarding, as her principal function was to be seduced by a young man intent upon taking Holy Orders in the Anglican Church, an act that flings him into such a turmoil of guilt that he instantly deserts her and embraces Catholicism and celibacy. Yet Pamela, pronounced the *Derby Evening Telegraph*, succeeded in being 'deeply moving.'[30]

Spotlight, founded in 1927, is a directory of actors, each entry consisting of a photograph, a résumé and a note of proficiency in languages and accents, and widely used by casting agents. Wanamaker told Osborne and Creighton that he thought *Personal Enemy* had its merits but producers might consider it too anti-American. Leslie Twelvetrees agreed to Osborne joining the Playhouse company, probably a result of his acquiescing to the wishes of a valuable but disconcertingly restless leading lady than being impressed by Osborne's distinctly patchy curriculum vitae.

He arrived in Derby over the weekend of 16-17 January (earlier than Pamela had previously anticipated) and moved into her rooms at Ashbourne Road. As soon as he had unpacked, he began a week of rehearsals for his first appearance as Valentine, a dentist, in Bernard Shaw's *You Never Can Tell*. He was playing opposite Pamela as Gloria Clandon, a young woman with whom Valentine falls in love. Gloria, however, a zealous social reformer and a Shavian 'new woman', scorns such emotional involvement as irrational and irrelevant. Almost immediately, Osborne realized how humiliatingly ironic both the title of the play and their characters were.

In his memoirs, he records that a week after his arrival he suffered an excruciating toothache, whereupon he visited a dentist recommended by Pamela, who extracted two teeth. That night, 25 January, he strode on to the stage for his first performance as Valentine. Soon afterwards—Osborne is imprecise on the chronology of events, but it is likely to have been sooner than later—he learned that the dentist who had treated him was 'not only rich [and] a member of the

Theatre Committee, but, before going to work on my teeth, had, it seemed, made me the town cuckold.'[31] This was a tremendous shock. Having squirmed beneath the drill of a dentist subsequently revealed as his wife's lover, Osborne had become the injured party in every sense.

Joe (Joseph S) Selby, the man who had lent Pamela the money for an evening dress, was a forty-eight-year-old dental surgeon who had returned to practice in Derby following war service with the Army Dental Corps and attaining the rank of Major. A veteran of *Ding Dong*, an amateur concert party group giving annual performances in which he sang comic songs and did conjuring tricks, he was a well-known local figure and a leading light of the Rotary Club. He had also been a moving force in the creation of the Playhouse in 1952, and remained an influential member of the theatre's governing board. Although the name of the dentist with whom Pamela had had an affair was never divulged, Osborne developed a virulent animosity towards Selby that continued long after he, Osborne, left the Midlands for London. Emotionally vulnerable at the best of times, the revelation that he had been betrayed—as he saw it—by his wife instantly soured their relationship and reawakened Osborne's conviction, seldom dormant for long, that the potential for treachery lurked in every encounter he made.

At twenty-four years old, Osborne took a broadly romantic view of marriage in that it entailed a total commitment between two people. Perhaps, and this would have been conventional at the time, he might have expected to be the dominant partner, whether or not he actually formulated this in words. He was stunned to discover that as far as Pamela was concerned, he had been under a misapprehension. Moreover, his wife seemed curiously ambivalent about the incident and bafflingly indifferent to the predicament in which she had placed him. From the moment he met her, he had thought there was something elusive about her, a quality he could not define, but this had been part of her attraction. Now, however, she seemed an entirely different woman than the one he thought he knew. 'Ever since I have been up here she seems to have deliberately gone out of her way to treat me like a stranger,' he complained to Creighton.[32] The events of his first week at Derby sparked not only Osborne's dislike of Selby, but also his lifelong animosity of Shaw, a dramatist he later denounced as 'the most fraudulent, inept writer of Victorian melodrama ever to gull a timid critic or fool a dull public'.[33]

A retaliatory but half-hearted and brief affair of his own with an actress in the company failed to have the impact on Pamela he hoped. He was further disconcerted to discover that Pamela, despite being frequently exhausted by rehearsing and performing each day, and despite her complaints about the company and the plays in which she was appearing, was otherwise becoming more assertively self-confident each week. As 'Pamela's star rose like the weekly returns,' it seemed ever more certain that a successful career lay ahead of her and above all else, she was determined upon it.[34] Her growing professional assurance and apparent lack of sympathy towards him added to Osborne's sense of isolation, defeat and resentment of all things Derby.

It is impossible to know what precisely prompted Pamela's infidelity, just as it is impossible to know what explanation she offered her husband and what was said about his own vengeful little dalliance. Nothing of this is referred to directly in the surviving correspondence between them. On the face of it, the letters she wrote to her husband in London tell one story and her actions in Derby another. It appeared that in the short time she had been in the Midlands and perhaps even before, she had concluded that her marriage, entered upon as a great adventure, had been a mistake in that the kind of commitment that Osborne, and perhaps both of them, wanted was incompatible with her ambition. In the light of later events, it may also be that she had realized that an emotional and sexual partnership with a man might be incompatible with her nature. What Osborne perceived as Pamela's almost wilful disinterest, a quality he later transferred to Alison in *Look Back in Anger*, was not cruelty, as he thought, but an attempt to conceal emotional struggles within herself that confusion and reticence prevented her from attempting to explain. Perhaps at this stage she did not fully comprehend her doubts and was convinced her husband would not either. Perhaps this is why Alison in *Look Back in Anger* appears a rather unresolved character.

In the fraught atmosphere of their claustrophobic room at Ashbourne Road, the Osbornes began to quarrel furiously, occasionally violent arguments triggered ostensibly by her anxiety over money or by his accusing her of casting him aside. For much of the time, Pamela was in a state of considerable anxiety, exacerbating her propensity to asthma, a condition which in any case was hardly alleviated by their both being smokers. Convinced there were conspiracies against him afoot,

Osborne rifled through her belongings while she was out, searching for evidence of intrigues and treacheries. Sundays, when there were no performances and little to do apart from the laundry and learning their lines for the next morning's rehearsals, marked the lowest point of their week. It forms the opening of *Look Back in Anger*:

> JIMMY: God, how I hate Sundays! It's always so depressing, always the same... Always the same ritual. Reading the papers, drinking tea, ironing. A few more hours, and another week gone. Our youth is slipping away... [35]

Osborne's 'Sunday evening glooms' were sometimes alleviated by visits from John Dexter, whose presence would be transformed into Webster, one of *Look Back in Anger's* many offstage characters.[36]

> JIMMY: I like him. He's got bite, edge, drive—
>
> ALISON: Enthusiasm.
>
> JIMMY: You've got it. When he comes here, I begin to feel exhilarated... [37]

More often, however, Sundays were spent in the company of John Rees, a fellow Playhouse actor two years their elder and who had a room below the Osbornes at Ashbourne Road. A shrewd, stocky Welshman, 'a kind, gentle person who would do anything for anyone,' Rees had spent part of his childhood in an orphanage after his father had been convicted of bigamy and sentenced to prison.[38] He had subsequently trained as a boxer during National Service and later graduated from the Central School of Speech and Drama. Rees could not help being aware of the difficulties between Osborne and Pamela even if he did not quite understand them, yet he enjoyed their company and did his best to diffuse the tension between them. He became the model for Cliff in *Look Back in Anger* who mediates between the Porters, banters with Jimmy and flirts gently with Alison. At other times, Osborne reverted to his Bridgwater practice of relaying furious reports of his predicament to Anthony Creighton in London.

JO to Anthony Creighton ms letters Texas

[various dates January-May 1954]

'... I don't know what is the matter with Pam, I simply don't... I can only feel that everything between us is over... old Osborne's just in a panic at the moment...'

'....Oh she is a different girl from the one we waved off at St Pancras last year. I detest being with her, particularly alone...'

'... I told her on Monday night that she was a FAKE and a PHONEY— about the biggest.'

'... Every time I look at Pam, for instance, I could beat her head in... I just want to see the back of her—for good...'

'... her own words: "You see, when I'm working, you must understand I'm a different person..."'

'... We go to and return from the theatre separately, sleep separately. The only misfortune is that we are obliged to share the same roof and meal table...'

'.... That pusillanimous, sycophantic, sniveling, phlegmish yokel, that cow has gone off to London for the weekend... you've no idea how sinister it all is....'

'... I brought out that trump card I've kept all this time: the letter she wrote to Mummy all those months ago ("you may think I'm a bit of a flop as a person but at least I'm an actress, etc.") Was she shaken!.. I was enjoying every moment of it. She tried everything... But it was no use... A few more truths smashed home and it was a knock-out... a very real triumph for me'.

'... Only EIGHT more weeks to go... I can look forward quietly to the day when Pam is only something belonging to my past. I want a CLEAN SLATE...'

'...Pam will have at least £1000 (a family legacy) in her pocket in a few months' time, and I feel quite unscrupulous about trying to get my hands on at least some of it... Afterwards, when it suits me, she can go HANG...'

'... Now that things are clear-cut between Pam and myself, we are getting on better than we've done since I came up here... Two more weeks and Derby will be over... What a waste it has all been.'[39]

A resolution had been reached: things were 'clear cut.' Pamela was adamant: she needed time to be alone and think; besides, she was intent upon her career and had decided her independence was intrinsic to it. She and Osborne would separate. They had appeared in twenty-four plays together, including *The School for Husbands*, a Molière adaptation by the American playwright Frederick Jackson, in which they played husband and wife: 'Pamela Lane... self-possessed, shrewd and scheming', while 'John Rees and John Osborne are a quite happily-cast comedy team.'[40] In *Harvey*, a threadbare comedy by Mary Chase: 'Pamela Lane and John Osborne are excellent as social climbing relations,' and in *The Little Foxes*, a family drama by Lillian Hellman, Pamela Lane appeared 'the incarnation of ambition and greed,' while Osborne's 'obnoxious son' was 'particularly good.'[41] The season ended in the second week of July, the final production being *Nothing but the Truth*, a 1920 American comedy by Robert Montgomery in which a stockbroker accepts a bet to tell nothing but the truth for twenty-four hours. Despite having collected some reasonable reviews, Osborne was not offered a contract for the following year, and neither did he wish to prolong his stay. Pamela would return to Derby after the summer. Meanwhile, she 'went on holiday to Switzerland with the dentist' and Osborne took the train back to London alone.[42] She had left him a note, in much the same manner as Alison does Jimmy Porter:

JIMMY: *(Reading ALISON's letter.)* My dear, I must get away. I don't suppose you will understand, but please try. I need peace so desperately, and, at the moment, I am willing to sacrifice anything just for that. I don't know what's going to happen to us, I know you will be feeling wretched and bitter, but try to have patience. I shall always have a deep loving need of you.[43]

They were 'Pamela's own words as surely expressed as she had "dull and boring,"' recorded Osborne in his memoirs.[44]

The following two letters from Osborne to Pamela are difficult to date precisely. However, their content suggests they were written during the period of his leaving Derby for London. That neither is written on conventional notepaper suggests improvisation and perhaps hurry, or merely lethargy. The first is written on the reverse of a half-sheet of company notepaper headed: 'Building and Allied Trades Enquiry Bureau, London', the second on pages torn from the cheap exercise books of the kind Osborne used for his writing.

JO to PL ms letter n/a n/d BL

Thursday

Pam, my dear—

I just haven't the courage or strength to go through with it. I simply cannot bear the thought of any more pain again. Whatever else I feel, I am afraid. Call it cowardice, but there is nothing I can do about it. This whole business has made me feel so ill and unhappy. I can't write anymore. Try to forgive me

Johnny

JO to PL ms letter n/a n/d BL

It's nearly an hour since you went and I still can't move. But of course I must. I sit here looking around your room, seeing those very familiar things I have known for years, and I simply can't believe that this at last is really it—the unequivocal end, and no turning back. There are no uncertainties, no more vague dreams, not even the cruelty of hope. Someone—I forget who—said to love without hope was to love without fear. Anyway, as I say, sitting here, it seems impossible. Even now, I don't seem to be able to accept it. But of course, it <u>has </u>happened, it's time and it's inescapable. It's very stupid to feel stunned after all that has happened. Even so, it's not easy to write off nearly four years of one's life. But that is just what I must do, and I mustn't sit here writing to you. It's too late—there's nothing more to say. This is really goodbye then. I really did love you too much, didn't I?

Goodbye darling. Bless you.

B

■ ■ ■

Osborne returned to his old room at Caithness Road. Back in Derby in September, and apparently undaunted by the collapse of her marriage, Pamela 'swept through' *Waters of the Moon*, N. C. Hunter's 1951 drama in which a group of elderly guests and the glamorous, cosmopolitan Lancasters are trapped by a blizzard in a Dartmoor hotel, giving 'what must be one of her best Playhouse performances of this or any other season'.[45] Watching her a week later in the title role of *Hedda Gabler*, a local critic observed that 'from her first entrance, one feels that here is a dangerous woman indeed. The voice is curt, the eyes flash menacingly, and gradually the portrait is built up bit by bit, until in the end one feels a sort of sympathy for the wretched Hedda.' [46]

Meanwhile, in London, 'I didn't feel liberated from Pamela,' Osborne reflected later. 'The prospect of divorce never entered my sometimes wild projections for the future as [in October] I moped around the Welsh villages on an Arts Council tour of *Pygmalion*... I began to feel her all-too-accountable desertion would resolve itself... Pamela would come back. Our marriage would not be a closed incident, nor an open—or, worse, healed—wound. I felt oddly content to wait on events...'[47] By the end of the year, this simple strategy of inertia had resulted in a fragile truce. Osborne and Pamela, now minus the dentist, began writing again and occasionally seeing each other both in Derby and in London. He applied for his usual seasonal work at the Blythe Road Post Office and set aside part of his unemployment benefit to pay for a ticket to another production of *Hedda Gabler*. From an exchange of letters in late 1954, only one from Osborne appears to survive.

JO to PL ms letter n/a n/d BL

Friday 4.30
[Caithness Road]
[late 1954]

My darling,

This has got to be a short one, as I seem to have mis-timed everything to-day. Tony and I are going to see 'Hedda Gabler' tonight, 10/6 seats! Our 'lodger' is taking us. I'm hoping we can get him to take us to 'Separate Tables' sometime.

Thanks so much for your letter. Everything is a little unreal. I almost wonder if you were really here on Monday. I'm having a few problems to face at present, which I shan't explain now, but it's not making life easier.

I've heard no word from the Post Office yet. However, I suppose it will be alright. We haven't let the room either. Ah well! As usual, I am meeting trouble half-way.

It's so strange writing to you after so long—twelve months almost since I wrote a letter. God, what a hateful year it's been. You can beat 1954 from my calendar.

Unemployment seems to be yelling from the housetops, and I wonder if I'll ever work again. I don't think the future could be more vague, could it? In every way. One makes decisions, resolutions, but have they any meaning in and relation to circumstances? I don't know.

Although Monday was such a wonderful repeal, it was also rather a terrible let-down. I think we were left somewhere up in nowhere-in-particular and one feels frustrated and at a loss. One is like a general, suddenly presented with an army, but no idea where the battle is—or, perhaps, what it is about.

But when I am with you again it surely must run itself out. [sic]

For the first time I've managed some work. God, what torture it is! It never leaves me alone. I have sat down most of the day sometimes, and at the end of it feel utterly spent, without having achieved anything. However, I have begun to make a little progress this week—after such a long time—and that has helped to make me feel easier.

Forgive me if I seem to be burning at a rather low power. Seven days stand between us still, and I feel a little strung up still.

I do hope Johnny is alright. How absurdly difficult it all is! With each appearance of hope, new barriers seem to arise. Wish to God I were coming up tomorrow. I am very much in need of you and your help and inspiration particularly.

I've almost forgotten what it's like to sleep with you. Till later, darling

My love

Johnny

According to the pocket diary note he reproduced in *A Better Class of Person,* Osborne saw *Hedda Gabler* at the Lyric Hammersmith on 4 May 1955. However, this is a misattribution, as the production, which opened 8 September 1954, transferred to the Westminster Theatre in November and in the new year played at two other venues in London before a European tour, closed at the end of March. On 4 May 1955, Peter Brook's production of Anouilh's *The Lark* was running at the Lyric, Hammersmith. As Osborne also complains of 'no word from the Post Office yet,' it therefore seems likely the above letter was written in the autumn of 1954, despite his assertion that 'it's been twelve months almost since I wrote a letter.' Perhaps he discounted or merely overlooked his two previous, undated letters.

The important point, though, is that this production of *Hedda Gabler* was the first time that Osborne saw George Devine. The future founder and artistic director of the English Stage Company, was playing 'an endearing, innocent-seeming Tesman' opposite Peggy Ashcroft's Hedda.[48] According to Irving Wardle, Devine's biographer, the production, which had arrived from Dublin where it had been genially greeted as an uproarious comedy, was 'carefully situated between the world of mutton-chop whiskers and the present.'[49] Yet the Derby and the Lyric productions alerted Osborne to a play to which he would later return, preparing his own adaptation for Jill Bennett in 1972. *Separate Tables* by Terence Rattigan, starring Eric Portman and Margaret Leighton, opened at the St James's Theatre on 22 September 1954. The Caithness Road 'lodger' was 'a youngish Pakistani businessman' who had been searching for cheap temporary accommodation in the area.[50] The 'work' was *Epitaph for George Dillon,* which Osborne was writing in collaboration with Creighton. For the identity of 'Johnny,' see the 1955 letters below.

However, Osborne at least remained both intensely vulnerable and volatile. A Christmas or New Year gift of money from Pamela, or a previous incident for which the gift was intended as a peace offering, so affronted him that he fired off a scathing response:

JO to PL ms letter n/a Texas

13 February 1955

My dear,

Thank you very much for the two pounds. A sudden inexplicable fortune out of the blue—I am very grateful indeed.

I say 'inexplicable' because there was no note with the money, and I cannot understand what moved you to send it to me. It's difficult to believe concern for me to be your nature. On the other hand, expensive gestures of contempt are hardly in your line either. However, I suppose I should give up trying to work out your weird emotional processes and content myself with the fact that you were good and kind enough to send me this money.

Perhaps you were irritated because, although I was not too proud to accept your money, I wasn't able to return your rather cosy expression of fraternity in your last letter. Make no mistake—for the money I am sincerely grateful. But your setting up as a kind of emotional soup kitchen for your grubby husband is something else. If you had any understanding or real—and not simulated—feelings at all, you must know what a bitter taste this kind of watery gruel must have. What you may put in a registered envelope and send to me, I accept but spare me the cheesy charity of your feelings. Again, thank you for the money.

[Unsigned]

His spirits were lifted by a cheery wave from the nomadic Patrick Desmond, the director of *The Devil Inside Him*, who had pitched his managerial tent at the Harrogate Grand Opera House and agreed to produce *Personal Enemy*. Rehearsals began on 22 February before opening for a week's run on 1 March. Osborne and Creighton went up for the first night, and again for the closing night on Saturday, after which the play disappeared from view until after Osborne's death. In Derby, meanwhile, Pamela gave 'a finely subdued performance' as Catherine in Rattigan's *The Winslow Boy*, followed by one of 'well sustained vigour,' as Amanda Wingfield in Tennessee Williams' *The Glass Menagerie*; 'completely at home in the role of a mother to whom frustration has become life itself.'[51] Twenty-five years later, she would play the same part at Leicester.

At the end of March, Osborne sent *Epitaph for George Dillon* to Desmond, who promptly sent it back, presumably in the belief that he could afford to lose money on two plays by Osborne but no more. At the same time, Pamela left Ashbourne Road, where John Rees continued to live, and moved to an attic flat with sloping ceilings and a dormer window in a three-story Georgian terrace at 114 Green Lane. It was at this flat, within the sound of the bells of St Peter's Church and which Osborne visited, that they agreed their separation would be permanent. It was also the flat that he later confirmed to Pamela that he 'had in mind' as the setting of the play he was beginning to write and which within a few weeks would become *Look Back in Anger*.[52] During the first week of June, he typed the final draft on the portable Olympia typewriter that Pamela had given him as a wedding present.

Osborne subsequently and understandably denied that *Look Back in Anger* was autobiographical. 'No, not a bit,' he told an interviewer soon after the play opened. 'It's so easy to overpersonalise these things.'[53] Yet if the play's attic flat setting is reminiscent of Green Lane, the evidence of Osborne's letters to Creighton and of the notebooks Osborne kept at the time reveals that the entire basis of the play and much of the characterization, events and atmosphere are transposed directly from his experiences of life at Ashbourne Road. Jimmy Porter is clearly a self-portrait of his creator, while Pamela is the origin of Alison, a character who embodies the suppressed feelings, the confusion and the tension that Osborne perceived in his wife but probably could not as yet fully explain. Alison's background, though, her father being a civil servant recently returned from India, is markedly different from Pamela's and through this Osborne adds to their marital struggle a patina of the class conflict so many young people were talking about at the time. However, Colonel Redfern, to whom Jimmy is generally sympathetic, voices sentiments that might not have been wholly dissimilar from William Lane's, while Jimmy's resentment of Alison's mother accurately reflects Osborne's hostility towards Mrs Lane. The character of Helena is possibly almost entirely fictional, although the circumstances of her arrival and her intervening on the side of Alison have their origins in an occasion on which an actress friend of Pamela's came to stay for a few days. She was also a Roman Catholic, and seems to have upheld a moral code that provoked Osborne's hostility. Finally, almost thirty years later, Osborne privately acknowledged the autobiographical basis of the play to Pamela, describing it as 'a pretty anguished love letter,' although one that was 'put together with some skill, I hope.'[54]

Yet 'writing and finishing *Look Back in Anger* presented no purge or lasting comfort', he reflected, 'no justification by either faith or works.'[55] He remained dejected and bewildered that the 'unique prize' he had carried away from Bridgwater had in turn carried herself away from him. At the same time, he conceded that by writing it, 'I had addressed myself to events in some way…'[56] And it appears that writing the play had indeed diluted Osborne's bitterness, as he made a further attempt at a reconciliation with Pamela that summer. She too made conciliatory overtures. A hesitant line was drawn beneath the immediate past.

■ ■ ■

The following two letters are clearly consecutive, and although undated, were written before June 1955, when Osborne left Caithness Road. Their tentative reconciliation was taken a significant further. While the identity of 'Johnny' in the late 1954 letter above and the following two letters is not stated, circumstantial evidence suggests this to be John Rees, who, like Osborne, was known as 'Johnny' by his friends in Derby.

Little is known of the precise association between Osborne, Pamela and Rees, other than at Ashbourne Road they were close friends and grateful for each other's company. However, the following letters suggest that Rees, although a largely benevolent influence and looked upon kindly by Osborne and Pamela, was also a complicating and potentially destructive presence in their lives. The letters suggest that the erotic undertow to the protective, tactile quality of the affection between Cliff and Alison and the resentment this provokes in Jimmy in *Look Back in Anger* may not be entirely fictional. 'I wouldn't be at all surprised if John had had an affair with Pamela,' reflected one of Rees's relatives many years later. 'He was probably cheering her up after Mr O's departure.'[57] As there is no clear evidence of an affair, this is speculation, but it may be that by moving from Ashbourne Road to Green Lane, Pamela not only sought a fresh beginning away from the room she had shared with Osborne and which had been the scene of so much unhappiness, but also wanted to distance herself from Rees as well.

Another visit by Pamela to Caithness Road produced a letter from Osborne in which it seems that he and Pamela had embarked upon an intensive bout of mutual soul-searching of which Johnny had been a principal feature. A crisis appears to have been confronted and a resolution agreed.

JO to PL ms letter n/ d BL

Caithness [Road] Tue 3.30
[1955]

My darling,

I do hope you got back alright. You must have been worn out my dear. I wonder if your back is any better. I got home last night dazed and utterly exhausted. Fortunately, Mouse was in bed and asleep, so I was able to be on my own and without any cross-examinations. I looked in the mirror and was horrified. I know I was looking rather a weed, but I hadn't realized just how much. What a mess! Hope to God I look a little better when you see me again. After the mirror shock I staggered into bed, but didn't get to sleep for some time. Perhaps it was the up-roar of the day abetted by the brandy—anyway, my mind and blood were racing as soon as I lay down. I heard four o'clock strike, and thought of you in Derby.

When I woke up I felt tired but refreshed and got up almost as soon as Mouse had gone.

Today everything is different. It is an utterly different day to the ones that have made up these past weeks. Perhaps neither of us seem to be really much better off. What is going to happen I don't know. I can't tell whether we shall be able to make each other happy or not. At least one can be cer-tain that failure can never be quite so bitter the second time. All I know is that when I was with you again yesterday, not even the strength of all my old fears could prevent me wanting you all over again, and today I am feel-ing more peace than I have known for many, many months.

You know me as I am. You should know what the difficulties will be like, and whether you can overcome them. In fact, your picture of the future must be clearer than my own. After all, you have my case history in front of you. I have not changed. We will not be together on the old terms and I shall not know what to expect. With you, you will know, very largely, what life with me is likely to be like.

Please don't misunderstand me and think me patronizing or pompous but I think you may have grown up in these last months. Don't be insulted. Tony has always said that you have never grown up, and the day came when I had to say that he was right. Learning to love is not easy.

You certainly grasped the difference between Johnny's love and mine. You made the point that if he were a Christian Scientist and you detested CS or—worse—were indifferent, he wouldn't mind as long as you slept with him regularly and observed outward loyalties. I think this attitude of mine has always baffled you. Perhaps I can explain it a little. I used to think: 'How can I expect any truth or honesty in her feelings for me when she has no deep, violent convictions of her own about anything?' With her feelings it is all 'done by mirrors', reflecting other peoples' passions and opinions—rather dimly. In my case, she has merely held the mirror closer, and the image is even muddier. Those old existentialists speak a lot of truth when they point out that our lives seem dominated by choice—with a capital C. In everything, we are implicated in a matter of choice—even in love we have to make up our minds which side of the barricades we are to be.

You used to make the mistake—I believe—of identifying deep passionate need with weakness, and despising it. Certainly I wanted strength—your strength. That is not to say that I had none of my own. Weakness is not the only quality that seeks out the strength of another. Surely, there is a kind of burning virility of mind that sees something as powerful as itself, strength seeking out strength. The strongest creatures of this world are the loneliest… The voice that cries out does not have to be a weakling's. It may be that of the artist, the visionary.

Perhaps this is claiming a lot for myself. I am only trying to clear away an old stumbling block.

All I know at the moment is that the sickness in my heart has gone. Yesterday, I was on my own. Today, it seems I have a wife. I can't wait to be with you again. I thought I might come up on the evening of Saturday week, and stay three or four days.

Oh, darling, I hope you are alright. I hope you are coping with poor Johnny. I must go now. Mouse will be home soon. I'll write later. I do love you.

Johnny

PL to JO ms letter n/d Texas

Playhouse
Derby
Wednesday 6pm
[1955]

My darling,

I don't know what to write. What can I say?

I've just come back to my digs after walking through the town for two hours, scarcely knowing where I was going. I've hardly slept at all since I saw you. I'm so tired, but intensely happy.

Thank you for your letter, my darling—I keep reading it over and over again to prove to myself that all this has actually happened. I should like to write back to you about love, strength and weakness—there is so much I want to say to you and hear from you. But I can't write it now—my mind has been full of it for two nights and days—I can't sort it out properly today from the tangle of joy. I don't think I look any different from usual, except perhaps rather haggard—the delight hangs heavily right through my body and makes me look rather depressed if anything, I think. Oh. God, I'm impatient to see you again. I long for you. By Saturday week this hot mist will have cleared from my head and I shall be able to talk to you soundly, clearly, with a quieter love, about ourselves, where this will lead and what we are to do. Just now I am almost mad with relief at getting way from the death of the last months and having reached—at last—the centre of your love.

I have told Johnny—I think he knew something had happened as soon as he saw me. He cried for an hour and I could think of nothing to say, nothing adequate at least. He says he is glad and relieved for my sake. He's staying away from me more now, trying to absorb it all, I think, and there is nothing I can do but leave him on his own for as few days until I can get near him again. He was so glad to see me back I could hardly tell him what had happened, but it was the only thing to do. He said today that he was looking forward so much to seeing you again. He meant it of course, he's too sincere to make sacrificial gestures.

I can't write any more, I'm almost too tired to hold the pen. I can't wait to hear from you, darling. I love you so.

Pam

These appear to be the last letters sent to and from Caithness Road. On 1 June 1955, Osborne and Creighton moved to the *Egret*, an old Rhine barge moored on the River Thames near Chiswick, and which Creighton had bought with a legacy from his mother who had died the previous year. With no acting work in the offing and hoping to make some money while sending *Look Back in Anger* to Patrick Desmond and a list of other agents, Osborne 'gambled on horses.'[58] But not only did he draw a blank with the agents, the horses failed him as well. In August, however, his luck turned and the play was accepted by George Devine at the English Stage Company and scheduled for production at the Royal Court Theatre in Sloane Square the following May.

By December, Osborne had completed another play, *Love in a Myth*, later reworked as the basis for *The World of Paul Slickey* and having completed his Christmas stint at the Blythe Road Post Office, confidently opened his 1956 pocket diary on 1 January with the terse entry of '16 [weeks] to *Look Back in Anger*.'[59] Pamela, meanwhile, was still at Derby, her performance in the title role of Shaw's *Candida*, acclaimed as 'magnificent... a truly Shavian performance that puts to flights our latent impatience with the author's sermonizing.'[60] Thirteen years later, she would play the same role in Wales.

The spring and summer of 1956 produced decisive changes for both of them. On the weekend of 24-25 March, Osborne visited Pamela in Derby. She was appearing in Bridget Boland's *The Prisoner*, a 1954 drama set in an unnamed Eastern European country released from Nazi domination only to be suppressed by Communist rule and in which she played what was then termed the love interest. As she and Osborne walked away from the theatre on Saturday evening, Pamela, exasperated after months of unbroken work, remarked bitterly that she hoped the theatre would burn down.[61] Within a few days, and to their astonishment, her wish was granted.

On Monday, 26 March, Pamela opened in *The Wick and the Wax* by Alex Deane Wilson, a prominent local Liberal and 'for many years closely associated with Mr. L. du Garde Peach and his famous village theatre at Great Hucklow' in the Peak District.[62] The play was set in 'the living room of the vicarage in the village of Black Gate' in 1665, five years after the Restoration of the Monarchy, and the stage was generously stuffed with props borrowed from most of Derby's antique shops.[63] Unfortunately, and because this was a world premiere, the *Manchester Guardian* had been induced to send a reviewer, who the next morning solemnly pronounced that the play 'did without, or failed to find, any effective theatrical device' whatsoever.[64] The following night, a fault in the theatre's 'frighteningly dangerous electrical system' of labyrinthine cables caused a blaze that reduced the Playhouse interior to ruins.[65] The company was forced to disperse. Charles Workman, the character actor, moved to Sheffield, while Leslie Twelvetrees, the director, became producer for the Penn-Ross Players at Redcar on the north Yorkshire coast, a resort 'where rep,' warned *The Stage*, 'has always had an uncertain existence.'[66]

■ ■ ■

A week after the blaze, on 2 April, the English Stage Company opened its inaugural season at the Royal Court, with George Devine's production of Angus Wilson's *The Mulberry Bush*, while Tony Richardson, Devine's assistant director, began rehearsals of *Look Back in Anger*. A week after that, Pamela joined the Repertory Company at the Theatre Royal, York, as leading actress. 'Pamela Lane has just arrived from the scene of the tragic fire at The Playhouse, Derby,' sympathized a programme note. 'Although she has had to leave many friends behind, we hope that it will not be long before she feels "at home" with us'.[67] Her York debut a week later was as Jane Pugh in *Clutterbuck*, a 1946 comedy by Benn Levy, the Labour Member of Parliament for Eton and Slough, a successful playwright and a scriptwriter for the Alfred Hitchcock film, *Blackmail*. A convoluted variation on Coward's *Private Lives*, the play involves the Pughs and the Pomfrets, married couples on board a luxury liner who encounter another couple, whereupon both husbands discover that the other has had a pre-marital affair with the third woman, while the wives discover they have had similar relationships with the third man. It was, sighed *The Sketch* on its original London run, 'extraordinary nonsense.'[68]

The Theatre Royal was a daunting building standing on the site of a medieval hospital and decked out with a Victorian Gothic frontage incorporating a line of archways from above which gazed stone likenesses of leading Shakespearian characters. Inside, there was a red plush auditorium, which, 'in the interests of public health,' advised a note printed in the programmes each week, was regularly 'disinfected with Jeyes Fluid.' In this rigorously hygienic environment the company specialized in comedies, occasionally but not too often interspersed by something more serious but not too demanding. The essential aspect of York's repertoire was that it was comprised of recent West End hits, the staggering success in London of the following week's show being loudly trumpeted in the programmes. 'Next week's play is a skilfully constructed farce which played to capacity houses for over a year at the Wyndham's Theatre, London,' represented the house seal of approval. Sometimes, a local warranty was added: the next week's 'recent comedy success hit London by storm and is guaranteed to provide a week of solid laughter for York.' So relentlessly enthusiastic were these signals that if the best that could be dredged up about a play was that 'when it was produced in London last July, the critics gave it a warm welcome,' it sounded a distinctly dodgy proposition.[69] The critic for the *Yorkshire Evening Press* was similarly eager to point out in his previews which London star had originated each successive leading role. This tactic simultaneously implied that the local actor was both understudying someone more luminous but was at the same time more than equal to the job. After she had been at the Theatre Royal for several weeks, the *Press* heralded Pamela's appearance in the title role of *Mrs Willie*, Alan Melville's 1955 family drama, with the proviso that: 'Pamela Lane's part at York Theatre Royal next week was written for Yvonne Arnaud.'[70]

Over the next eight months, Pamela would appear in twenty-eight plays, Denis Neill 'at the piano' at every performance. He must have been worn out. Most of the productions were supervised by Geoffrey Staines, the company's 'talented and energetic' director, and in most Pamela appeared opposite John Barrie, a sturdy character actor thirteen years her elder, or Dennis Spencer, both of whom went on to long careers in repertory and achieved some incidental television prominence in *Z Cars*, a long-running crime series.[71]

On 8 May, Pamela was four plays into the season and appearing as 'a visitor,' in fact an ex-mistress returning supposedly from the dead to confront her former lover and his 'charming' wife, in Philip Mackie's thriller, *The Whole Truth*.[72] That same evening, just over two hundred miles to the south, Pamela's estranged husband was sitting in the circle at the Royal Court Theatre, watching the world premiere of *Look Back in Anger*, a play that told the whole truth, at least as he saw it, of his own marriage. Mackie's play was reassuringly set in the Hampstead home of a film producer, Osborne's in the unfamiliar territory of an attic flat in the Midlands rented by a university graduate running a market sweet stall.

Over the following weeks, while Pamela appeared in 'riotous comedies' and 'topical thrillers,' judging the May Queen competition at New Earswick Folk Hall and being photographed for the local paper eating a bacon butty in support of the city's Bacon Week, *Look Back in Anger* and its creator became the talk if not of the town, then of London's cultural journalists and gossip columnists.[73] Having been nowhere, John Osborne was suddenly everywhere. Hardly a day passed without his name looming up in the national press. His photograph peered from the arts pages, the earnest discussions as to his credentials as a spokesman for post-war youth spilling over into the editorials. Headlines in the popular papers proclaimed him an Angry Young Man while reporters wanted to know why he lived on a houseboat and implored him to confide in them about his relationship with Mary Ure.

His voice leaked from the wireless and his face, once staring from audition photographs now appeared looking thoughtful on television. Everywhere he was profiled and interviewed and asked for his opinions on matters judged to be of national cultural importance. You would have had to have been quick, though, to actually catch *Look Back in Anger* itself, as it closed after a week to make way for the next productions in the English Stage Company's repertoire. On 4 June, it returned to the Royal Court for a short run. In York, Pamela had arranged to take a week off, and instead of appearing in John van Druten's 1925 drama, *Young Woodley,* a once-controversial piece in which a public schoolboy falls in love with his headmaster's wife, she travelled down to London to see *Look Back in Anger.*

She could not have avoided the reviews and some of the coverage, although Osborne himself had not told her much about the play. 'She said that before seeing it,' recalled Richard Digby Day, 'she knew something of it from friends, but seemingly no real detail.'[74] This was arguably both cowardly and callous on Osborne's part, and after the performance Pamela scurried across Sloane Square with very mixed feelings. While there are no verifiable contemporaneous accounts of her reaction, several unreliable and probably apocryphal stories survive as hearsay.[75] Many years later, though, Pamela herself recalled that although she had been 'thrilled' that Osborne had written a play that was making his name, 'something John and I always hoped might happen,' the 'personal side loomed rather large.'[76] Watching a lightly-fictionalised account of her own marriage on a public stage, and a version of herself being played by Mary Ure, her husband's new lover, had been deeply disconcerting. The very real possibility that both she and Osborne would be associated with Alison and Jimmy Porter placed her in an invidious position. Osborne might be making his name, but Pamela had yet to make hers. She was twenty-six, a successful repertory actress intending to make her own mark in London, and yet all she hoped for might be compromised if she were identified, as she may well have been, as the model for Alison, and 'that association haunt me down the years.'[77]

Fortunately, audiences and cultural commentators were looking the other way, preoccupied by the play as being emblematic of contemporary reality and by Jimmy Porter as a young, post-war Everyman, while the popular press was equally absorbed by Osborne's relationship with Mary Ure, two new stars in the making. Nobody worried about Osborne's wife, now back in York and rehearsing the following week's Repertory Company production of Michael Brett's 1955 comedy, *Lucky Strike*. Nobody enquired whether the actress playing the 'obstinate, feather-brained' and newly-widowed Mrs Salesby, attempting to run her late husband's factory despite the opposition of a roguish trade union leader, might in reality be the origin of Alison in *Look Back in Anger*. Instead, lamented *The Stage* critic, *Lucky Strike* was a play in which 'middle-class suburban snobbery pervades almost every line.'[78] It was not a charge that could be levelled against *Look Back in Anger*.

Pamela resolved to say little either in private or public about either the play or her husband, and maintained this position for much of her life. In 1959, a journalist preparing an article for *Woman's Own* on Mary Ure's love for Osborne ('women everywhere love a rebel. And in John Osborne, with his tall, romantic good looks and brilliant talent, they found a new idol'), recorded Pamela as saying that: 'I don't begrudge John his success. He deserves it. My ambition is to succeed on my own, not by trailing in his wake.'[79] She appears to have ducked further questions, if indeed there were any. Osborne himself, probably with an eye for the integrity of the play and his own reputation as much as Pamela's, always asserted that *Look Back in Anger* was a fiction, adding, rather unconvincingly, that Jimmy Porter was essentially a comic creation.

Within weeks, he had left Creighton and the *Egret* to move in with Mary at a house she had bought in Woodfall Street, off the King's Road not far from the Royal Court. With a success on his hands, a home in Chelsea and money pouring into his Post Office Saving Account, the days of weekly repertory and the Blythe Road Post Office were clearly over and he was on his way up in the world. Celebrated, discussed and denounced in equal measure, the Angry Young Man and his views about anything and everything to do with Britain and the times in which they lived continued to be very much in demand. The *Observer* petitioned him for his thoughts on the plays of Tennessee Williams, the *Evening Standard* wanted him to review films and television, while weekly magazines queued up for his opinions on almost anything from romantic love to his favourite food. Provocative, illuminating, infuriating, he seemed, at twenty-six-years old, irresponsibly talented.

He was flourishing socially as well. As one half of what the press was calling a Golden Couple, he was hobnobbing with such luminaries as Arthur Miller and his then wife, Marilyn Monroe, Laurence Olivier and Vivien Leigh, and Richard and Sybil Burton. 'There are going to be about three great English writers in this century,' Mary assured him, 'and you are one of them, my dearest.'[80] Many critics and columnists, while not going quite that far, agreed he was very much worth watching, although much less so when he appeared on the Royal Court stage as an actor. On 26 June, he could be seen alongside most of the *Look Back in Anger* cast in two roles in the fifth play of the English Stage Company season, Nigel Dennis's *Cards of Identity*, an eccentric comedy, observed Irving Wardle, that 'slashes away at psychiatrists with apparently complete enjoyment.'[81] Reviewers largely chose to overlook the Angry Young Man's performances as Dr Scavanger and Second Aunt.

And yet, 'I had no idea of what pain I might have inflicted on Pamela,' Osborne wrote later, 'and reflected on it daily.'[82] By now, they had decided to divorce. On 2 August, Osborne equipped himself with a lawyer, opting for Oscar Beuselinck, a pugnacious personality and a brilliant courtroom negotiator industriously building up an impressive show-business client list from offices in Ludgate Hill. In order to protect Osborne and Mary's public reputation, it was decided that he should sue Pamela for adultery, which was technically fair enough, if not quite gentlemanly. Anxious that the process should be as speedy as possible, Osborne travelled to York to see Pamela on Sunday 5 August. The previous evening, she had appeared as Harriet Sterling in the final performance of *Sweethearts and Wives*, a 'hearty Naval comedy' set in Malta and 'all very English indeed,' written by the husband and wife team of Gilbert and Margaret Hackforth-Jones, he being a submarine commander as well as a purveyor of patriotic marine adventures.[83] Pamela had spent much of Sunday learning her lines for *The Love Match*, an 'uproarious comedy' by Glenn Melvyn, first produced in 1953 and according to the programme notes, guaranteed to make audiences 'ache with laughter.'[84] Comedy, in the opinion of the *Yorkshire Evening Press*, was Pamela Lane's strongest card.

'She met me on the station platform and we went into the buffet,' Osborne remembered in his memoirs. 'I told her about Oscar and the technical complications of adultery. My train back to London was due in half an hour. I felt I could easily have persuaded her into an unresolving bed. She had heard that I was living with Mary and asked me if we intended to get married. I said, truthfully, that it was possible but not definite. She said nothing to this but told me that she had not been well lately, having had an abortion… She saw me on to the train and absent-mindedly kissed me goodbye.'[85]

While there is no evidence other than Osborne's autobiography to support either this or his two previous claims that Pamela had terminated a pregnancy, incidents he might easily have omitted, the fact that she approved what he had written before publication suggests that his recollection is correct.

JO to PL: ms letter on English Stage Company headed note-paper. BL

Tuesday
envelope postmarked 7 August 1956

My dear,

I must thank you for Sunday. You were so helpful and it wasn't easy for either of us. I am contacting my solicitor today, and I expect you'll be hearing from him fairly soon. I know that the sooner we get the whole affair behind us, the easier life will for both of us. And this way certainly seems the quickest and least painful. Don't forget to contact me at any time if you find any problems. But apart from that, if I can somehow help you in any way, I should like to very much.

I thought you seemed so very much older—I don't mean physically (I thought you looked as good as ever).

Obviously things haven't been easy for you, but I dare say you are richer for it. I only hope you will find the things you need. You may not have to wait so long—one spends one [sic] [one's life] making compromises. Above all, emotional ones. Bless you, my dear. Please remember: you are free and always welcome to come to me if you wish. Look after yourself.

My love

Johnny

Precisely what Osborne meant by writing that 'obviously things haven't been easy for you,' and his hope that 'you will find the things you need,' is not immediately clear as no other record remains of their meeting in York and what was said apart from Osborne's brief account in his autobiography and the letter above. He may simply have been referring to Pamela's thoughts about her career and acknowledging that, in the occupations they had chosen, 'compromises... Above all, emotional ones' were inevitable. Or he may have been referring to the misgivings and confusion Pamela had about her relationships with men, which she had attempted to confront in Derby, perhaps had attempted to explain to him then, and perhaps again later. Yet despite the emotional quandary in which they found themselves, his tone continued to be affectionate and reassuring.

JO to PL ts letter on English Stage Company headed notepaper BL

August 27th [1956]

Pam darling,

I rang up my solicitors today and found to my dismay they had done nothing. I expect you've been wondering when they would contact you. Anyway, you should hear this week now, and let's hope we can get it over as quickly and painlessly as possible. I think they will send a chap up to get a statement from you. Anyway, don't worry. It should be pretty straightforward. One thing—for heaven's sake don't let anyone else see these letters I'm writing to you. It wouldn't help either of us at all! Another thing—quite sincerely—I shouldn't feel any qualms about letting Joe Selby's head roll. I've heard a great many revealing things about this gentleman in the last couple of weeks. He seems quite a professional as far as this kind of thing is concerned. Don't forget to let me know when you change your address, so that I know where I can contact you. I am going to Spain next week, but will be back to rehearse the Brecht on the 17th. If you're in London, please give me a ring. Do hope you're well and life is being a little easier. Tony [Creighton] sends his love. He often talks about you. Look after yourself

Love

Johnny.

The allusion to Joe Selby implies there may have been a possibility of his being named in a divorce court, which would have compromised his position socially, professionally and as a member of on the Derby Playhouse board, who were then appealing for money to rebuild the theatre, which the owners, a family of tanners, had not insured. From the letter below, it appears that Selby had offered to pay, or contribute to, the costs of a divorce action.

Osborne was about to take a holiday in Spain with Mary Ure. They were due to return for rehearsals at the Royal Court on 17 September for *The Good Woman of Setzuan*, the company's first venture into the world of Bertolt Brecht, the German playwright who only a month previously, had died, aged fifty-eight, of a heart attack in East Berlin. His company, the Berliner Ensemble, visited the Palace Theatre between 27 August and 15 September, their repertoire of *Mother Courage*, *The Caucasian Chalk Circle* and *Trumpet and Drums*, Brecht's adaptation of Farquhar's *The Recruiting Officer*, causing huge interest. This was the first time the Ensemble had visited Britain and therefore the first opportunity for London audiences to see Brecht's dramatic techniques on stage.

JO to PL ts letter on English Stage Company headed notepaper n/d BL

Wednesday
[September 1956]

Pam darling,

Many thanks for your letter. Had a hell of a rush during the past 3 days, and haven't managed to 'phone my solicitor. I wonder if they've got on to you yet. I do hope so. Dexter says he spoke to Selby the other day, who was unusually curious about what I was doing now, where I was living, with whom, etc. I don't know whether you have told him what is happening but I do hope you are going to be firm about it. All I want is a quick, speedy, unsensational divorce. I don't want anything from Joe S. I am quite prepared to pay for the whole thing. If I don't press right ahead now, the legal position will be very difficult. Anyway, as we both agreed, we cannot be tied together in this way any longer. Don't forget, if you have any problems or complications, write to me. I'm just off to Spain, but will be back on the 17th.

The Berliner Ensemble is an unforgettable experience. Do see it if you can. I feel I shall never be quite the same again. Sat up all night Sat[urday] and Monday eating and drinking with some of the company—had a great time. I'm longing to get away. Feel utterly spent and exhausted. Tony [Creighton] is having quite a time in the south of France. He won't be back until the 11th I think. Look after yourself

Love

Johnny

JO to PL ms letter on English Stage Company headed notepaper ms n/d BL

Monday
[mid-September 1956]

Pam darling

So sorry about all these telegrams. It's just that I'm anxious to get all this business out of the way for both of us. It's rather hanging over my head at the moment. Can't understand why you didn't get the solicitors' letter. Perhaps he didn't send it—I think he's a bit of a horse.

Anyway, Tony [Creighton] tells me that you will be down here from Thursday to Monday. This seems the ideal opportunity to get it all done. All you need to do is go along to my solicitors' and make a statement and have it witnessed etc. I have made arrangements about this so will you please ring CIT 6392 and ask for MR BARWICK sometime on Thursday preferably in the morning. Then you can arrange a convenient appointment. He is expecting you to ring. All you have to do is explain who you are. I'll try and ring you myself on Thursday. Let me know if there's a theatre or something you'd like to see and maybe we could go on. Friday or Saturday if you're here.

I'm doing this during rehearsals, must go and post it quickly. Was very sorry to hear you hadn't been well. Not looking after yourself, I expect. You're very naughty. Hope to see you soon.

Love

Johnny

The rehearsals were for *The Good Woman of Sectzuan*. Having opened at the Theatre Royal, Brighton, on 15 October, the production transferred to the Royal Court Theatre on 31 October. Directed by George Devine, the production starred Peggy Ashcroft as Shen Te/Shui Ta, while Osborne appeared as Lin To, a peasant. The actors were additionally coached by Helene Weigel, Brecht's 'most official wife' according to Osborne, and Paul Dassau, a composer at the Berliner Ensemble, but 'it seemed to me as daunting as doing a Japanese Noh play in weekly rep,' Osborne reflected. 'To a couple of dozen willing but unequipped Anglo-Saxon actors, Brecht remained little more than the image of a bitten-off haircut and the sprout of a long cigar butt.'[86]

Osborne's concern about Pamela's health refers to her being taken ill during a performance of Agatha Christie's *Appointment with Death* on 8 September, when at a moment's notice the stage manager took over 'the large part of the redoubtable Lady Westholme.'[87] The following morning, it was announced that Pamela was suffering from 'gastric trouble and nervous exhaustion,' and that she would have 'a second check by her doctor today.'[88] In any event, and whatever her troubles, she was up and about by Monday, and giving 'a smooth and delightful performance' in the title role of *Mrs Willie*. This was a melodrama set in Sussex, to where Mrs Willie, the former queen of a Balkan state, has understandably withdrawn after her husband had been assassinated 'in bed—with a machine gun.'[89] It was written by Alan Melville, a former BBC war correspondent turned playwright and the chairman of *The Brains Trust*, a radio programme in which a panel of prominent personalities debated political and moral issues suggested by listeners.

Just over two months later, at the end of November, and having played Mrs Erlynne, the 'society beauty' in Wilde's *Lady Windermere's Fan*, a part in which, promised the previous week's programme, 'there is little doubt this talented actress will add to her laurels,' Pamela left the company.[90] After eight professionally successful months and immediately before the Christmas pantomime, her departure appears rather abrupt. No public announcement seems to have been made in the local press and it seems as though she did no stage or any other work for almost four months. Nor does there appear to be any surviving correspondence between her and Osborne since his letter in September until after their divorce the following in April. She dropped out of sight.

■ ■ ■

In January 1957, Osborne was at the Savoy Hotel, being presented with an *Evening Standard* award for the year's Most Promising British Dramatist. Two months later, in March, and in the less glamorous surrounds of the Intimate Theatre at High Wycombe, much the same claim was being made for Norman Andrews, in whose first play, *Gilt on the Gingerbread*, Pamela appeared in the leading role of Mrs Blackstone. The theatre had been recently converted from a swimming pool by 'four ex-servicemen with repertory experience,' and Pamela probably got the job because she knew Neil Gibson, the company's director, who had directed *Duet for Two Hands* at Derby.[91] The almost furtive launch of another new dramatist alerted a watchful critic for *The Stage*, but he arrived at the Intimate only to be disappointed. Whatever qualities Andrews might have, he judged, he was clearly unable to construct a credible plot. That the mysterious stranger who so beguiles 'the wealthy and attractive Mrs Roger Blackstone' that she 'invites him first to stay for dinner and then spend the night under her roof,' turned out merely to be a lonely but amiable salesman for an interior décor company, was, he thought, a considerable let-down.[92]

On 9 April, Osborne's divorce action against Pamela was heard at the Law Courts in the Strand. Yet, as he remembered it thirty-four years later: 'I had gone on vaguely hoping I would hear from her. Some vagueness of purpose or even forgetfulness would surely delay the final resort to the court... Surely Pamela, sphynx, muddler and arch-procrastinator could be relied upon to equivocate triumphantly at the last moment?'[93] Pamela, however, had not equivocated and neither was she in court. Instead, she was 'sustaining the romantic interest' in High Wycombe, appearing as Second Officer Mary ("Paddy") O'Brien in Basil Mason and John Elliott's *Little White Horses*, 'a charming little comedy' set in a Naval supply office and being given its first outing at the Intimate Theatre.[94] However, if there was ever a likelihood of Selby's name appearing both in court and in the press, it was averted. John Rees, in a Cliff-like gesture, had consented to Osborne and Pamela's proposal that he be cited by Osborne as co-respondent. Whether he technically qualified for the role, while possible, is unknown, yet he made his entrance, confirmed his testimony and made his exit. On cue, Osborne duly uttered his own lines, admitted his subsequent adultery with Mary Ure, and his petition was accordingly upheld.

■ ■ ■

The following day, 10 April, Osborne's divorce case was splashed across the newspapers. Although only her name and profession appeared, it turned out to be some of the most extensive national press coverage Pamela would ever have. That night, as she soldiered on sustaining the romantic interest as "Paddy" O'Brien in High Wycombe, *The Entertainer*, Osborne's second play for the English Stage Company, opened at the Royal Court. As Laurence Olivier, the nation's most lauded Shakespearian actor and Hollywood film star had decided to ally himself with the new and controversial to play Archie Rice, the down-at-heel music hall comedian, the occasion attracted huge interest. The audience's arrival was filmed by Independent Television News and Osborne was interviewed for the programme broadcast later that evening. Within a year, and due in great part to

Osborne, the English Stage company had established itself as a leading force in London theatre and its reputation was flourishing further afield both at home and abroad. Unfortunately, the same claim could not be made for The Intimate Theatre, which shrivelled into bankruptcy and closed its doors in the summer. The management blamed its demise not on the repertoire, mostly comprised of wobbly new comedies, nor its dwindling audiences, but on continued petrol rationing that prevented them getting to the theatre in the first place.

On 11 August, Osborne and Mary Ure married at Chelsea Register Office. By this time, Pamela had joined a repertory company both closer to London and on a more secure financial footing. *Look Back in Anger* had begun cropping up at the more adventurous regional repertory theatres, including the New Theatre at Bromley, where it was such a 'resounding success' that it had been hurriedly revived.[95] Successfully avoiding her former husband's play, Pamela joined the Bromley company as leading lady, stayed for a year and appeared in sixteen productions. Like York, Bromley specialized in energetically recycling recent West End successes. *Look Back in Anger* had been an audacious gamble, a brush with the contemporary youthful spirit that had luckily paid off. Otherwise, the management took few chances with their audiences, who knew exactly what they liked and expected to see it. In the year that Pamela was at the New, the sole concession to the more highbrow among the local audiences was Molière's *School for Wives*. Molière's plays had been popular at Derby too. They had the advantage of being regarded as classics, which struck a serious note while not being entirely serious in themselves, and provided a welcome showcase for the stage designer and wardrobe department. Audiences liked decorated sets and approved of a good display of costumes. The absence of both was just two of the aspects that made *Look Back in Anger* such a risky proposition.

Pamela made her Bromley debut in *Subway in the Sky*, a thriller by Ian Main set in Manhattan, in which she played Dinah Holland, 'a woman of character and strength,' noted a critic, 'if not great intelligence,' who shelters a US Army deserter accused of murder and treason.[96] The following week, she played Myra Hood, one of the glamour roles in *Mrs Gibbons' Boys*. This was an American comedy by Joseph Stein and Will Glickman in which the peaceful life of an elderly widow is disrupted by the arrival of her two convict sons and their girlfriends. Despite being forced to close only five nights after its Broadway premiere in 1949, the play had stealthily crossed the Atlantic to make an improbable second life for itself in British weekly rep. From having appeared in a play that a theatre had closed, Pamela advanced to a play that had actually closed a theatre. *It's the Geography that Counts,* a crime thriller by Raymond Bowers, had opened the previous year at the St James's Theatre in London's King Street and ran happily for several weeks until the theatre was declared unsafe and demolished. In the comparative security of Bromley, Pamela played Mercia, the woman holding the final piece of evidence in a case in which a man attempts to implicate his younger brother as the murderer of their wealthy mother. And so it went on.

The Entertainer, meanwhile, transferred from the Royal Court to the Palace Theatre, Olivier still playing Archie Rice and Osborne still of enormous interest to the cultural and gossip pages. Pamela, of no interest to either, went home to Bridgwater for Christmas. Her marriage had distressed her parents and the relationship between the Lanes and their headstrong daughter had been frosty since, but perhaps it was more with feelings of sympathy that they watched her open the letter from her solicitors, M. M. Rossfield and Company, of York, informing her that for their part in negotiating her divorce and consulting the Ace Detective Agency to investigate her estranged husband on her behalf, they demanded a fee of £6.

In February 1958, *The Entertainer* joined *Look Back in Anger* in New York, while *Epitaph for George Dillon,* its title abbreviated to *George Dillon,* transferred from the Royal Court to the West End. Osborne flew to New York, where he was again extensively interviewed and photographed, before taking a holiday in Paris and Jamaica. Pamela, meanwhile, was back at Bromley, wading her way through *The House by the Lake,* by Hugh Mills, a murder mystery and 'a decided success in its dogged way,' conceded Philip Hope-Wallace in *The Guardian,* which had opened at the Duke of York's Theatre the night after *Look Back in Anger* opened at the Royal Court.[97] A 'pseudo-psychological thriller with murder, emotional blackmail, hypnosis, hyoscine, threatened suicide and family skeletons among the ingredients,' explained *The Stage,* it featured a cast of characters who were all 'far from normal.'[98] The leading role of Janet, 'a hysterical wife who becomes an unwilling accessory after the fact,' had been played in London by a 'hand-wringing' Flora Robson.[99]

In Bromley, Pamela surely wrung her hands as well, for despite its limitations, the New Theatre took great pride in its leading ladies so authentically recreating West End star roles that it was only a matter of time before they graduated to becoming West End stars themselves. In September, Pamela became the fifth successive leading actress to leave Bromley for London. *A Day in the Life of...* a quirky comedy by Jack Popplewell, a prolific lyricist and light dramatist, opened in Nottingham before descending upon the Savoy Theatre in the Strand the following month. A play in which John Mallorie, a not particularly likeable music publisher, 'begins his day in the bed of his mistress and ends it in the bed next to his wife,' its principal, perhaps sole, attraction was that it provided a plum part for Alfred Marks, a heavily-built comic actor, or, as *The Guardian* put it, 'a very decided personality and a distinguishable figure'.[100] Pamela played Laura, Mallorie's forbearing but fitfully-faithful wife. On the First Night at the Savoy, a bouquet of flowers awaited her at the Stage Door:

JO to PL florists' card n/a n/d BL

[1958]

Very good luck for tonight darling.

All love

Johnny

It was Osborne's first communication with his former wife since their divorce, and one that might be seen as carefully neutral: simply a playwright wishing an actor good fortune, although there is no record of Osborne going along to see a performance. Marks dominated the reviews, but Pamela edged into the final paragraph of *The Guardian*'s notice as having 'made the best of [her] moments.'[101] *The Times*, however, failed to notice her at all. 'I'm glad to see they've said good things about her,' declared Osborne to the *Woman's Own* reporter interested in the lighter aspects of his relationship with Mary Ure. 'She's very talented—and very brave.'[102] This was rather different to the tone he used to Lynne Reid Banks, whom he met by chance one day outside the Royal Court. When she asked about Pamela, he replied dismissively: 'Oh, she's gone. I rubbed a few of her rough corners off for her.'[103]

Flimsy at it was, *A Day in the Life of...* had a respectable run, which was more that could be said for *The World of Paul Slickey*, Osborne's next venture, a musical satire on gossip columnists and the press which he both wrote and directed. After a turbulent national tour during which the cast, supported by urgent letters from audiences, appealed in vain that he re-write it, the show opened at the Palace Theatre on 5 May 1959, to mutinous audiences and disastrous reviews. Besieged by collapsing ticket sales, the producers surrendered and closed the production after seven weeks. But as the blazing comet of Osborne's professional reputation spectacularly faltered, his private life was providing rich pickings for the gossip columnists he had mocked on the stage. By now, his marriage to Mary Ure was collapsing, although they contrived to maintain an outward façade of contented domesticity. Osborne, however, had begun a relationship with Jocelyn Rickards, the costume designer for Tony Richardson's film version of *Look Back in Anger*, due to open in September. Taking advantage of Mary appearing as Desdemona in *Othello* at Stratford, Osborne escaped with Jocelyn to France and Capri, his holiday arrangements and a lurking photographer's surreptitious snap of the getaway couple avidly recorded by the popular press.

David Pelham, who had produced *The World of Paul Slickey*, chose a more cautious investment for his next project. *Last Day in Dreamland* and *A Glimpse of the Sea* was a double bill of plays by Willis Hall that opened at the Lyric Theatre, Hammersmith in November. It turned out to be another glimpse of Derby, as Charles Workman appeared in the first play as the owner of seaside amusement stall and Pamela in the second as the mistress of an adulterous husband, while John Dexter directed both. Like Osborne, Hall was a dramatist of the moment. His first play, *The Long and the Short and the Tall*, about a group of British soldiers in Malaya during World War II, had made a great impression when directed by Lindsay Anderson at the Royal Court Theatre a few months earlier, and he was busy working on a stage version of *Billy Liar*, Keith Waterhouse's novel about a northern undertaker's young clerk who invents alternative lives for himself. *A Glimpse of the Sea*, wrote Irving Wardle in the *Observer*, was 'a piece of *verismo* partly in the spirit of *The Long and the Short and the Tall* and partly under the aegis of Rattigan.'[104] It featured Tony, a married businessman and Jean, his lover, played by Pamela, being pursued to a down-at-heel seaside hotel by Penelope, Tony's wife, 'unusually cool and a great deal more malicious than she knew she could be,' remarked *The Times*.[105] In real life, Mary had chosen not to pursue the adulterous Osborne and Jocelyn abroad, but in retrospect it seems strangely prescient that Penelope, the character of the pursuing wife in *A Glimpse of the Sea,* not only has the same name as Osborne's third wife, Penelope Gilliatt, but was also played by Jill Bennett, the woman who in real life would supplant her.

As well as appearing at the Lyric, Pamela was rehearsing for Mrs Darling in *Peter Pan* at the Scala Theatre in Charlotte Street, off Tottenham Court Road. Stage adaptations of J. M. Barrie's story had been performed in London almost every year since 1904 and the show had evolved into a Scala tradition, the annual announcement of who would play that year's Peter causing a hectic popping of flashbulbs and breathless paragraphs in the press. In 1959, the production was even more anticipated than usual as the title role was played for the first time by the eighteen-year-old Julia Lockwood, the daughter of Margaret Lockwood, one of the most popular of British film stars and herself a previous and much-admired Peter. Julia Lockwood was also the star of *Please Turn Over*, a comedy film in which the hairdresser daughter of a respectable suburban accountant is revealed to have written *The Naked Truth*, a novel purportedly revealing the scandalous secret lives of her neighbours. Mr Darling and Captain Hook was played by Richard Wordsworth, a great-great-grandson of the poet and a tall, aquiline actor with a distinguished track record at the Old Vic and Stratford.

Peter Pan represented a considerable advance for Pamela. It presented her with an almost certain opportunity of being reviewed nationally in a good supporting role, and of staking a claim on a part to which if need be she could return for a few years yet. It also introduced her to actors such as Julia Lockwood and Richard Wordsworth who were well-known in the business and who became close friends.

The production opened on 18 December for an assault course of a season, twice-daily for six-weeks, and indeed secured Pamela her first review in *The Times*. 'Pamela Lane's Mrs Darling is by no means a sweet cypher,' judged the anonymous critic, 'but Richard Wordsworth's Mr Darling knows his place, which is in Nana's kennel, too well from the beginning.'[106] Yet critics agreed that it was an 'irreproachable' production, 'with all the colour, movement and spectacle that has delighted children for more than half a century.'[107] Coincidentally, it was directed by the same man who had directed Osborne's first two plays, none other than Patrick Desmond.

The 1960s

■ ■ ■

■ ■ ■

In retrospect, Osborne liked to depict Patrick Desmond as a slightly disreputable, even spivvish figure. In fact, the two men got on very well.[1] Certainly Desmond was an opportunist, yet like many directors of the time unattached to a repertory theatre—and he tried hard to become attached and sometimes succeeded—he had to be. It was his very proficiency, the sheer range of what he and many like him did that gave him an air of impermanence, if not inconsistency. He turned his hand to almost everything short of painting the scenery. As a 'play doctor,' he supplied emergency lines to plays in need of perking up, he masterminded hastily assembled national tours of thrillers, he agented, he acted, he managed and he directed almost anything, anywhere.

'He was my mentor,' remembered Julia Lockwood. 'My Svengali. He was very creative and hard-working, and wanted Peter Pan played much more straightforwardly than usual, almost as if a child might play it. I was tall, so he cast the other main parts tall; it was one of the reasons he chose Pamela and Richard Wordsworth. And I thought Richard was the best Captain Hook. He had a nonchalance that none of the others had.'[2] Despite *The Times* noting that his Mr Darling seemed to be too peremptorily consigned by his onstage wife to the dog kennel, Wordsworth and Pamela began an affair that lasted as long as the production. 'Everyone knew,' recalled Lockwood. 'They were enchanting together, and Pamela was enormously popular. Everyone fell in love with her. All the pirates. Even the Lost Boys.'[3]

Once the show closed at the Scala at the end of January 1960, the company set off for a three-month national tour. As this was the centenary of Barrie's birth, they opened in Scotland, playing Dundee, Glasgow, Aberdeen and Edinburgh before crossing the border and winding their way through the northern English cities. A few months earlier, Osborne had taken advantage of Mary Ure appearing at Stratford to escape to France with Jocelyn Rickards. Now, in February, after Mary left for New

York to appear opposite Vivien Leigh in a revival of Christopher Fry's *Duel of Angels*, he took the opportunity to leave Woodfall Street. Moving in with Jocelyn at her flat in Lower Belgrave Street in Belgravia, he quickly established what he described as 'a stable base of loyalty and affection.'[4] *Duel of Angels* was being shampooed and styled into a sleekly prestigious show. The costumes, Mary told him, were designed by Dior, who got prominent billing, which was far more than the wardrobe department of *Peter Pan* could ever envisage.

Despite Pamela's brief attachment to Richard Wordsworth and Osborne's newly found domestic tranquillity with Jocelyn Rickards, they established contact again as soon as he had unpacked his bags at Lower Belgrave Street. This seems to be their first exchange of letters since Osborne's bouquet had arrived at the Savoy Theatre stage door sixteen months previously at the end of 1958. The divorcees were getting on so well they were planning to spend a few days together when the *Peter Pan* tour arrived within easy reach of London.

JO to PL ms letter n/d BL

29 Lower Belgrave St

[March 1960]

Pam darling,

I shall try to come up to Coventry, but I'm not yet certain whether I shall be able to. However, I shall certainly come to Brighton for most of the week. I don't know the best arrangement for our accommodation, or what you may have already fixed. Anyway, unless you can think of something better, I suggest the following: I shall book a double room at the ROYAL ALBION for April 10th in my own name, and you can book a single room in your name. I think this is the easiest and most convenient. (Naturally, I shall pay as I know you wouldn't have gone to all the expense yourself.) Can you do this right away. Please let me know. Do hope you're well. Longing to see you.

Love

Johnny

PL to JO ms letter n/d Texas

Opera House
Manchester
28th March [1960]

Darling—

Brighton would be better than Coventry, as we do matinees every day at C. But I rang the Royal Albion and can't get a single room for that week, because it's Easter. Can you suggest something else?

The other thing is—we don't play the Monday in Brighton, so I shall travel down from London on the Tuesday morning, the 12th. I don't know where to suggest we stay—but will leave it to you to let me know what you decide.

Are you feeling good and working well?

I shall see you soon.

Love

Pam

JO to PL ms letter n/a BL

29. 3. 60

Darling,

It's difficult, isn't it? I'd forgotten all about Easter. I've actually booked a single suite for myself at the Royal Albion from Sunday to Thursday. I think it would be a mistake to cancel that now, as I've tried all the other hotels in Brighton. I suggest therefore that you fix up something for yourself independently and we'll try and make do. Only, make it for the Sunday, as I'd like to get away, and I can take you down at the same time. I'm off again to Paris now, trying to set up a deal for 'Taste of Honey'. But I'll be back by the weekend. Please ring me (SLO 4944) any time early next week. Do hope you're alright.

See you soon

Love

John

Osborne and Tony Richardson were co-directors of Woodfall Film Productions, the company that had produced the film of *Look Back in Anger* and was then making *The Entertainer*. The film version of *A Taste of Honey*, Shelagh Delaney's play which had premiered at the Theatre Royal, Stratford East, in 1958, would be their third project. Additional funds were secured from Bryanston, a consortium of sixteen investors and a subsidiary of British Lion. The film was released in 1961.

The Royal Albion, one of several white-painted Regency hotels on the seafront, occupies a prime position opposite Brighton Pier. Ever since the day trips he had taken with Nellie Beatrice, and since he had lived there with Stella Linden while writing *The Devil Inside Him* in 1949, Osborne had loved the bracing, fish-and-chips atmosphere of Brighton. Even though the town was infamous as a destination for illicitly amorous weekends, hotels that prided themselves on their good standing frowned at unmarried couples—including, presumably, those recently divorced—suspected of occupying the same room. Osborne's management of their accommodation requirements suggests he too considered a certain propriety to be necessary, at least in the hotel register. That week, he saw *Peter Pan* and he may, as he walked along the seafront, have thought that he was doing sufficiently well to reward himself with one of his favourite things in Brighton: a good fish lunch. He had emerged more or less unscathed from *The World of Paul Slickey* the previous year, *Look Back in Anger* was generating healthy royalty cheques from Britain and from abroad, films were being made, the Royal Court was anxious for a new play and he was putting the final touches to *A Subject of Scandal and Concern*, his first television play. Starring Richard Burton, it would be broadcast on 6 November.

Although increasing television and film production provided new opportunities, Osborne and Pamela, trained as stage actors, were uneasy with the technical requirements of both. Osborne never felt entirely at home writing for television. While happy to be a director of Woodfall, he had shied away from writing the additional dialogue demanded by the film versions of *Look Back in Anger* and *The Entertainer*, although he later flung himself into writing the script for Richardson's 1963 film of Henry Fielding's *Tom Jones*. Pamela's excursions into the film world were both brief and anonymous. She secured two fleeting, uncredited appearances in 1960, firstly in *Moment of Danger*, directed by László Benedek in which Trevor Howard starred as a jewel thief on the run in central Europe, and secondly in

The Millionairess, a comedy directed by Anthony Asquith, tenuously derived from Bernard Shaw's play (or more accurately, commented one critic, the title) and starring Sophia Loren as an heiress and Peter Sellers as an Indian doctor. The following summer, a skilled observer might have glimpsed her in the background of Michael Anderson's *The Naked Edge*, a thriller starring Deborah Kerr and Gary Cooper in what turned out to his last film, in which a wife suspects her husband of murder. 'Only the man who wrote *Psycho* could jolt you like this!' promised the posters outside the cinema. But if film work was not getting Pamela very far, neither, for the moment, was the stage. For eight months after the end of the *Peter Pan* tour in March, her diary was dispiritingly blank.

And so began the 1960s. The subdued grey of the 1950s suddenly burst into full colour as in 1964, the country elected a Labour government and a later much-mythologized decade of social change and liberalization blossomed with optimism and youth and with London at its heart. Yet while these were years of extraordinary professional success for Osborne, they were crushingly disappointing for Pamela. As the decade began the future seemed so promising, yet these would be years of fits and starts and of fleeting hopes caught on the wing followed by disillusionment and unemployment.

■ ■ ■

JO to PL ms letter n/a BL

7 November 1960

Darling,

I'm so sorry to hear that things are difficult. I'm now in management with Oscar Lewenstein, as you may know, and if I can give you a push at the right time, I certainly will. Let's try and meet again sometime.

Love

John

Oscar Lewenstein was a theatrical producer involved with the Royal Court. A former member of the Communist Party and still a committed socialist, he had been instrumental in securing the Berliner Ensemble's visit to London. Pamela was hoping that Osborne might use his contacts to secure her a part either at the Royal Court or in one of Lewenstein's own productions. But nothing seemed forthcoming and in November she began rehearsals for her second *Peter Pan*, opening at the Scala on 16 December. This year, it was directed by Toby Robertson, a Cambridge University graduate and former actor who was now one of the producers of *Armchair Theatre* for Independent Television. Once again, Pamela invested 'some character into Mrs Darling, which is not easy,' remarked the *Illustrated London News*, while Julia Lockwood again played Peter, displaying 'remarkable grace in her flying.'[5] Donald Sinden appeared as an urbane and impeccably articulated Mr Darling and a dashingly malicious Captain Hook.

In anticipation of Mary's return from America, Osborne had re-installed himself at Woodfall Street. An electrical fault resulting in a small house fire in January 1961 presented them with a convenient opportunity to separate without too much loss of dignity. Mary took a flat of her own near Sloane Square, while Osborne returned to Jocelyn and Lower Belgrave Street. From there, he wrote to Pamela:

JO to PL ms pc n/a BL

17 Jan 61

I've just looked in the paper, and I see that your play [*Peter Pan*] finishes on Saturday. Everything seems specially different at the moment. I've been working very hard, feel full of fatigue. Anyway. I've been thinking of you and, frankly, wanting you again. I can think of nothing I'd rather like more than seeing you alone again, and being together, as we were in Brighton. If I picked you up after the show on Saturday, would you care to go somewhere—if only till Sunday? I can arrange it. If you'd like to, would you just ring Oscar Beuselinck and say to go ahead with the arrangements, that you're agreeable. If not, just say you can't make it. I'll understand. Hope you're well.

Love

John

Peter Pan was due to close at the Scala on 21 January before going on its usual three-month tour. Osborne was 'working very hard' researching and writing *Luther*.

Whether or not he managed to whisk her away for a night or two is unknown, but in any case, Pamela was reclaiming something of the 'dashing life' she remembered from her student days. She enjoyed *Peter Pan* and the company of her fellow actors, busily supervising fiendishly intricate word games to engage the younger members of the cast when they were not needed on stage. While on tour, instead of travelling with the main group each Sunday to the next venue, she and Julia Lockwood frequently jumped on the night train to London to spend a day and a night in town before joining the company on Monday. 'She was wonderful to be with,' recalled Lockwood. 'She drew people to her. She was very clever, very sexy, and we had a lot of fun going to parties together.'[6]

Once the tour ended in the spring and the magic of never growing up was consigned to storage, Pamela returned to London and a rented flat at 27 Holland Park Avenue. She moved in with Hazel Coppen, an actress six years her elder, whom she had met in Bromley and with whom she had kept in touch. Pamela had resolved a question with which she had struggled for several years, perhaps as long ago as Bridgwater and her days at RADA, but certainly during her spectacularly disastrous marriage. Not only was her independence vital to her establishing a career, but it seemed that her nature was such that the emotional security she sought might rather be found with a woman, with whom her sexuality might also be equally—or better—satisfied.

Pamela may have had earlier intimacies with women, but had not previously lived with another woman. Due perhaps to her natural inclination for reticence, or the legacy of her upbringing where outward appearances were judged to be vital, or the weight of prevailing moral convention, an important consideration for one who might be in the public eye, or perhaps a combination of all this, there was nothing overt in Pamela's relationships with her female partners, and little was revealed to others. She may have discussed her emotional confusion with Osborne, in many ways the person to whom she was closest and who, it might be argued, deserved her confidence, but otherwise her friends were left to infer and draw their own conclusions. A lively, sociable woman, Pamela managed to be simultaneously unforthcoming in matters she considered private. 'Her sexual preferences were not immediately apparent to me,' recalled Richard Digby Day, who met her a few years later in 1968 and subsequently knew her very well. 'They rather crept up on one over time, never directly expressed, at least to me. Eventually one understood. In a theatre company, for instance, Pamela was at the centre of things yet essentially private, although not secretive. I imagine this was always the case from Bridgwater onwards.'[7]

From Holland Park Avenue, Hazel set out for Richmond, where she was appearing in *This Is My Life*, a crime thriller by Philip Weathers, while Pamela advanced warily towards the television studio. She had secured a couple of minor roles, one in an episode of *Deadline Midnight*, a series set in a daily newspaper office, and another in the airline drama *Flight 447 Delayed*, in which she played a passenger. But although she made occasional television appearances over the years, Pamela's career on the small screen, as in the cinema, never really sprang into life. There were odd days here and there in the studio or on location, but her final screen appearances were too brief and too incidental to make a lasting impression. Hazel was much more successful. Beginning in 1961 with an appearance in an episode of *The Avengers*, the jauntily stylish spy series starring Patrick Macnee and Honor Blackman and an essential element of that irreverent decade, she went on to appear in most of the popular series of the times. At the same time, the theatre provided a steady supply of supporting roles, mainly in the regions and occasionally in the West End. On the radio, she became a regular component of *Waggoners' Walk*, a long-running series set on an eponymous street in Hampstead and broadcast daily in fifteen-minute bursts. Like Pamela, like many actors, Hazel Coppen was never a prominent name or an immediately familiar face in the public mind, but unlike Pamela, she was seldom out of work.

On 18 June 1961, almost three months after finishing in *Peter Pan*, Pamela stepped on to the stage at the Royal Court. Perhaps this engagement was the result of the 'push' that Osborne indicated he might give in his letter of 7 November the previous year. If so, it had been a long time coming and proved hardly worth anyone's trouble. *Empress with a Teapot* was unveiled for one night only in one of the theatre's regular 'Sunday night without Décor' productions, in which uncertain new plays were flung before an audience not knowing what to expect. *Empress* was written by the Australian poet and playwright, B. R. 'Bertie' Whiting, a former aide-de-camp to Lord Mountbatten in India and devoted bee keeper who had mailed the typescript from Italy, where he judiciously elected to remain. An oddball comedy in which a middle-aged man assumes the character of his deceased mother while dispensing tea and sympathy to the residents of his Kensington lodging house, Pamela appeared as Gloria, a woman intent upon setting up a company catering for the vices of businessmen. It was a 'vague' piece, complained *The Times*, the author having no idea, once he had dreamed up his characters, of what to do next.[8] Although the play 'intermittently took wing,' conceded Irving Wardle in the *Observer*, 'with Pamela Lane's rip-roaringly maternal tart,' the first night turned out to be the last and Pamela never appeared again at the Royal Court.[9]

As rehearsals were then underway for *Luther*, she and Osborne probably met, although there appears to be no record of their having done so. A week later, on 26 June, *Luther* opened at the Theatre Royal, Nottingham, before transferring to Paris and on 27 July arriving at the Royal Court, its critical reception decisively restoring Osborne's professional reputation battered by *The World of Paul Slickey*. Pamela dispatched the first of what would become her customary first night good luck telegrams.

JO to PL ms pc n/a BL

31. 7. 61

Thanks so much for your first night greeting. I was so delighted to get it. I'm going abroad for two months tomorrow. Let's meet when I get back. Do hope you're well and alright.

Much love

John

Osborne and Jocelyn were planning a holiday in the south of France as guests of Tony Richardson, who had rented a villa hidden among pine woods near Valbonne. Osborne's convoluted private life, which the popular press delighted in making public, was becomingly whirlingly chaotic. Although he and Mary were now estranged, the 'stable base of loyalty and affection' at Lower Belgrave Street was already compromised by his new attachment to Penelope Gilliatt. Like Pamela,

Osborne was then thirty-one. Jocelyn was thirty-seven and Penelope twenty-nine. Socially, if not from the absolute top drawer, Penelope was very close to it, and a very 1960s woman who had made her own way. A daughter of Cyril Conner, formerly a barrister and a director of Overseas Broadcasting for the BBC, she had been educated in the United States and returned to London to become film critic of the *Observer*, sharing a house with her husband, Dr. Roger Gilliatt, a prominent neurosurgeon, in Lowndes Square. But: 'I have never loved anyone so profoundly and completely as I do you,' Jocelyn protested.[10] Yet: 'I love you deeply & furiously & with total attention,' proclaimed Penelope.[11]

One of Penelope's attractions for Osborne, apart from her intelligence, vivacity and enviable social assurance, was that, like Pamela, she had red hair, a quality he thought hypnotically fascinating. While Osborne sunned himself in France with Jocelyn, he wrote almost daily to Penelope, who was in Venice reporting on the film festival. Between screenings, she composed rapturous replies. 'I feel utterly invaded by you, as though every kind of physical sound barrier has been crashed,' she confirmed.[12] In early September, Osborne flew to Venice to join her before returning to Valbonne and Jocelyn, with whom he travelled back to London. No sooner than he arrived than he bolted, evading Mary and abandoning Jocelyn, and going to ground with Penelope at his newly-acquired country house, The Old Water Mill, in Hellingly, Sussex. The bewildered Dr Gilliatt and the disconsolate Jocelyn, blameless both, remained in London.

While the press provided a fulsome and illustrated commentary to this frenetic activity, *Luther* transferred to the Phoenix Theatre in the West End. Pamela, meanwhile, was scraping by for the second year in succession with little acting work. After such an optimistic beginning in the regions, providing her with a bundle of enthusiastic reviews, her appearances at the Savoy, Hammersmith, the Scala and the Royal Court had failed to generate the interest of London producers. Her agent sought auditions, while Pamela sounded out her gradually widening professional network, but to no immediate avail. Theatre work had stalled, while film and television seemed to be non-starters. Therefore, as many actors did in similar circumstances, she resorted to casual work. It was something she would be obliged to do many times in the future.

In later years, giving seminars for groups of visiting American acting students provided a vital and dignified lifeline, but now and for several years to come, she signed up with an agency conducting market research surveys. The advantage of this was that it was easy to take time off for auditions; the disadvantage was that it was joyless work involving her standing on shopping streets armed with a clipboard and a list of questions, accosting passers-by on their views on various products and other incidental matters. Pamela discovered her career to be developing two separate strands. Over the next few years, she became familiar not only with much of the landscape of western drama, especially the more remote valleys visited solely by weekly rep, but also fully briefed on the particular qualities people expected from a biscuit and the criteria on which they chose a vacuum cleaner. It was on one of these forays in the autumn of 1961 that she came down with a rampaging cold that developed into pneumonia, scuppering another return to *Peter Pan*.

Julia Lockwood did not appear at the Scala either that year, although she was working again with the irrepressible Patrick Desmond. He had not forgotten *The Devil Inside Him*, the play by Osborne and Stella Linden that he had produced in Huddersfield twelve years previously, and, digging it out of a drawer, decided both to appear in and direct a lightly revised version at the Pembroke Theatre in Croydon. It opened on 8 January 1962, with Michael Williams, playing Huw, and Julia Lockwood and Richard Wordsworth, another *Peter Pan* veteran, in the leading roles. Osborne agreed to the production on the condition that neither the original title nor his name were used, and therefore *Cry for Love* was credited to Robert Owen, the name presumably borrowed from the eighteenth-century Welsh social reformer and utopian. Stella Linden, having long since left both Desmond and Britain for obscurity in Mexico, was probably entirely unaware of it. London critics failed to identify the play as having been previously performed under another title, or that it was the work of Britain's most talked-about dramatist rather than a worthy but unknown Welsh playwright. It was, announced *The Times*, 'a serious and ambitious work' providing 'three immediately powerful acting roles.'[13] The following month, the production transferred to the Empire Theatre, Sunderland, coincidentally the theatre where, while on tour with *No Room at the Inn* in March 1948, Osborne had begun writing the play. *Cry for Love* 'seldom rises above women's magazine level,' warned *The Stage*, 'although this fact is in itself enough to commend it as a commercial proposition.'[14] Evidently, Desmond thought so too.

By now, after only a single night's stage work in a year, stints of market research and several weeks of incapacity, Pamela, never the best of domestic economists, had plunged catastrophically into debt. She had not seen much, if anything of her former husband for some time, but on 2 February, she telephoned him and appealed for his financial help. Three days later, he wrote to his accountant from Sussex:

JO to Walter Strach ts letter Texas

The Old Water Mill
5 February 1962

Dear Walter,

I had a rather distraught telephone call from my first wife, Pamela Lane, on Friday, and feel I must do something to help her. She is not the sort of person to ask for help easily so I know she must be under some considerable pressure. Apart from being unemployed for quite some time, she has recently been very ill with pneumonia. She has recovered, however, and is now working for Air France.

Best wishes

John

Having arranged for a substantial £250 (about £4890 at 2018 rates) to be transferred to Pamela's bank account, and insisting that should she require more, then she must ask, Osborne returned to completing *Plays for England*, a double bill comprising two short plays, *The Blood of the Bambergs* and *Under Plain Cover*.

JO to PL ms letter BL

[The Old Water Mill]
17 May 62

My dear Pam—

I'm wondering if you're alright. Do let me know. I'm going to Hamburg tomorrow but I will be back in about ten days. Why don't you come down here and rest for a few days sometime? We'd love to see you. Hope you're alright.

Much love

John

Osborne was flying to Hamburg with others from the Royal Court to promote the work of the English Stage Company. 'We' were himself and Penelope. Unlike Mary Ure, Penelope welcomed both Anthony Creighton and Pamela, who were issued with open invitations to stay for a weekend, while she also did much to reconcile Osborne with Nellie Beatrice, whom Mary had found embarrassing. *Plays for England* opened at the Royal Court Theatre, on 19 July, which Pamela commemorated with another first night good wishes telegram.

JO to PL ms pc BL

The Old Water Mill
25 July 62

Bless you for the telegram. You are a good girl. Thank heavens it's all over once again. I'm rather pleased with them. When are you coming down? Hope you're well.

Lots of love

John

Within a few weeks, though, Pamela found work at the Theatre Club in Leatherhead. In common with Derby Playhouse and many regional theatres, the Theatre Club had abandoned weekly repertory in favour of fortnightly production and a correspondingly longer rehearsal period. This allowed local audiences more time to relish the works of Jean Anouilh, the French playwright who was enjoying a considerable London vogue and was also a firm favourite in Leatherhead. In fact, Anouilh was the nearest thing the Theatre Club got to a house dramatist. On 4 September, Pamela appeared as the Countess in *The Rehearsal*, a 1950 play in which the residents of a chateau rehearse their production of Marivaux's infidelity comedy,

The Double Inconstancy, and by pretending to be someone else, reveal their true selves. The following month, swathed in a nineteenth-century dress like a heavy curtain, she played Natalia Petrovna, the leading role in Turgenev's *A Month in the Country*, directed by Hugh Cruttwell who was married to Geraldine McEwan, who had played Jean in the West End run of *The Entertainer.* Cruttwell himself would later become an influential Principal at RADA. As the 'self-willed Natalia who regards the workings of her conscience as the greatest of her misfortunes,' reported *The Stage,* 'Pamela Lane exploits a wide range of restrained emotions with a sure touch.'[15]

On 14 November, Osborne and Mary Ure were divorced. He spent Christmas with Penelope in Sussex while on Boxing Day, Pamela returned to the Lyric, Hammersmith, to embark on a four-week, twice-daily run of Maurice Maeterlinck's *The Blue Bird*, a musical fairy tale that 'even the centenary of its author's birth,' observed *The Stage,* 'makes an insufficient excuse for its revival.'[16] *The Times* was more charitable, drumming up the Christmas spirit by applauding the heaving overboard of the 'heavy German morality' in favour of pantomime and declaring the story of Tyltyl and Mytyl, two children searching for the blue bird of happiness, to be 'an exotic addition' to the season.[17] Pamela, though, playing the unrewarding role of Mother Tyl, failed to gain a mention.

She and Osborne remained in intermittent correspondence, each addressing the other in restrained, rather formal terms: 'My dear John,' 'My dear Pamela,' as though unsure of their ground. At the end of April 1963, he sent her a copy of the newly-published *Plays for England*.

PL to JO ms letter Texas

27 Holland Park Avenue
W11
6 May 1963

My dear John,

Thank you for the Plays—I <u>was</u> pleased to have them.

Reading them for the first time was a tremendous pleasure, you know, and almost a shock: I mean, to discover real English in the theatre when most writers seem hell-bent on manipulating it to death. Perhaps you won't always be a lone revivalist, a one-man restoration act, but you certainly are at present, and it grows more apparent with each play. (Very sexy, too, not dull and boring at all.)

I'm sorry to have been out of touch for so long, I haven't meant to be, of course, it's only that things have been stupidly difficult and demanding but we must meet again soon.

Take care of yourself,

Much love

Pam

Her 'very sexy' comment refers to *Under Plain Cover*, which includes several passages celebrating women's underwear, a subject in which Osborne had a playful, rather juvenile interest. In later years, this would be something that Pamela shared. 'Dull and boring' echoes her verdict on one of his earliest writing efforts.

Just over a fortnight later, on 25 May, Osborne and Penelope married in Sussex and returned to live in London, expensively setting up home at 31 Chester Square in Belgravia, the mortgage and comprehensive renovations funded mostly from his share of the producers' profits of *Tom Jones*, which opened on 26 June. A cheerful pastoral romp, the film caught the spirited irreverence of the times and broke box office records, the revenues boosting Osborne's burgeoning bank account and easing him towards becoming a millionaire before the age of thirty-five. In addition to owning an imposing home in Belgravia and a weekend retreat in Sussex, he now felt able to fully indulge his passions for travel, fashionable clothes, expensive cars and, in the country, for riding.

In Holland Park and intermittently employed, Pamela could only imagine such a charmed life. In June, she appeared briefly in *Charlie is my Darling*, an episode of the *Love Story* television series of one-hour romantic dramas, this time at least achieving a screen credit, if only as 'woman with child.' In November, almost a year since her last stage appearance, she was at the Theatre Royal, Stratford East, which, under Joan Littlewood's fiercely anti-Establishment leadership, rivalled the Royal Court in its reputation for invigorating new plays. Brendan Behan's *The Quare Fellow* and *The Hostage* had been produced there, as had Shelagh Delaney's *A Taste of Honey* and Lionel Bart's cockney musical *Fings Ain't Wot They Used t'be*, which had transferred boisterously into the West End. *The Albatross*, the script that Pamela held in her hands, came with an intriguing authorial pedigree. Howard Koch moved in glamorous Hollywood circles, having contributed to the screenplay of *Casablanca*. He had also written the 1938 radio adaptation of H. G. Wells' *The War of the Worlds,* which in Orson Welles' delivery had convinced more gullible listeners that alien spaceships really were landing nearby, resulting in widespread alarm. However, '*The Albatross* is not going to touch off any panic-stricken stampede in the neighbourhood of Angel Lane,' *The Times* critic reassured his more apprehensive readers, 'but is in its own way just as much a stunt as its predecessor.'[18] A ponderous exhumation of the lives of Charles and Mary Lamb and hopefully bound for Broadway, it failed to survive London's arctic critical blast. 'If the principals [who included Nigel Hawthorne] have little opportunity,' pronounced another reviewer, 'then the remainder [who included Pamela as Fanny Kelly, an actress to whom Lamb unsuccessfully proposed] have none at all.'[19] Yet again, Pamela's contribution to the exercise was overlooked by the press.

There was no alternative that Christmas but Mrs Darling, *Peter Pan* and the Scala. Several other regulars were returning, including Julia Lockwood as Peter, while Patrick Desmond, his cigar blowing noxious fumes, was once again directing. The veteran comic actor Alistair Sim advanced as 'a most ferociously fearful Captain Hook,' hoisting the Jolly Roger first in London and then on yet another three-month national tour.[20]

JO to PL ms letter n/a BL

16. 12. 63

My dear Pamela,

Glad to hear you're back among the fairies.

This is simply to send you my love and hopes for you in '64. I think of you often and wonder how you are. Perhaps we might lunch one day. Anyhow, take care.

As ever,

John

As the *Peter Pan* tour negotiated its familiar buccaneering path through Scotland and northern England, *The Third Secret* loomed up on the nation's cinema screens. This was a reasonable film-noir directed by Charles Crichton, whose forte was Ealing comedies, in which a newscaster investigates the mysterious death of his analyst. Pamela again walked on and off, unnoticed and uncredited, somewhere behind a cast led by Richard Attenborough and Jack Hawkins. In Cardiff in March with *Peter Pan*, she received a cautiously optimistic letter from Osborne:

JO to PL ms letter n/a BL

9 March 1964

My dear Pamela,

I'd hoped we might meet during Wimbledon Week, but I was in bed for most of it. I had to have shots for cholera and all sorts of things and they made me feel pretty ghastly. Also, I [have] just finished a new play and that felt a little like emerging from the bottom of a well after several months. Anyway: I would have rung you, but I always feel it might be very inconvenient for you at home so here I am writing.

I have to go to New York on the 17th and a week later I'm taking off to India for a couple of months. Sounds a bit exotic but I've not had a real holiday for about two years and I can write my new play (I hope) there. So—there doesn't seem much likelihood of seeing you before the summer. I hope you're alright. I often think of you, as you must know. My heart remembers so much of you. Look after yourself. Don't forget—you always have one friend.

As ever

J.

'Wimbledon Week' refers not to the Tennis Championships, which take place during July, but to *Peter Pan* playing at the theatre there for a week as part of its tour. Osborne had taken inoculations against a fleet of diseases prior to his holiday in India with Penelope. The play he had recently completed writing was *Inadmissible Evidence*, in which Bill Maitland, a relentlessly self-destructive lawyer, charts his own failure. The 'new play' would become *A Patriot for Me*, the story of

Alfred Redl, an officer in the Austro-Hungarian Army during the 1890s, whose homosexuality results in him being blackmailed into spying for Tsarist Russia. Perhaps work on *A Patriot for Me* had made Osborne more acutely sensitive than usual to divided loyalties, hence his caution about telephoning Pamela at Holland Park Avenue. The presence of Hazel Coppen, he thought, might make it 'inconvenient.'

Towards the end of April, he and Penelope arrived in India, staying at the fabulously located—in the centre of a sapphire-blue lake—and fabulously expensive Lake Palace Hotel in Udaipur. A picture postcard was promptly dispatched to Pamela in London:

JO to PL ms pc n/d BL

[April 1964]

This is where I'm staying on [sic] this beautiful place in the middle of a lake. The temperature is 90 degrees in the shade. Went for an elephant ride yesterday!

Hope you're well and alright. I'm managing to do some work. Did I tell you I've finished a new play? I'd like you to see it. Shouldn't be too long. Look after yourself.

Love

John

While they were in India, news arrived from the Academy Awards in Los Angeles that *Tom Jones* had won four Oscars, including one for Best Picture and one for Osborne in the Best Adapted Screenplay category. Osborne and Penelope arrived back in London in the early summer.

JO to PL ms letter BL

Woodfall Film Productions

August 1ˢᵗ 64

My dear,

I shall be in London fairly frequently from August 10ᵗʰ as I'm rehearsing for the re-opening of the Court. Would you care to have lunch one day? I'd love to see you. It's been so long.

With love

As ever

John

The rehearsals were for Anthony Page's production of *Inadmissible Evidence*, starring Nicol Williamson, and due to open in September.

JO to PL ms pc n/a BL

[London]

12. 8. 64

What about <u>dinner</u>, Wednesday the 26ᵗʰ 9pm at BOULESTIN'S (Southampton St?) Or lunch Thursday the 27ᵗʰ 1pm at RULE's (Maiden Lane?) Dinner would be nice. But as you like. Just finished my <u>other</u> play yesterday. Quite exhausted. Rehearsals for present are going fine. Dying to see you.

Love

John

Boulestin's, its interior decorated with circus-themed murals and formerly owned by the French connoisseur, *bon viveur* and writer, Marcel Boulestin, was once known as the most expensive restaurant in London. It closed in 1994. Rules, which remains open and has the distinction of being the oldest restaurant in the capital, serves traditional British food and specialises in game. Both were appropriate venues for an Oscar winner to be seen dining. The 'other' play is *A Patriot for Me*; the 'present' enterprise is *Inadmissible Evidence*.

JO to Pl ms pc n/a BL

[London]

24. 8. 64

Ok why not lunch on Friday then—12.45 at RULES. Ring HYO 3866 and leave a message with the Woodfall secretary.

Love

John

On 9 September, *Inadmissible Evidence* opened at the Royal Court to largely celebratory reviews. Pamela saw it and admired it hugely. As she seems to have had no acting work since the end of the *Peter Pan* tour in the spring and she was once again finding it difficult to make ends meet, Osborne arranged with his accountants that she receive a share of the royalties of *Inadmissible Evidence*. At the end of September, though, things picked up, and Pamela joined the Meadow Players at the Oxford Playhouse for two plays.

Close to the University colleges and the Ashmolean Museum, the Playhouse was directed by Frank Hauser, a forty-four-year-old Oxford graduate and a former director in the BBC radio drama department. When Hauser arrived in 1956, the Playhouse's reputation was negligible, but eight years later and by dint of 'prompt, brave and imaginative action' in programming a sprightly mix of classical plays and world premieres, it was flourishing.[21] Pamela appeared first as Myra Arundel, 'purring and preening, like a smugly attractive cat on a rug,' in an 'eminently stylish' production of Noël Coward's *Hay Fever* directed by Tony Tanner, a former West End revue actor turned director.[22] This was followed by Miss Linde in Ibsen's *A Doll's House*, directed by Robert Chetwyn, a former actor embarking on what would become a successful directorial career.

Before Pamela left for Oxford, she and Hazel moved from Holland Park Avenue to Kilburn, renting what the landlords described as a garden flat on the lower ground floor of a stucco-fronted two-storey Victorian villa. According to Osborne's recollections, Pamela's home-making skills, last seen in action in Derby, quickly transformed number 23a Priory Road, with its living room and two bedrooms, into a 'very cosy Tiggywinkle basement.'[23] The general effect of snugness, prompting Osborne's memory of Mrs Tiggy-Winkle, the industriously domestic hedgehog in the children's stories by Beatrix Potter, was augmented by a generous scattering of the Wedgwood china and porcelain that Pamela had begun to collect. Number 23a became Pamela's home for the rest of her life. The first indication of Osborne visiting her there is his diary for 3 February 1965, when Hazel was conveniently on tour. 'Pamela's flat, 11.30 am,' he noted laconically. 'Once again, easy glide between sheets.... Bland still upon bland, but quite affectionate. Says the weekly sums she got from her piece of *Inadmissible Evidence* have kept her going. Quite a large sum when I think of it—£200 a month [equivalent to about £3500 in 2018] at least. No, more. And then there'll be America'.[24]

While their few days in Brighton two years earlier were not without their romantic moments, this appears to have been their first sexual encounter since, although there is no indication in the letters that it was more than a single, commemorative incident. Eight days later, Osborne confirmed further financial arrangements to help Pamela through her post-Oxford period of unemployment:

JO to PL ms letter n/a BL

11. 2. 65

Pamela love—

 Hear things are being difficult one way and another. I'm so sorry. I'm setting something in train immediately which may help a little. I hope so. Look after yourself. Let's meet soon.

As ever

Love

John

Just what was difficult 'one way and another' is not immediately clear. Osborne was probably referring to her failure to find consistent find acting work, but there may also have been complications in the relationship between Pamela and Hazel. As anxious as ever about her ability to earn money, Pamela was aware that disparity between incomes might threaten even apparently stable relationships. The 'something in train' was confirmation to his accountants that Pamela would receive a percentage of the profits from the imminent West End run and the anticipated New York transfer of *Inadmissible Evidence*.

A fortnight later, on 24 February, Penelope Gilliatt gave birth to Osborne's daughter, Nolan, at a private nursing home in Welbeck Street in Marylebone. The following month, on 17 March, *Inadmissible Evidence* opened at the Wyndham's Theatre in the West End, with Nicol Williamson still playing the leading role.

PL to JO telegram Texas

17 March 1965

WISHING YOU A REPEAT SUCCESS TONIGHT PAM

JO to PL ms postcard n/a BL

March 22nd [1965]

My dear Pam,

Bless you for the telegram. It went quite well, although the first night audience was pretty frightful. See you soon, I hope.

Much love

John

Pamela was working in television again, credited and with a few lines of dialogue. On 26 February, she had appeared as the Sister in a hospital scene in *Dixon of Dock Green*, the reassuring and long-running police series, and on 9 April, maintaining the hospital theme, she cropped up as Mrs Drayton in an episode of *Emergency Ward 10*, the seemingly never-ending medical drama series. On 20 April, she was back at the Oxford Playhouse for something more substantial, the world premiere of *A Heritage and its History*, adapted from Ivy Compton-Burnett's 1959 novel by Julian Mitchell, who only six years earlier had graduated from the city's university. Compton-Burnett was then seventy-one and a dauntingly imperious figure ensconced in a Kensington flat famous as the scene of her intimidating tea parties. This was the first of her novels to be dramatized. The story is set in a grand house somewhere in southern England, where the ageing, wealthy, but unmarried

Sir Edwin Challoner is surrounded by an avaricious extended family impatiently waiting for him to pass away in order to get their hands on the loot. Pamela played the supporting, but in terms of the plot, pivotal role of Rhoda Graham, a young woman whom Sir Edwin marries, much to the family's consternation. Her subsequent brief affair with Simon, Sir Edwin's married nephew, results in a son to whom Sir Edwin declares himself the legal father, thus doing the grasping Simon out of his anticipated inheritance.

It was, on the face of it, a strange choice for the liberalizing 1960s. Compton-Burnett's novels, almost always about upper-class late-Victorian or Edwardian families, contain a lot of dialogue but are not immediately theatrical. To some critics, this was the play's great flaw. A 'slow, stately production' of 'overriding emotional bloodlessness,' with a cast that included Alan Howard as Simon, Hauser's production lumbered on to Cambridge and on 18 May, docked uneasily at the Phoenix Theatre in the West End.[25] Apart from *Peter Pan*, it was Pamela's first West End appearance since *A Day in the Life of…* just over six years earlier. But unfortunately, 'one cannot believe a single thing,' complained the critic of *The Stage*.[26] It was 'an interesting display of costumes', conceded another critic, but the characters inside them 'never lived.'[27] But the play 'demands concentrated attention,' argued the anonymous critic of *The Times*, indignantly. With the melodramatic ingredients of 'marriage, seduction, incest and death,' it was 'a remarkably effective' production, a 'combination of high comedy and Greek tragedy' that 'grips and amuses.'[28] The play and Alan Howard cornered the reviews. Again, Pamela was largely overlooked.

At the Royal Court the following night, 19 May, Osborne watched the curtain go up on something as far removed from *A Heritage and its History* as it was possible to get. *Meals on Wheels* was a chaotic satire on all things English by Charles Wood, set on the stage of a variety theatre that looked as if it might be an offcut from *The Entertainer*. Having concluded that while everyone at the Court agreed the play should be produced, nobody could make sufficient sense of it to be confident of taking it on, Osborne had decided to direct it himself. The result was that critics and audiences failed to make much of it either. 'Presumably the play is making a statement about social repression,' hazarded *The Times*, pointing out that this was a tentative verdict arrived at only in hindsight.[29] J.C. Trewin in *The*

Illustrated London News, though, was not one to spend time in retrospection. It was 'an incomprehensible waste of everybody's time,' he snapped.[30]

Penelope Gilliatt, however, who had gone along to *A Heritage and its History* as theatre critic of the *Observer*, loved it, and said so the following Sunday. It is 'really about what is expected of us, by ourselves, by others and by the process of life,' she explained mystifyingly, and compared it to the monumental stature of Greek tragedy. The play called for 'the manners necessary at Mycenae' and the actors caught the technique superbly. It was all a marvellously sustained display of *style*, and style was very important to Penelope. Scrutinizing the stage for wife number one, she noted the presence of 'Pamela Lane as a novice in the family who begets her husband's nephew's child, perhaps through nerves,' but said no more.[31]

JO to PL ms letter n/a BL

21.6.65

Pamela love

Will come and see the play as soon as I can. Everyone tells me how good you are. So glad you got some nice notices too.

Also; you'll be getting some of the profits from Inadmissible in a few days, so buy yourself some new knickers or something. Hope all's well. See you soon.

Much love

John

A Heritage and its History was still running on 30 June, when Anthony Page's production of Osborne's much-heralded *A Patriot for Me* opened at the Royal Court, starring Maximilian Schell as Redl and controversially confirming Osborne as the pre-eminent dramatist of the day. This was also the evening on which Osborne and Anthony Creighton met for the last time. Since Osborne had become an Angry Young Man and moved in more exalted circles, Creighton's career had retreated quickly into the twilight. Acting work had more or less dried up. With Bernard Miller, an American friend, he had written *Tomorrow with Pictures*, a play about the editor of a fashion magazine and which had begun life at the Lyric, Hammersmith in 1960, but after a brief West End run had vanished, never to be seen again. Still insisting that a theatrical future lay within his grasp, he had bumped along on a series of temporary jobs while draining the royalties account from the Royal Court, West End and American productions of *Epitaph for George Dillon*. In the meantime, Creighton had become an increasingly heavy drinker and consequently socially unpredictable. His loud and injudicious derision of *A Patriot for Me* at the first night party resulted in an infuriated Osborne having his inebriated former collaborator ejected from the building. Thereafter he cut Creighton out of his life altogether. They never met again.

Across town at the Phoenix Theatre, however, ticket sales had been disappointing and the producers had decided to cut their losses when a surprising surge at the box-office resulted in a temporary reprieve.

PL to JO ms letter n/a Texas

19th July 1965

Thanks for your card—the play's been put back to run, anyway for a couple of weeks, I shouldn't think for longer.

I hope your week in the country did you good and you were able to work <u>and</u> recover from Patriot: it looks as if it will keep Tynan and McCarthy going for a bit.

I hope you're all right—I think of you.

Nothing yet, by the way, from Inadmissible—should there be? But I suppose it's not likely to have gone astray.

Come and see me when you can

All love

Pamela

Mary McCarthy was an American novelist and critic who had written an article for the *Observer* on 4 July, attacking *A Patriot for Me* as 'tiresome and predictable' and that 'harangue and repetition' comprised the 'basic plot of the Osborne play.' Kenneth Tynan wrote a feisty response, published under the headline of *Missing Osborne's Point* on 18 July.

JO to PL ms pc BL

The Old Water Mill

23.7.65

You should have got some money from I.E. today. Sorry about the delay. Inefficiency somewhere. See you soon. So glad about the play.

Love

John

JO to PL ms pc BL

The Old Water Mill

27. 7. 65

Thank heavens you've got it at last. Don't know whose idea it was to send it to your agents. Don't let them charge you commission!

[unsigned]

Just over a week later, on 7 August, George Devine, who was playing Baron von Epp in *A Patriot for Me*, came offstage after the performance and suffered a heart attack. He was taken to St George's Hospital, where he stayed for two months, a distraught Osborne among those anxiously following his progress.

JO to PL ms pc BL

The Old Water Mill

13.9.65

Horrified to read your play is closing. Everyone tells me how good you are in it. I'm down here all this week <u>trying</u> to work and recover from PATRIOT. However, will try and come and see you in it if I possibly can.

Lots of love

John

A Heritage and its History closed at the end of September. Despite his assurances, Osborne probably never got around to seeing it. That he had not taken the opportunity to do so early in its run suggests reluctance, possibly the result of fearing that he would dislike it intensely. Two months later, in November, he went to New York for the American opening of *Inadmissible Evidence* at the Belasco Theater. Pamela, unemployed and market researching again, wrote on his return:

PL to JO ms letter n/a Texas

Dec 21 [1965]

My dear John,

Thank you more than I can say for making 1965 so easy and comfortable for me: the income from Inadmissible has been welcome beyond words. I meant to write thanks before this, but you were in America and there didn't seem much point, if you weren't going to get the letter anyway: but I've never stopped being glad and grateful.

New Year again, which only means, I suppose, renewing all that I wish for you always.

My love to you and Penelope—

Ever

Pamela

Penelope and Pamela had met, probably at The Old Water Mill, although it is not clear when. As Pamela's valediction suggests, they were on good terms, although Penelope was unaware of their sexual encounter in February, or any others there may have been. While *A Patriot for Me* won Osborne his first *Evening Standard* Best Play of the Year Award, the occasion was overshadowed by grief. Having returned home from hospital in October, Devine died of a second heart attack on 20 January 1966. He was sixty-five. His death was a tragedy for many and especially so for Osborne, to whom Devine was not only the man who had fostered his work, but was also a father figure. As Tom Godfrey, Osborne's real and revered father, had also died in January twenty-five years previously, the first month of year often became one of morbid memory and despondency.

■ ■ ■

In progressively liberal and optimistic times, if you were young and talented, the prospects for success were more plentiful than ever. Or at least that was the coming idea. Osborne and Pamela were thirty-six in 1966, at the older end of the spectrum considered youthful, but while he was confidently surfing the wave of opportunity that he had played his part in creating, she appeared to have missed the current altogether. Like many actors, she found herself adrift of the theatrical changes for which the late-1960s would be remembered: the emergence of new dramatists, the proliferation of fringe theatres and 'alternative' theatrical events, and the arrival of a new generation of actors not all of whom possessed Home Counties accents and were thereby well-equipped for the kind of plays being produced at the Royal Court and now elsewhere as well. Even the abolition in 1968 of state censorship of the stage had no immediate effect on her career. By and large, regional theatres remained cautious in the face of such momentous events.

Once *A Heritage and its History* closed in September 1965, Pamela did not work in the theatre again until the following summer. Apart from a second appearance in *Dixon of Dock Green* on 26 February, again playing a Matron in yet another hospital scene, she was reliant on casual work and her former husband, who continued to send her cheques ranging from £50 to £200 to supplement a depressingly unpredictable income.

Pamela headed a register of the needy. Although it no longer featured Anthony Creighton, Nellie Beatrice was on the list and had been the recipient of weekly cheques ever since her son had started work. Initially, these were necessarily modest, but after the success of *Look Back in Anger* she received a £40 monthly allowance, which in 1961 he increased by a further £25 a month, making £780 a year (equivalent to £16,300 in 2018.) Moreover, she became a regular weekend guest at The Old Water Mill. Now that he was wealthy, Osborne was financially generous. Sonia McGuinness, his secretary, was well-paid and her birthday and those of others close to him were never overlooked. Actors in his plays received gifts. He also responded to appeals from the representatives of good causes—a donation to a theatrical trust in Jamaica, aid for the victims of the Biafran War— and from various relatives, including the luckless Uncle Jack in Salisbury. At the same time, he discreetly came to the assistance of friends and those he had worked with who found themselves unexpectedly in financial need. Medical bills were quietly paid here, arrears of rent remedied there.

JO to PL ms letter BL

[The Old Water Mill]
9. 3. 66

My dear—

I've been meaning to write and see how you are. Also to find out if you have changed your address yet. I think you said in your last letter that you might be moving in March. Would you let me know? Also the phone number. I wonder if you'll be alone or as before.

The last few months have been rather glum for me. Principally because of poor George's long illness and then his death. He was a unique friend to me and I loved him dearly. Things seem very different now that he's gone.

I am coming up to London next week as Nolan is having a minor operation for hernia [sic] she had when she was born. It would be lovely to see you again for a few hours—or even less. Hope all is well for you. Let me know how you are—and where.

As ever

My love

John

The reason why Pamela thought of moving is unclear. If there were difficulties with Hazel, these had apparently reached a crisis point. In the event, however, both women remained where they were.

Bereft by the loss of Devine, Osborne also felt overwhelmed by Penelope, whose ferociously critical intellect and relentless social zeal had left him feeling professionally and socially lacking. In compensation, he had begun a relationship with Jill Bennett, who had played Countess Sophia Delyanoff, a leading role in *A Patriot for Me*. They had known each other socially for some time. A photograph exists of a lunch party given by Osborne and Penelope at The Old Water Mill in

1962, in which Osborne is pouring wine for their guests, including Jill, shown beaming at the camera. Paradoxically, although Jill appeared far more spontaneous and easy-going than Penelope, she was equally socially well-connected. Her family owned rubber plantations in the Malaysian peninsula, while she had been sent to boarding school in Surrey before going to RADA. While Penelope had begun to suspect her husband of having an affair, she had as yet no idea with whom. Losing his professional and emotional bearings, Osborne flailed in indecision. Having telephoned Pamela several times and failing to get a response, he dispatched an urgent postcard instead:

JO to PL ms postcard n/a BL

24.4.66

I've been ringing you but no answer. Perhaps you're away or working. Anyway, if you can please do ring me anytime (SLO 1520) but preferably before 11am as I'm rehearsing. I thought we might go to the theatre.

All love

John

Perhaps they did. In July, Pamela left London for Edinburgh, where she was due to appear in David Mercer's *Ride a Cock Horse* at the Traverse Theatre, as part of the Edinburgh Festival Fringe. Founded three years earlier, the tiny Traverse in the city's Old Town occupied an upper floor of a long-abandoned brothel once known locally as Kelly's Paradise. Osborne was meanwhile following the rehearsals for *A Bond Honoured*, his adaptation of Lope de Vega's *La Fianza Satisfecha*, starring Maggie Smith and his old friend Robert Stephens and which opened in John Dexter's production at the National Theatre at the Old Vic, on 6 June. Although Mervyn Jones in the weekly *Tribune*, a long-standing Osborne ally, preposterously declared it to be 'a work of genius that will last as long as the English language,' the daily newspaper critics united in a chorus of derision: 'pretentious bunkum,' declared the *Daily Mail;* 'delirious,' cried *The Times*. [32] A month later, the popular press was reporting the collapse of Osborne's marriage to Penelope and his liaison with Jill Bennett. Pamela, on the other hand, had unpublicized troubles of her own. Her difficulties, either over work or at Priory Road or both, were continuing and she was feeling bewildered and downhearted.

PL to JO ms letter Texas

TRAVERSE THEATRE CLUB
LAWNMARKET
EDINBURGH 1
18th July 1966

My dear John,

I've been thinking of you lately. I hope you're all right.

I hear you and Penelope have separated—if it was a bad time for you, which it must have been, I'm terribly sorry.

That isn't really why I'm writing, though.

For months I've felt—what is it?—oppressed, alone, and I can't overcome it by myself, though I've tried. I've found myself wanting to call on your strength, as I used to do, and I can't get this need out of my mind. Forgive me, your own resources may be low for all I know. All I want is to be assured that your love and friendship which you once offered me, are still mine for the asking, if I have to? It's too much to assume after so long.

I'm up here rehearsing 'Ride a Cock Horse' for this tiny theatre. I don't know if you [have] ever been in it. It holds about fifty seated on two sides of the acting area, which is about ten feet square. They're doing 'Six Characters in Search of an Author' this week. I'll go and see it tomorrow. I long to know how they all get on the stage.

I don't know where you are—will send this to your London address.

Much love—

Pamela

Six Characters in Search of an Author is an absurdist play by Luigi Pirandello, first produced in 1921. Pamela had written to Osborne at Chester Square, where Penelope and Nolan, who was now fourteen months old, remained after Osborne moved into a flat in Prince's Gate Mews with Jill Bennett. Alarmed by her letter, Osborne dispatched a telegram to the Traverse:

JO to PL telegram BL

20 July 1966

MY DEAR JUST GOT YOUR LETTER MY NUMBER IS KENSING-TON 1072 STOP I AM AT 33 PRINCES GATE MEWS STOP FROM FRIDAY TO MONDAY MORNING AT HELLINGLY 325 STOP PLEASE RELY ON ME STOP

If Pamela telephoned, then it was from Edinburgh, as she was appearing throughout the Festival and did not return to London until September. *Ride a Cock Horse* opened on 2 August. A 'long, difficult play' in which Peter, an adulterous, alcoholic writer, 'a sort of Jimmy Porter and Billy Liar combined,' eventually suffers a breakdown, it was directed by Stephen Frears, later a prominent film director but then recently graduated from Cambridge.[33] David Burke played Peter opposite Pamela as Nan. The critic from *The Scotsman* found it all intensely irritating. The writing allowed the main character such 'self-indulgence,' he observed, that 'the most insistent response' was merely one of 'embarrassment.' His sympathies lay not with Peter but his 'desperate wife,' where there was at least the respite of 'a really persuasive performance from Pamela Lane.'[34]

After the play closed on 19 August, Pamela remained in Edinburgh, appearing in the chorus of Euripides' *The Trojan Women*, which opened as part of the official Festival on 29 August in the appropriately gaunt setting of the city's Assembly Hall, usually the meeting place for the General Assembly of the Church of Scotland. Frank Dunlop's modern dress production, which starred Flora Robson, whose hand-wringing Pamela had once emulated in Bromley, as Hecuba, drew parallels with the escalation of American troops in Vietnam. 'Never was the waste and utter futility of war expressed so forcibly in dramatic terms,' commented *The Stage*. 'Dunlop's production has all the immediacy of a documentary.'[35]

A Greek tragedy of sorts had meanwhile enveloped Osborne in London, as a distressed Penelope at Chester Square battled to save her marriage and Jill, in Kensington, energetically laid claim to Osborne for herself. 'I have such a terror that I shall never see you again,' cried Penelope.[36] But: 'I've never felt so loved as you make me feel,' urged Jill, adding that: 'I'm glad you've accepted my final offer of marriage.'[37] Exhausted by overwork, the anxiety of meeting professional expectations and his habit of postponing decisions in his relationships with his lovers and hoping either that they would be made for him or things might resolve themselves of their own accord, Osborne, like Peter in *Ride a Cock Horse*, suffered a breakdown. His distressed wife delivered him into the care of the private Regent's Park Nursing Home, where doctors diagnosed severe strain and depression and psychiatrists prescribed sedatives and gentle, therapeutic conversation, not something at which Osborne excelled. Oscar Beuselinck, his lawyer, who knew all his client's affairs both professional and personal, was hurriedly instructed to act as gatekeeper, preventing the news of Osborne's predicament from reaching the press and only revealing it, on a strict 'need to know' basis, to a chosen few. Pamela, who in September returned from Edinburgh to London, was one of those entrusted with a guarded telephone call.

PL to JO ms letter no year date Texas

23a Priory Road

NW6

KIL 0352

September 14th [1966]

My darling—

I've only just heard from Oscar that you're feeling ill. I don't know anything about it or where you are, but if you'd like to see me, just ring or write or wire me here.

Please don't fail to call on my friendship if you need it, at any time. I remember you well and love you very much.

Yours ever,

Pamela

Pamela may have gone to see him, but with Penelope and Jill also visiting and each taking elaborate precautions to avoid the other, admittance to the patient was an intricate manoeuvre demanding constant vigilance and the most adroit judgement. Perhaps Pamela summoned her actor's sense of timing and succeeded. At one point, though, she sent an exploratory telegram, to which Jill replied on a postcard.

Jill Bennett to PL ms pc n/a BL

[London]
21 Oct 1966

Dear Pamela,

It was sweet of you to send the wire. Thank you—it's all settling a bit now—would you like to come and see it? John's better—and it would be lovely to see you again. Thank you

Love and fond wishes

Jill

Whether Pamela and Jill had met since 1959 is unclear. 'It' was *The Storm*, an adaptation by Doris Lessing of Alexander Ovstrovsky's 1859 play in which Jill was appearing as the scandalous Katerina in John Dexter's production at the National Theatre at the Old Vic. In November, and discharged from the nursing home, Osborne flew to Jamaica for a recuperative holiday, arriving back in London a few weeks later pronouncing himself fully restored. By this time, he and Penelope had agreed on a divorce.

After many months without work, Pamela was back at the Leatherhead Theatre Club, appearing on 29 November for two weeks in Henry Arthur Jones's *Mrs Dane's Defence*, a 'woman with a past' play first produced in 1900. This was followed by another eight months without stage work, her income again supplemented by market research and cheques from Osborne.

Nowadays, they would often meet for restful and nostalgic lunches at West End restaurants such as Boulestin's or Rules, where the hefty cost of the meal signalled that a certain elegance was required in their guests. Osborne had a taste for fashionable suits and ties and spent freely both in Carnaby Street and Savile Row, while Pamela, despite her much more limited means, also took great care in her appearance and devoted time and attention to prepare for their meetings. Her hair and make-up were by now very different to the audition photograph she had provided for Derby Playhouse. She looked a lot younger, for a start. Both she and Osborne were of a generation who spent their twenties looking like their parents and their thirties catching up with looking like themselves. Nowadays, Pamela's somewhat unruly hair was sometimes coerced into a quite expensive bob, while her make-up drew attention to her best features: wide, expressive eyes, strong cheekbones, delicately sensuous mouth. Her wardrobe included a lightweight A-line coat, fashionable at the time, and another in vivid jade green. Julia Lockwood, who had a flat at the other end of Priory Road to Pamela's, would often notice her friend pass by the window 'dressed up to the nines. I knew then that she was off to meet John for one of their lunches.'[38]

By this time, Osborne and Jill had moved into a house he had bought at Chelsea Square, a fifteen-minute walk away from Penelope, who remained with Nolan at Chester Square.

JO to PL ts letter BL

30 Chelsea Sq

London

17 April 1967

Dearest Pamela,

I'm dictating this note to you in a hurry as I only got your letter over the weekend and in case you are pressed I thought it would be better to get the enclosed off to you as soon as possible. I do hope it will help you out. If you need more, or any sort of help at all, do let me know.

Much love

John

The 'enclosed' was a cheque. On 31 August, Pamela appeared in another episode of the *Love Story* television series. She was in Leatherhead at the time, for two plays that would take her through until the end of November. On 4 September, she opened in *Let's Get a Divorce!*, an adaption of Sardou's 1880 farce in which an elderly, indifferent husband is married to a younger, indulged but neglected wife whose quest for divorce runs aground on the improbable sands of the couple discovering true love. It was directed by Hugh Paddick, an actor best known for the radio comedy series *Round the Horne*, and who had appeared in the London production a year earlier. Pamela, however, was more concerned by an intimidating demand for arrears of rent. Osborne quickly dispatched another cheque to avert a threatened eviction:

JO to PL ms letter BL

30 Chelsea Square

17. 10. 67

Darling—

Enclosed as promised. If you need more while I'm away, do please ring Sonia. She'll help. Don't lose heart. Will see if I can be of help. I'll be back Nov 4th Take care

With love

As ever

John

Sonia was Sonia McGuinness, Osborne's secretary, a trusted confidante who was with him between 1960 and 1971, typing the final drafts of his plays and his daily business correspondence. Osborne was on his way to Turkey to join Jill, who was on location for Tony Richardson's film of *The Charge of the Light Brigade*, in which she was playing Mrs Duberley. Crisis averted, Pamela returned to Leatherhead.

PL to JO ms letter n/a Texas

1 November 1967

My dear John,

A thousand thanks for keeping the home fires burning. Bless you, the worst of my worries are over. You are a good thing.

Love

Pam

A week later, on 6 November, she opened in *The Luck of the Navy* by Clifford Mills, a pseudonym shrouding the figure of Emelie Clifford, whose dramatic specialty was fervent, even jingoistic patriotism. Mills had been responsible for *Where the Rainbow Ends*, a flag-waving Christmas show first staged at the Savoy Theatre in 1911 and which had been such a hit that it returned for many years. *The Luck of the Navy*, a 1917 comedy in which 'straight but stupid' British Naval officers outwit 'crooked but clever' Germans, was designed to help the war effort by bolstering the pride and resolve of its audiences.

Once a popular but now a justifiably forgotten sub-genre of English theatrical history, the Naval comedy worked mainly on the principle that goofiness is no impediment to rectitude, and both are qualities that not only make the British so lovable, but invincible as well. *The Luck of the Navy* was the third of these things, after *Sweethearts and Wives* at York and *Little White Horses* at High Wycombe, in which Pamela had appeared. On its first production, explained *The Stage*, *The Luck of the Navy* was 'regarded as exciting, thrilling, rollicking, human, and calculated to go "straight to the heart of a British audience."' But even though 'the villains are splendidly led by Pamela Lane, whose ability to change from a hard-faced spy to a charming society hostess on the instant is admirable,' hearts and audiences, like many other things, had since changed.[39] It paid the rent, though, and in Pamela's present circumstances, that was what mattered.

JO to PL ms letter n/a BL

Nov 9 67

Pamela darling

Just got back. Delighted to hear from you and that you're working. Glad you liked the 'Times' piece. I got some fun out of it. You <u>must</u> come round here soon. I'll ring you next week.

Lots of love

John

'The *Times* piece' was an article published on 14 October. Ostensibly a review of two books, *The Rise and Fall of the Well-Made Play* by John Russell Taylor, which 'takes us trippingly through the Landseer school of dramatists, from Scribe through Pinero to Rattigan,' and *Theatre at Work* edited by Charles Marowitz and Simon Trussler, 'a collection of reprinted pieces from the mercifully defunct theatre magazine, *Encore,*' Osborne used the article to bemoan the state of contemporary theatre criticism. On 4 December 1967, he and Penelope were divorced. She was awarded custody of Nolan, whom she later took with her to New York, where she had been appointed film critic for the *New Yorker.* She retained the house at Chester Square, staying there on her visits to London.

JO to PL ms letter n/a BL

19. 12. 67

Darling—

Smashing to see you last night—and recovered.

I'd like to have brought you a present but I feel the enclosed wd be better and you can do as you wish with it. I hope you can buy something you need or covet. Do come for a meal in the New,

Take care

Love

John.

■ ■ ■

The following year, 1968, was one of upheaval for both Osborne and Pamela. At the beginning of the year, Elspeth Lane, Pamela's mother, died in Bridgwater at the age of sixty-eight. On 10 April, Tony Richardson's Woodfall film of *The Charge of the Light Brigade* opened to muted enthusiasm. This had not been a happy experience for Osborne. His initial screenplay had become becalmed by copyright complications, with the result that Richardson turned to Charles Wood to provide an alternative, the incident causing an angry breach between Osborne and his old collaborator. Just over a week later, on 19 April, the disgruntled playwright married Jill Bennett. The break with Richardson, however, was not the only thing to put his nose out of joint. Pamela had strenuously advised her former husband against marrying Jill, believing (correctly, as it turned out) that they were entirely incompatible. Osborne, whose loyalty to any woman with whom he happened to be in love was at the outset absolute, bridled. Although Pamela was a former wife, a close friend, confidante and occasional lover, he considered that she had intruded uninvited into his private affairs. As if badly stung, Osborne quickly retreated. Their friendship cooled, and they would not see each other again for over a decade.

On 23 May, *Time Present*, Osborne's new play, opened in Anthony Page's production at the Royal Court. Pamela may have been startled to discover that the leading character, a brittle, rancorous, pregnant, largely unemployed actress in her early thirties—although claiming to be twenty-nine—had the same name as herself and, moreover, was being played by Jill Bennett. Yet there is little similarity between the fictional Pamela and her real-life counterpart; if anything, the character is more plausibly a shrewd distillation of Jill herself. *Time Present* was followed at the same theatre on 3 July by *The Hotel in Amsterdam*, again directed by Page, in which Laurie, played by Paul Scofield, a jaded, insecure writer whose opinions broadly coincide with his creator's, and five others congratulate themselves on escaping the professional and emotional tyranny of KL, a film producer. This unseen character was assumed, correctly, by those close to Osborne to be his vengeful attack on Tony Richardson.

Both plays were celebrated at the *Evening Standard* Awards, Jill winning Best Actress for essentially playing a version of herself in *Time Present* and Osborne Best Play for *The Hotel in Amsterdam*. But while Harold Hobson, the theatre critic for *The Sunday Times* and a long-standing and perceptive Osborne supporter, declared *The Hotel in Amsterdam* to be 'the best contemporary play in London,' there was also a widespread undertow of misgiving.[40] Mary McCarthy had protested after *A Patriot for Me* that Osborne was becoming predictable. *A Bond Honoured* had been widely denounced. Now the mutterings were louder and more insistent. The Angry Young Man of the fifties, it was said, had failed to adapt himself to the liberalizing, classless spirit of the sixties. Pamela was merely 'a feminine Jimmy Porter,' complained Ronald Bryden in the *Observer*, 'heaping scorn on contemporary Britain,' and there was Laurie, 'with his prejudices,' grumbled Benedict Nightingale in *Plays and Players*, 'his mistrust of the world… his fear of spiritual impotence, his anxieties about becoming older and staler…'[41] Elsewhere, other voices were making much the same point. Osborne, it was suggested, was not as radical as had once been thought and was now revealing himself in his true if unappealing colours. 'Thus do the angry young men of 1956 turn into the Edwardian high Tories of 1968,' concluded Martin Esslin sadly.[42]

In July, as *The Hotel in Amsterdam* opened at the Royal Court and *Time Present* transferred to the West End, Pamela was in Bournemouth, the scene of her parents' 1923 honeymoon. It was a resort still renowned for its seafront palm trees and a population of the comfortably retired upper-middle class augmented by summer visitors attracted by the town's reputation of being much more refined than Brighton. She joined the Summer Theatre Company, directed by Richard Digby Day, an ambitious twenty-eight-year-old 'ebullient extrovert,' born in Cardiff and 'the first student of direction RADA ever had.'[43] Pamela and Digby Day would collaborate several times in the future, and become lifelong friends. 'She was a very impressive woman,' he recalled many years later, 'and at her best, she was an absolutely outstanding actress.'[44]

The company was stationed at the Palace Court Theatre, a curious building with a vaguely Egyptian façade near the promenade. There was ruthless competition for Bournemouth's holiday cash that summer. The Winter Gardens was quaking from 'the noisiest show on the south coast' as the singer Tom Jones 'thundered through his favourite songs,' while at the Pier Approach Baths, 'stars of previous Olympics' were splashing about in an aquatic version of *The Adventures of Robinson Crusoe*, a show featuring rather more carefully choreographed diving than that conceived by Defoe. Down the road at the Pavilion, audiences deterred by deafening pop and a swimming pool extravaganza were being soothed by 'the restful humour' of Dickie Henderson, a television light entertainer topping the bill of a 'clean and cleverly balanced' variety show providing 'oceans of fun and merriment.'[45]

Those opting for the Summer Theatre discovered more economical, even threadbare fare: a comedy and a murder mystery performed by the same four actors whose 'splendid teamwork' was nevertheless earning 'warm praise from theatre-goers.' Pamela appeared as Sheila, a befuddled, deceived wife, in Alan Ayckbourn's *Relatively Speaking*, a 1965 comedy of mistaken identity in which a jealous boyfriend visits his girlfriend's older lover and his wife innocently assuming them to be her parents. In J. Lee Thompson's *Murder Without Crime*, a hugely successful thriller involving 'dark doings at a Mayfair flat,' she played Jan, another wife obliged to deal with a situation not encountered in most marital relationships. After a quarrel with her husband, Jan leaves the apartment and much of the play, while her husband has a night on the town, returning in the company of a nightclub hostess whom he murders when Jan telephones to announce that she is on her way home for reconciliation. 'Drama, cynicism and revenge [are] ingeniously blended,' enthused *The Stage*, 'as the mystery of the body in the ottoman is cleared up.' [46]

Both plays were directed by Michael Winter, Digby Day's assistant. Digby Day himself left Bournemouth that autumn to lead the English-speaking section of the Welsh Theatre Company at the New Theatre in Cardiff. From there, he summoned Pamela to play the title role in Shaw's *Candida*, opening on 11 November and afterwards going on a Welsh tour. When she returned to London, a terse note arrived from Osborne, seemingly their first communication since Pamela's appeal against his marrying Jill.

JO to PL ms letter n/a BL

12 Dec 1968

I don't like sending you £—but I'm sure you'd rather this than sand or something. Anyway, a quid New Year an' a' that.

With my love. And from JB.

John

JB was Jill Bennett, with whom Osborne spent Christmas at Chelsea Square. Although there was considerable cause for optimism in his embarking on what he called a 'new life' with Jill and *The Hotel in Amsterdam* following *Time Present* into the West End, where it was joined by a revival of *Look Back in Anger*, he was also more than usually anxious.[47] Dismayed by the critical doubts over his work and, since the death of Devine, uncertain of his future at the Royal Court, he was also worried about money. One day in February 1969, he returned from a distressing lunch with Walter Strach, his accountant, who had informed Osborne that instead of being comfortably cushioned by the royalties from his plays and from *Tom Jones*, as he had assumed, he was actually in debt, already owing £50,000 in tax and £40,000 to his own production company (equivalent to £775,000 and £620,000 in

2018.) Money was leaching away and had been for a long time. In the year ending January 1968, for example, Osborne's 'personal expenses' amounted to almost £15,000 (£245,000) while slightly more had been splashed out on renovations at Chelsea Square. Then there was the Bentley, the crates of champagne that he and Jill ordered without a second thought, his expensive divorce from Penelope and the maintenance for Nolan, the secretary, the chauffeur, the house in the country and the housekeepers. It was all costing much more than he ever contemplated. In fact, he had never contemplated it at all. That, his accountant pointed out and Oscar Beuselinck sadly confirmed, was precisely the problem.

Digging in at Chelsea Square, Osborne hurriedly drew up lists of how he might save and how he might make money. The Old Water Mill was quickly sold and at Jill's prompting, he resuscitated his dormant acting career, appearing with her in three short television plays. Financial necessity enabled him to overcome his old aversion to Shaw by appearing as Beerbohm Tree in Richard Huggett's *The First Night of Pygmalion*, a television play speculating on Shaw's encounter with the fiery Mrs Patrick Campbell, and broadcast on 23 December 1969. Much needed royalties arrived from the New York transfer of *A Patriot for Me* in which Maximilian Schell, who had become a close friend, reprised the role of Redl, while the following year Osborne pocketed a fee for playing Maidanov, a poet, in Schell's film *First Love*, based on Turgenev's novella, *Erste Liebe*. At the same time, Osborne dashed off *The Right Prospectus*, a television play and his first for ten years. Yet even these measures, added to the still lucrative royalties from his plays, were insufficient to avert the crisis hurtling towards him. Pamela, meanwhile, who appears to have done no stage work after the Welsh tour of *Candida* finished at the end of 1968, was also facing a more than usually tightly budgeted Christmas and New Year a few miles away in Kilburn.

The 1970s

■ ■ ■

■ ■ ■

The communications blackout that Osborne imposed between himself and his first wife continued throughout and beyond his marriage to Jill Bennett. During this time both he and Pamela were beset by personal difficulties and immersed in debilitating professional struggles, Osborne flinging himself into writing potentially well-paid but exasperatingly unsold film screenplays, Pamela coping with stretches of unemployment. Yet at the end of the decade they emerged from their separate troubles to encouraging signals that a brighter future, both for their careers and their friendship, lay tantalizingly ahead.

By the time *The Right Prospectus* was broadcast to argumentative reviews on 22 October 1970, Pamela was about to return to Cardiff, where a month later, on 23 November, she opened as Maria Wislake in Richard Digby Day's revival of Frederick Lonsdale's 1926 comedy, *On Approval.* This very English play, in which society widow Maria Wislake hauls her young admirer off to her Scottish country house to road-test him as a possible husband, was the inaugural production at the Welsh Theatre Company's Studio Theatre, a converted Mission Hall near the city centre. Although it has its share of snappy dialogue, ('a dinner party lasts two hours, marriage has been known to last two years,') the play almost certainly influenced Coward's altogether snappier *Private Lives* four years later, with the result that the latter has more or less eclipsed the former. Nevertheless, Digby Day's effervescent production was admired for its 'fine sense of style,' and Pamela for giving a 'dynamic performance.'[1]

Meanwhile, Osborne, desperate for quick money, was continuing to revitalize his acting career, signing up for a few days' filming on *Get Carter*. An atmospheric and sadistic gangland thriller set mostly in Newcastle, directed by Mike Hodges and starring Michael Caine as a professional assassin on the trail of his brother's killer, Osborne cornered a few scenes as Kinnear, a crime overlord. It was his most successful screen performance, silkily sneering and 'wholly convincing,' acknowledged the *Observer*, when the film was released in March 1971.² At the Royal Court, where Anthony Page had succeeded George Devine as artistic director, *West of Suez*, Osborne's latest play, opened in Page's production a few months later on 17 August. Set on a former British colony in the Caribbean and starring Ralph Richardson as an elderly writer lamenting the changes in his life, it failed to mollify those convinced that Osborne was travelling further to the political right. And yet, countered Harold Hobson in *The Sunday Times*, it was 'one of his finest plays.'³ It was 'about the decaying of tongues,' explained Osborne, 'not just of colonial empires but emotional empires too.'⁴

Osborne's own emotional empire was in a precipitously perilous state. At the same time as his professional confidence, buckled since the death of Devine, collapsed still further under concerted critical assault, his marriage to Jill was acrimoniously disintegrating, and not only privately behind the doors of 30 Chelsea Square. Waiters at the more refined Belgravia restaurants were beginning to find them unnerving guests, their unrestrainedly loud bickering hijacking the hushed, soothing atmosphere conducive to expensive dining. What had begun for Osborne as a larky respite from keeping pace with Penelope's professional and social expectations had become soured by a combustible combination of his anxieties and vulnerabilities, and Jill's volatility and neuroses. Pamela had been right. He and Jill were essentially, catastrophically, incompatible. He resorted to tablets to buck him up, tablets to calm him down, and more and more wine, vodka and champagne. He was becoming alcoholic. Over the next six years, holed up in his study and surrounded by bottles and bills, he despairingly noted the appalling debris of their marriage and the simultaneous decline of his health in a series of journals. He wrote of the rows, frequently fuelled by drink, the insults, the mutual denigration, the occasional violence. He sagged under bouts of obliterating migraine, monitored skin rashes suddenly flaring a volcanic red before inexplicably fading, endured sleepless, sweating nights and hours of bleak despondency, drinking and struggling with work. And still the bills fluttered through the letter box.

He thought of ringing Pamela, but decided against it. He consulted an array of doctors, quarrying out assessments, fishing for second opinions and scrutinizing possible remedies. There was Patrick Woodcock, a doctor with a predominantly show business list whom he treated at his private surgery in Tachbrook Street, behind Victoria Station, a man so fascinated by his patients that a consultation tended to turn into a brisk discussion of the latest plays and books. In search of a diagnosis for chronic pain, he consulted Dr Mason, a specialist who sought advice from Dr Brian Piggott in Weymouth Street, who 'prefers to use the rather vague term of inflammatory anthropathy until further x-rays have been done', and made appointments for him in Wimpole Street and Harley Street.[5] A further batch of consultants at University College Hospital administered more exploratory tests. A West End acupuncturist silently probed.

In the autumn of 1971, while Osborne was making befuddled inventories of his various symptoms, Pamela made her first venture into Shakespeare since leaving RADA almost a quarter of a century earlier. She joined the New Shakespeare Company, a bucolic organization braving the vagaries of the English summer by performing at the Open Air Theatre in Regent's Park. Richard Digby Day's productions of *Romeo and Juliet* and *A Midsummer Night's Dream* were setting out on a national indoor tour and in September, Pamela took over the roles of Lady Capulet in *Romeo and Juliet* and Hippolyta in the *Dream*. Gary Raymond, who had played Cliff in a Royal Court revival of *Look Back in Anger* in 1957 and again in the film version, played 'a wise and compassionate' Oberon in the *Dream* opposite his wife, Delena Kidd, but as so often, Pamela's name eluded the national press.[6]

Back in London, Osborne fought on, preparing a version of Ibsen's *Hedda Gabler*, a play, he declared, by which 'I have been fascinated for a long time,' probably from having seen both Peggy Ashcroft and Pamela playing the title role.[7] Anthony Page's production, starring Jill Bennett, opened at the Royal Court on 28 June 1972. Considering that, apart from modernizing a few phrases, Osborne's work amounted to little more than emphasizing the tone he hoped the production might adopt, it was diplomatically billed as being 'adapted' (rather than translated) 'by John Osborne.' 'He has not imposed himself on *Hedda Gabler*,' acknowledged Harold Hobson in the *Sunday Times*. 'He shows there is something in *Hedda Gabler* that has imposed itself on him. It is a perception of boredom as being one of the most powerful activating forces in human nature.'[8] Almost six months later, on 4 December, *A Sense of Detachment* opened at the same theatre. An anarchic, freewheeling semi-cabaret outlining Osborne's current perception of England as a land of decency slithering into one of self-serving brutality, it failed to impose itself on almost everyone. It was the last of his plays to be produced at the Royal Court.

In January 1973, as he sank further into despondency and alcohol, Osborne might have blearily watched Pamela in *Fitton v Pusey*, a three-part drama in the *Crown Court* television series. She played a supporting role as the wife of a retired Army Major fighting a libel action against a military historian accusing him of dereliction of duty during the Korean War, the conflict that had formed the backdrop to *Personal Enemy*, the play he and Anthony Creighton had written all those years ago. He was beginning to conclude that the theatre in general had no place for him anymore. Confirmation of this came the following year when *A Place Calling Itself Rome*, a contemporary interpretation of Shakespeare's *Coriolanus*, became the first of his plays for twenty-three years to fail to find a producer.

At the end of August, Pamela was back in Leatherhead, where the Theatre Club had metamorphosed into the Thorndike Theatre and moved into new premises. 'Hidden behind a street-front of commercial mediocrity is [architecturally speaking] one of the best theatres of the 1960s,' asserted the Twentieth Century Society, approving an unusual reversal, the conversion of a 1930s cinema into a 500-seat theatre. The company may have moved, but it had not abandoned its beloved Jean Anouilh, 'the most popular playwright in the esteem of their audiences,' acknowledged *The Stage*.[9] A sample of the dramatist's seemingly inexhaustible output continued to be programmed each season and on 18 September, Pamela appeared as Lady Hurf in *Thieves Carnival*. She was 'distinctly right,' thought *The Stage*, 'as the diversion-seeking older woman from whom love has departed, leaving nothing in its wake.'[10] Immediately afterwards, while Osborne in London planned more film screenplays, Pamela returned to York for the first time, professionally speaking, for almost twenty years, for a run of three plays that would take her into the middle of the following year.

■ ■ ■

Joyce Kay was a primary school music teacher, sixteen years Pamela's senior and now aged fifty-nine. They had met almost twenty years previously in 1956, when the Kay family had answered one of the Theatre Royal's regular appeals in the local newspaper for rooms to let. They had a spare room at their home in Lumley Road, a five-minute walk from the theatre, could run to the late supper stipulated by the theatre management, and Pamela, recently arrived in York, became one of their first lodgers. Now, seventeen years later, she returned to the same house where, her parents having died, Joyce lived alone. During the intervening years, she had continued to go to Theatre Royal productions, become a bastion of the York Schools' Music Association and was a vice-President of York Opera, a relentlessly enthusiastic amateur group specializing in annual productions of operetta.

Through Joyce, Pamela became acquainted with a theatrical and musical network, largely comprised of women, the nucleus of which included Helen Wilkinson, a set designer at the theatre, Beryl Bunn, her assistant, Peter Clayton, a former stage manager and Jan, his wife, a dance teacher, Pauline Marshall, a co-founder of York Opera and a Gilbert and Sullivan devotee, and Clive, her equally musical husband. Apart from Pamela, the group's out-of-town members included Jean Alexander, an actress who had joined the Theatre Royal shortly after Pamela's departure. Clad in a pinny, headscarf and curlers, she had since imprinted herself upon the nation's consciousness as Hilda Ogden, the gossiping cleaner at the Rovers' Return pub in *Coronation Street*, television's longest running soap opera.

They established an agenda of meeting socially, lunching at each other's houses, block-booking musical events, gathering at Christmas and even, although Pamela never joined these, venturing on summer holidays together, favouring the classical music cruises operated by the P & O line. Although sailing was not in her line, music was and Pamela began spending occasional weekends and longer in York, taking in a concert or an opera at the same time. 'The Pamela Lane that we knew was a gracious, modest, almost self-effacing lady who could also be extremely amusing,' recalled Pauline Marshall. 'If she was in a room of people, she would soon gather a group around her, not because she set out to do so, but because people were drawn to her. She would entertain everyone with stories about the theatre.' Entertaining she might have been, but she was not entirely forthcoming. 'I had known her some time before anyone told me about her marriage,' added Pauline Marshall. 'I don't remember her talking about John Osborne at all.'[11]

In November 1973, Pamela appeared in David Storey's *Home*, originally produced three years earlier and an elegiac piece of 'gentlest intuition, sympathy and immediate observation,' thought Merete Bates, one of a growing band of arts correspondents for *The Guardian*.[12] A novelist as much as a playwright, mining the themes of family, work and industrial Yorkshire, Storey had come to prominence with *This Sporting Life,* a novel about a rugby league player, later transformed by Lindsay Anderson into one of the emblematic New Wave films of the 1960s. Anderson had gone on to direct several of Storey's plays at the Royal Court, including *Home.* Set in an institutional garden, furnished solely by a metalwork table and four chairs, where the benevolent Harry and the self-aggrandizing Jack, recalling disconnected snatches of the past, are joined by the unnervingly flirtatious Kathleen, laughing inappropriately at any remark that might inadvertently be construed as sexual, and the disconcertingly cynical Marjorie. It transpires that this rural idyll is deceptive, that these are the grounds of a mental hospital and the people four of the patients. Humanity and vulnerability lies in the detail, and as Kathleen, noted *The Guardian,* 'Pamela Lane rawly conveys the nervy abandonment of a woman broken.'[13]

While appearing in one of the finest plays of 1970, Pamela was rehearsing one of the previous year's finest and technically most adroit comedies. Alan Ayckbourn's *How the Other Half Loves,* deftly combines theatrical ingenuity with sharp insights into marriage and social class. Two adjoining living rooms share the stage, one belonging to Frank and Fiona Foster, an affluent company director and his wife, the other to Bob and Teresa Phillips, an up-and-coming employee and his socially militant wife, with the action taking place in each simultaneously. Fiona and Bob are pursuing a vigorous affair, and the play's most celebrated scene involves a dinner party given by both couples to a third, the Featherstones, whom Bob and Fiona attempt to use as alibis to cover their adultery. This time *The Guardian* was not present to record Pamela's adulterous Fiona, deviser of stratagems and juggler of divided loyalties, and the Theatre Royal records for this period are apparently lost. However, the following March, Robin Thornber, *The Guardian's* northern theatre critic, caught up with her at the city's Art Centre where she was reunited with Richard Digby Day, who was directing the northern premiere of Marguerite Duras's *The Lovers of Viorne.* Based upon a notorious French murder case, the one hundred-minute play comprises a series of interrogations into the motives of Pierre Lannes and Claire, his wife, convicted of the killing and dismembering a deaf-mute woman who kept house for Claire's cousin. According to Thornber, the performances, including Pamela as Claire, were 'as finely tuned as the writing. There was no curtain call at the end, not so much as a slap of applause. Not, I think, because the audience was unimpressed, but—and this is the ultimate theatrical compliment—because they were too stunned.' [14]

The absence of a curtain call was unusual but not unprecedented. Elizabeth Robins, the great American pioneer of Ibsen in London during the 1890s had done much the same at the end of the British premiere of *Hedda Gabler* in an attempt to preserve the illusion of Hedda as a real figure. Pamela's was evidently a compelling performance and in London, and considering that this was only the second production of *The Lovers of Viorne* in Britain, the first being at the Royal Court in 1971, it would have attracted considerable attention. But in those metropolitan-centred, pre-digital days, the great disadvantage facing Pamela and the many actors working predominantly outside the capital was of their work being overlooked nationally and unnoticed by London producers and casting agents. Critics in towns and cities across the country were regularly out and about, recording the fortunes of their nearby theatres for their local paper, but their readership was geographically limited. Regional productions were not given much priority by national daily newspaper editors for whom the world revolved about London, and there were as yet few journalists such as the indefatigable Thornber, who championed regional theatre and dictated his hand-written reviews from a public telephone to the newspaper's copy-takers usually within half an hour of the curtain falling.

The Guardian's reviews were widely read, as were those in *The Times*, but the fact that regional theatre reviews were both arbitrary and irregular was exasperating for repertory actors ambitious for wider recognition. Instead, they relied for wider coverage mainly upon *The Stage*, a weekly show business paper whose nationwide legion of critics provided extensive, though not fully comprehensive coverage. Generally, you could catch up not only with whatever was happening in Leeds, Newcastle, Nottingham or Exeter, but in Woking or Sunderland, Norwich or Torquay as well. There was, though, something about *The Stage*, a sense that because the paper was read exclusively by the profession, its reviews were more supportive than judgmental, more circumspect, more respectful, more cognizant of the actor's sensitivities—and usually all the actors were mentioned—than the more independent voices of *The Guardian* or *Times*.

Despite Robin Thornber and *The Guardian*, once Pamela walked off stage at the end of *The Lovers of Viorne*, she disappeared into her longest period of unemployment yet, as far as the theatre was concerned. She seems to have done no stage work for over three years. Presumably, she subsisted on casual work, supplemented, perhaps, by odd days working for radio or television.

Osborne too was discovering the sensation of not being in demand. Until recently, his theatrical territory had been Sloane Square and the West End. But as two more plays, *The End of Me Old Cigar* and an adaptation of Oscar Wilde's *The Picture of Dorian Gray*, joined *A Place Called Rome* and a series of film treatments on a reproachful pile of unproduced work on his desk, he felt a homeless outcast. In a bid to break the deadlock, he jettisoned Marjory Vosper, his agent of eighteen years, and turned to the formidable Robin Dalton of International Creative Management, who secured him a 'season' of his work at Greenwich. It was disappointingly off the beaten track, but she insisted that as the country was in the midst of an economic recession, it was the best that could be done and that he should be grateful. But *A Place Called Rome* was denied entry even there. Instead, a revival of *The Entertainer*, starring Max Wall and which Osborne directed, provided the bait for audiences which, it was hoped, would brave the winter evenings and return for *The End of Me Old Cigar* and *The Picture of Dorian Gray*. He had also sold two television plays: *Ms, or Jill and Jack* and *The Gift of Friendship*, both broadcast in September. But neither the Greenwich season nor the television plays drew wholly approving reviews. Pamela saw the new plays at Greenwich, as she saw all Osborne's work, and thought them disappointingly inferior to his earlier output. As Richard Digby Day later put it, she, like many others these days, identified 'a diminution of talent.'[15]

■ ■ ■

With the mid-seventies came a flurry of deaths. On 3 April 1975, Mary Ure, Osborne's second wife, died in London from an overdose of alcohol and barbiturates, aged forty-two. Five days later, Pamela's friend Hazel Coppen, after a lengthy struggle against cancer, died in hospital, aged fifty-one. Pamela was now alone at Priory Road. A few months later, on 14 September, William Ivor Lane, her father, died in Somerset. He was seventy-seven, and after a lifetime in the drapery trade, left an estate valued at £41,733 (equivalent to £321,000 in 2018). Pamela attended the funerals of her friend and her father, while Osborne avoided that of his second wife. The following year in London, Patrick Desmond, theatrical jack-of-all-trades, died aged sixty-eight. He had suffered a heart attack while on the bus home from buying food for his cats, and was discovered, still sitting upright in his seat on the upper deck, by the conductor when the bus ended its route at the depot. His cremation service at Golders Green Crematorium in September was enlivened by Sarah Churchill, a daughter of the wartime Prime Minister, a former Scala Theatre Peter Pan and an actress whose career was defined by her flamboyant lifestyle, singing *Home on the Range*, although neither Pamela nor Osborne were there to hear her.

Even though Osborne might have disparaged it, both he and Pamela were accustomed to Desmond's impermanent, opportunist world and were wary of institutions such as the Royal Shakespeare Company and the National Theatre, with their fortifications of dramaturgs, literary managers, supervisory committees and scrutinizing accountants, all of whom, in their eyes, potentially killed the experiment and spontaneity they believed essential to creation. The prospect of a production, though, got the better of Osborne's misgivings of the National, which had produced *A Bond Honoured*, and was still housed at the Old Vic. It was there that *Watch It Come Down*, Osborne's new play, starring Frank Finlay and Jill Bennett and directed by Bill Bryden, opened on 24 February 1976, before transferring a month later to the Lyttelton Theatre in the company's new South Bank building. A caustic and largely autobiographical examination of marital loathing, reflecting the social and moral disintegration that Osborne perceived all around him, the reviews were as scathing as he had come to expect. Peter Hall, the company's new artistic director in succession to Laurence Olivier, closed the production in June, pleading rapidly diminishing ticket sales.

By that time, Osborne had finally decided that he had had enough, not only of Hall and the National Theatre, but also of Jill and London, and escaped to Christmas Place, his newly-acquired, secluded Edwardian country house near Edenbridge in

Kent. As he was still inundated by debt, the house was a wild expense, yet Osborne had the knack of finding money when he most needed it. There were various bank accounts dotted about here and there, and all were plundered at one time or another. He even splashed out on the building of a swimming pool in the grounds.

He was joined at Christmas Place by Helen Dawson, who would later become wife number five and Osborne's eventual widow. A compact, forthright woman, they had known each other for several years. Ten years his junior, she was born in Newcastle upon Tyne, on 11 March 1939, the daughter and only child of Graeme Dawson, an accountant, and his wife. After school at Hunmanby Hall, a Methodist boarding school for girls in York (might she even have seen Pamela at the Theatre Royal?) Helen had read history at Durham University and spent a year at Brown on Rhode Island before returning to London, where she joined the *Observer* in 1960. Later, she became a drama critic and the newspaper's arts editor, in which capacity she encountered Osborne. They discovered they had family circumstances in common. Like him, Helen had suffered the early death of a parent. Osborne was ten when his father died, while Helen's mother had died when her daughter was in her early twenties. Coincidentally, in both instances it was the parent to whom the child was most devoted who had died. Osborne's veneration of the memory of his father was mirrored by Helen's of her mother, and his dislike of Nellie Beatrice by Helen's distrust of her step-mother, whom she considered responsible for coming between father and daughter to such an extent that they lost contact. This shared memory, and Osborne's misfortunes with Penelope and Nolan, did not prevent them, however, from hoping to become parents themselves. In their earliest months and years together, Osborne and Helen decided they would like children. Osborne hankered after more daughters, and as he was forty-five and she thirty-five, it was perfectly feasible for a few years yet. But the years went by and they were not successful.

■ ■ ■

Meanwhile, Pamela was still searching for stage work and as the summer of 1977 came to an end, she was finally successful. On 27 September, she reappeared at the Thorndike, Leatherhead, where the repertoire had taken a surprisingly daring departure, ambushing an unsuspecting audience accustomed to the works of Jean Anouilh with a rarely performed double bill of plays by Tennessee Williams. The umbrella title of *Garden District* shelters *Something Unspoken* and *Suddenly Last Summer*, plays originally performed in New York in 1958 at the height of the McCarthy era, and both dealing with formidable southern matriarchs confronting the spectre of homosexuality, largely implied but disturbingly close to home. In the first, Miss Gloria Scott, in her sixties, wealthy, elaborately dressed, anxious to be elected to the local branch of the Daughters of the Confederacy, demands that Grace, her long-term companion, admit the relationship that until now has remained unspoken between them; in the second, Mrs Violet Venable attempts to induce Catherine, her fragile niece, into submitting to a lobotomy in the hope that it might prevent her revealing the homosexuality and macabre death of her son, Sebastian. Yet the productions, directed by Joan MacAlpine, the Thorndike's new director, while much admired locally, passed unnoticed nationally even by *The Stage*, which for Pamela, a devotee of Williams and for whom the plays were important, was intensely disappointing. A few months later, *Tomorrow Never Comes*, a film thriller made largely in Quebec by Peter Collinson, was similarly overlooked for which Osborne, who in one of his quick sorties after cash played the part of a sleazy hotel manager, was deeply grateful. A few months later, on 22 February, Pamela was at the Liverpool Playhouse for a fortnight, making another rare excursion into Shakespeare, appearing as Gertrude opposite Christopher Neame's Hamlet, directed by Peter Watson, a former assistant to Richard Digby Day at the New Shakespeare Company. It too passed without comment.

Osborne and Jill were acrimoniously divorced on 10 August 1977. Almost a year later, on 2 June 1978, he and Helen married in Kent. She was the only one of his wives to formally take his name and renounce not only her own successful career in favour of his, but also London. Although Penelope had attempted a rural life at The Old Water Mill, her metropolitan instincts quickly got the better of her and the Osbornes had returned to London. Helen, though, liked the country and, moreover, had decided to make Osborne her mission in life. Her policy regarding her husband was one of fierce protection and seemingly infinite tolerance, and over the years she honed this skill to a fine art. Closeted in Kent, she drew him back from the further reaches of alcoholic self-destruction, successfully eliminating the vodka of recent years and reducing his wine intake. She cooked, organised his voluminous archives and his business correspondence, took over the typing of his manuscripts and generally defended him against the world. Friends soon observed him looking better than he had for a long time: bearded, pinkly cheerful, he seemed robust and, equally important, content. Other changes were made: the Osbornes set themselves up as hosts. Friends were invited. Even Nellie Beatrice, barred by Mary Ure, redeemed during the Penelope Gilliatt period but banned again during the Jill Bennett years, found herself reprieved yet again and the recipient of invitations to large, very English Sunday lunches of roast beef and Yorkshire pudding.

Helen's strategy was not entirely ironclad. She instigated a regime of guardianship, attention and nurture, but there was also a good deal of collusion. Jill had not been abstemious where alcohol was concerned, and neither was Helen. Osborne's champagne consumption remained virtually unchecked, and as a heavy smoker herself, she permitted him to continue incinerating himself with his favoured Turkish cigarettes. The alcohol and the nicotine became progressive as the years passed. Nor did the spending let up; or not yet. Each sympathetic to the other's foibles and prejudices, their often dyspeptic views of the world and many of the people in it dovetailed neatly and, like those of many couples, would become almost undistinguishable as time went on.

A couple of months after their marriage, a newly energetic Osborne was back in London and at the Royal Court, directing a revival of *Inadmissible Evidence*, once again with Nicol Williamson playing Maitland. 'I found it an overwhelming experience,' reported Michael Billington in *The Guardian*, 'a piece of emotional drama of frightening, skull-battering power.'[16] It is unclear whether Pamela continued to receive a share of the revenues and extremely unlikely that they met, as Osborne's postcard of 14 December the following year evidently breaks a long silence.

By the end of the decade, as Osborne was settling in to the country and his latest marriage, Pamela, after another year seemingly without stage work, was embarking at last upon a long-awaited resurrection of her theatrical career, and one that looked very promising indeed. In February 1979, she was at the Leicester Haymarket, playing Mary Tyrone in Eugene O'Neill's *Long Day's Journey into Night*, a monumental account of a single day in the life of a mutually destructive family bound together by guilt, recrimination, and dependence, governed by James

Tyrone, an alcoholic actor manqué, and his wife, Mary, despairingly addicted to morphine. Both leading roles are considered particularly challenging, calling for great reserves of both emotional insight and physical stamina to carry the audience through a lengthy evening. 'There can be few plays more aptly named,' added Charles Sigler, the critic of the *Leicester Mercury.* 'The subject is morbid, the vision bleak... [and the] final act stretches concentration to the limit, and beyond.'[17] However, he was relieved to discover that Scott Antony's production 'is deeply moving and the performances pure gold,' with Bob Cartland's Tyrone 'faultless' and 'Pamela Lane's dope-addicted Mary stunningly played.'[18]

Joining the Haymarket Theatre was a propitious move, as this, noted *The Stage*, was 'a theatre which has shot to the forefront of British regional theatre activity.'[19] Pamela would return regularly over the next five years. Wedged into a modern redbrick shopping centre, the Haymarket had opened in 1973 and boasted a clinically contemporary auditorium of exposed ceiling pipes, a thrust stage and, curiously for a new building, a theatre ghost, that of a young boy in a sailor suit thought to be the shade of a child who had drowned in a well deep below the foundations and who looked in occasionally on rehearsals. There was, though, another figure from the past stalking the corridors, this time reassuringly corporeal and whom Pamela recognised. This was Leslie Twelvetrees, the former Derby Playhouse director, who, after the fire in 1956 had managed a theatre in Redcar before returning to a revived Derby Playhouse during the 1960s, and had arrived in Leicester to become the Haymarket's first house manager.

Although Twelvetrees was now seventy and retired, like the theatre ghost he still looked in on the shows. He was among the last of his kind. Brought up as a child among musicians and actors, he had become a repertory theatre manager who also acted and directed. Many of the directors with whom Pamela had worked had previously been actors and some still were. Scott Antony, the director of *A Long Day's Journey into Night*, both acted and directed and in 1972 had starred as the French Vorticist sculptor Henri Gaudier-Brzeska in *Savage Messiah*, one of Ken Russell's frantically eccentric film biographies. Two years later, he had appeared in the more sedate *Dead Cert*, Tony Richardson's film version of the racecourse novel by Dick Francis.

But increasingly, actors and playwrights of Pamela and Osborne's generation were becoming aware of a further shift of the ground beneath their feet. With the fading of the regional repertory system, all-rounders such as Twelvetrees were fading too. So many younger directors and playwrights these days came equipped not with a repertory background but a university degree. Robin Midgeley was a case in point. The assertive artistic director at the Haymarket, Midgeley was six years Osborne and Pamela's younger and had graduated from Cambridge and joined the BBC drama department before moving into the theatre. At Leicester, he planned enterprising seasons combining revivals and new plays, funded by a combination of state subsidy and the lucrative revenues from touring musicals. In 1979, when Pamela arrived, a Leicester revival of *My Fair Lady* was politely entertaining British cities, while a new production of Rodgers and Hammerstein's *Oklahoma!* directed by none other than Oscar Hammerstein's son, James, was in the works and already pencilled in for the West End.

Seven months later, in September, Pamela returned to Leicester to appear first in *Caste*, a Victorian melodrama by T.W. Robertson first produced in 1867, and then the world premiere of *An Early Life* by Frederic Raphael. Both were to be directed by Michael Meacham, the Haymarket's associate director, an exact contemporary of Pamela with the more familiar background of a formerly having been an actor, while his management skills had been sharpened at the Citizens Theatre in Glasgow.

Caste is one of those titles familiar to readers of theatrical history as purportedly heralding the socially-observant theatre of Pinero, Henry Arthur Jones and Bernard Shaw, but as the play is so rarely revived the suggestion does not really mean very much. The plot involves George, who appalls his French aristocratic parents by marrying an impoverished ballet dancer, fathering a son and promptly departing with his regiment for India, where he is killed in action, leaving the child to be brought up by his grandmother. Pamela stepped forward as the Marquise de St Mauré, George's mother, 'grand and comically snobbish,' observed the actor Roger Davenport from his position as Captain Hawtree, one of the play's sprinkling of toffs. 'It's a difficult line to tread when the function of the part is to be an almost insurmountable obstacle to the course of true love. But she trod that fine line very skillfully.'[20] Pamela's 'autocratic presence' concluded one critic, enlivened a play that 'shouldn't be taken too seriously, but still retains its poignancy'.[21]

Davenport was one of a group of Haymarket actors with whom Pamela shared a house. 'Without dressing expensively, she had a quiet elegance and was attractively empathetic,' he remembered. 'We would talk while making tea in the kitchen, for instance, a little about Osborne as being a fact of her life, and of families and of relationships in general,' although nothing so illuminating as to be recalled years later. 'All in all,' he decided, 'she was very self-sufficient, likeable but just a little unknowable.'[22] Pamela did, however, volunteer her partiality for Wedgwood china, which fifteen years previously Osborne had noted as lending a Tiggy-Winkle cosiness to 23a Priory Road, but only as a prelude to explaining why she appeared so distracted at times. During the summer, burglars had broken into her home and had made off, among other things, with much of her prized collection. 'She was especially upset to have lost the china,' remembered Davenport.[23]

Just as *Caste* was about to open, something equally unexpected happened but this time welcome: after a decade's silence, a cheerful postcard arrived at the theatre.

JO to PL ms pc Christmas Place BL

Sept 14 1979

Darling

—— Have just read in the 'Guardian' where you are. Have thought of you so often and anxious to know if all's well with you. Please write and let me know how you are. Or ring—number above. I'm going to Italy on Monday until October 8th to work on my memoirs! (£—I'm afraid. I owe the Inland Revenue £120,000 [equivalent to £558,000 in 2018.]) I'm in spiffing form otherwise. I've lived in the country all the time for the past three years. It's rather splendid. Perhaps you cd come down for a restful visit?

Take care,

Much love

John

If Pamela replied, then the letter appears to be lost, although as Osborne's letter of 16 December 1980 makes clear, she wrote to him to mark his fiftieth birthday on 12 December. Since his arrival in Kent and at Helen's instigation, Osborne had been writing *A Better Class of Person*, the first volume of his autobiography, pocketing an advance that immediately went towards paying off his Inland Revenue debt. At the Haymarket, Pamela was rehearsing another maternal role, that of Lady Frances in *An Early Life*. Frederic Raphael was one of the writers of the moment, having won an Oscar for his screenplay of John Schlesinger's film *Darling* in 1965, while *The Glittering Prizes*, a novel tracing the lives of a group of post-war Cambridge graduates, had been transformed into a huge television success. *An Early Life* relates the story of Adam Morris, the central character of *The Glittering Prizes*, before he goes up to university. Raphael 'combines the abrasive wit of Shaw with the fundamental approach of Osborne,' declared a local critic, while Pamela's Lady Frances came fully-equipped with 'the dignity and forbearance one would expect of her class.'[24]

The leading role of Adam was played by Malcolm Sinclair ('not quite a flawless performance,' surmised the *Leicester Mercury*, 'but near enough to be worthy of acclaim,'), who had previously appeared as Jamie, the alcoholic elder son in *Long Day's Journey into Night*.[25] He and Pamela became friends and saw each other occasionally over the following years. 'She did mention Osborne to me, usually very affectionately,' he remembered, 'and while occasionally her eyes would look to heaven at some outrageous behaviour or comment of his, I never heard her blame him for anything to do with their relationship.'[26]

During the run of *An Early Life* a second, more insistent postcard arrived from deepest Kent:

JO to PL ms postcard n/a n/d BL

[autumn 1979]

Writing my memoirs. Played a daft priest in a movie last week. Also got two plays on ITV before Xmas. Do come down for a rest. <u>What's your address?</u>

Love

J

In a further money-making sortie, Osborne had played a cameo role as an Arborian Priest in *Flash Gordon,* Mike Hodges' next film after *Get Carter,* a wackily flamboyant space epic released at the end of 1980 and which survives as a collector's item for devotees of the bizarrely absurd. In the event, Osborne's television plays were broadcast in the New Year: *You're Not Watching Me, Mummy* on 20 January 1980 and *Very Like a Whale* on 13 February.

Pamela's decade ended in her exchanging one matriarchal role for another, but this time one altogether more wretched. In November, she was back at the Thorndike, Leatherhead, leading Joan MacAlpine's studio production of Sophocles' *Electra.* Despite the close proximity of the audience perched uncomfortably on the portico of Agamemnon's home, and a translation by E. F. Watling, a Sheffield schoolmaster, that 'did nothing for [the play], with ghastly English idioms scattered throughout,' she nevertheless 'made her mark,' thought *The Stage,* as Clytemnestra, the distracted Queen who murders her husband and in turn is killed by her son.[27]

Although the 1970s had in many ways been ruinous for both Pamela and Osborne, both were looking forward with newfound optimism. Osborne was preparing to deliver *A Better Class of Person* to Faber, his publishers, while Pamela was contemplating a return to American territory. And they were in communication once again.

The 1980s

■ ■ ■

■ ■ ■

Bulldozers were crunching down Sacheveral Street in Derby. The Playhouse on the corner, resurrected after the 1956 fire, had been closed since the mid-seventies when the acting company moved to a new theatre concealed within a modern shopping centre, its façade carefully designed to look as innocuous as the surrounding shops. The old theatre in Sacheveral Street had since suffered a brief, dingily humiliating afterlife as a cinema showing adult films before the demolition crews arrived, reducing the area to rubble as part of a slum clearance scheme.

Over a hundred miles to the south, Pamela sat on a beach, ruminating about being young again, about the possibility of living without social restrictions and considering the cautious appearance from behind the sand dunes of two human-sized, lizard-like amphibians. Was humanity evolving, she wondered, or devolving? It was May 1980, and she was making her second venture (after the Traverse in Edinburgh) into fringe theatre, appearing as Nancy opposite Patrick Westwood's Charlie, a couple on the edge of retirement, in the English premiere of *Seascape*, Edward Albee's 1975 play, at the Overground Theatre in Kingston-upon-Thames. Charlie longs to pause, rest, and claim his childhood dream of living in the ocean, whereas Nancy is agitated, edgily aware of passing time. When Charlie asks her why she so vehemently dismisses his need for tranquillity, she retorts that 'it's a healthy sign, shows I'm nicely alive.'[1]

Pamela and Osborne, celebrating their fiftieth birthdays, were similarly musing on past, present and future. They were looking older these days, spreading a little into late middle-age, time leaving its traces and professional and personal alignments shifting. Younger directors and actors were now looking upon Pamela as one of their elders. 'I saw her as an old lady,' remembered Jeremy Howe, then in his twenties and a director at the Mercury Theatre, Colchester, where Pamela would appear in the autumn of 1984. 'Heavy coat against the cold, capacious handbag…'[2] She seemed to some an emissary from the theatre of the past, 'the time when Laurence Olivier represented the model of what actor should be,' recalled the actor Paul Venables, then also in his twenties and who appeared with her in *Who's Afraid of Virginia Woolf?* at Colchester. 'There was the aura of another era about her. There was also a cachet because of John Osborne, although you didn't ask her about that. She looked a bit bruised, as if there had been hardships. She was always friendly, but at the same time slightly solitary.'[3]

Yet if this was a decade in which the characters Pamela played were more mature, they were also more substantial, and technically and emotionally more demanding. Between 1980 and 1984, she would play a formidable gallery: Mary Tyrone again, followed by Queen Elizabeth in *Mary Stuart*, Amanda Wingfield in *The Glass Menagerie*, Winnie in *Happy Days*, Claire in *A Delicate Balance* and Martha in *Who's Afraid of Virginia Woolf?*, women of harsh experience, beset by life's burdens. 'She really was an outstanding actress,' declared Richard Digby Day, who directed her as Elizabeth in *Mary Stuart*. 'She was not herself on stage, but she drew from reserves deep within her. She was a much better actress than Mary Ure or Jill Bennett, and many of the actors who were at the National or the Royal Shakespeare Company, but somehow she never had the chances they had.'[4] 'She was a marvellous actress,' agreed Malcolm Sinclair, who later became not only highly distinguished on both stage and television but the President of Equity, the actors' union. 'She should have had a much higher profile than she did.'[5]

Although still dogged by long and financially ruinous periods without acting work, these were Pamela's most accomplished years since the 1950s, in which she gave her finest performances and with a succession of roles in American plays, established a personal territory. 'She had that knack that a lot of American writing has of being able to go straight for the emotional jugular,' thought Jeremy Howe.[6]

Like Pamela, Osborne was throwing himself into work. He was content in the country and in a new marriage, and having completed *A Better Class of Person*, he was making notes on possible future plays. Yet who might produce them, or where, was another matter. His track record, he thought, should speak for itself, but somehow the theatre had changed and his reputation appeared to be of no consequence. Apart from his uncertain professional future, there were still debts to contend with and the matter of his health, which would never fully recover.

Yet after several years of silence, the touch paper of renewed contact lit at the end of the 1970s flared into life and during the first four years of the new decade a stream of increasingly intimate letters and cards blazed back and forth between them. They began seeing each other again, meeting for long, leisurely lunches at restaurants serving the traditional English food they preferred and becoming closer and more trusting than ever before. They became 'Bears' and 'Squirrel' again, meeting at Pamela's basement flat in Kilburn where their relationship quickly regained its sexual intensity. Osborne travelled to see her performances in Leicester, Colchester and elsewhere, his visits kept private, almost clandestine. They celebrated an alliance regained and proclaimed a love recaptured. It was a turn of events as surprising as it was unexpected, a sprightly, dashingly youthful resurgence, a liberating 'renewal of old but never neglected or forgotten feelings,' she declared.[7] 'What a triumph,' he agreed.[8] And then, suddenly, everything changed. In the autumn of 1985, a crisis upended everything, resulting in their taking stock and attempting yet again to decipher quite what each meant to the other and where each fitted in to the other's life. A year later, in November 1986, Osborne and Helen left Kent and moved north to Shropshire. The correspondence between the playwright and his first wife all but ceased.

■ ■ ■

At the Overground Theatre, Ned Chaillet, an American in London and Irving Wardle's deputy at *The Times*, sat critically in the audience at *Seascape*. It was 'a lightweight exercise,' he concluded, and 'hardly the stuff of Broadway success.' Pamela's performance, he thought, was 'relaxed,' and the theatre itself 'cheerful.'[9]

One of a rapidly proliferating number of London fringe venues, some above pubs, some in cellars, the Overground was indeed an improvised affair. Its first, short-lived incarnation had been in a large storeroom in a Kingston hotel run by 'a red-nosed alcoholic who frankly didn't give a damn whether we were there or not,' remembered the company's founder, the actor and director Alan Bryce.[10] With the aid of an amenable vicar, they set up a new home in a nearby church hall furnished with seats from an abandoned cinema and where *Seascape* was followed by *Long Day's Journey into Night*, in which Pamela reprised the role of Mary Tyrone. But while the Overground was technically in London and a fringe theatre of some note, the combination of distance and a long evening with Eugene O'Neill seems to have deterred national newspaper critics. Only the intrepid Peter Tatlow of *The Stage* ventured as far as Kingston, who declared that 'the *tour de force* came from Pamela Lane, who…changes from sweet charm to shaking temper and from neuroticism back to composure in a matter of seconds. Her whole demeanour expressed these changes in remarkable detail.'[11]

Both *Seascape* and *Long Day's Journey into Night* were directed by Angela— known as Angie—Langfield. She was thirty-seven, thirteen years younger than Pamela, a former actress and a member of staff at the Royal Academy of Dramatic Art, where she directed student productions. By the end of the seventies, she had also become an established director in fringe and regional theatre. She and Pamela would collaborate on five plays during the 1980s and became partners offstage, a relationship lasting until Pamela's death. But again, 'nothing was overt,' remembered Saul Reichlin, an actor with whom both women worked in Leicester.[12] As before, friends and those who worked with Pamela were largely left to draw their own conclusions. Pamela preferred discretion. Her relationships did not attract the attention of others and nor did she wish it, grateful that, unlike Osborne, she had neither the importance nor the notoriety to attract the inquisition of newspaper gossip columnists. While Osborne and Pamela probably spoke to each other about their respective partners over the years, there is no direct allusion to them in the surviving correspondence. Pamela commiserates with Osborne over the collapse of his marriage to Penelope and sends her regards to Helen, while both acknowledge their separate 'constraints,' but that is extent of it. Rather, the tenor of their letters suggests that they regarded Pamela's relationship with Angie and Osborne's with Helen as being quite independent of that between themselves.

In August, Pamela returned to the Haymarket Theatre at Leicester, this time for a substantial run of four plays comprising Mary O'Malley's *Once a Catholic*, Samuel Beckett's *Happy Days*, Alfred Bradley and Michael Bond's *Adventures of a Bear called Paddington*, and another Edward Albee, *A Delicate Balance*. These would take her through until the third week of March the following year, 1981. The local paper celebrated her return by publishing an admiring article enumerating the various accents she would be using.

Meanwhile, Osborne, again having ascertained Pamela's whereabouts from the listings columns in his newspaper, dashed off an urgent request:

JO to Pl ms letter on Brighton Metropole Hotel notepaper n/a BL

Addressed to Haymarket Theatre, Leicester

December 16th [1980]

Darling—

I don't have your [home] address. The last time you wrote to me (my birthday last year) you forgot to let me have it. I don't know how long you're at Leicester but could you let me know how I can contact you quickly?

The reason for this is that I have to, or rather, it would be helpful to me—get some written clearance from you on a short passage from my book, which is coming out next year. It'll only take a few minutes. So could you ring or write to me at home and let me know where I can send the material to you? I shld have it cleared for Faber and Faber by December 31st. Hope all's well. When are you coming down for a day or two?

All love

John

*In case you've forgotten: Christmas Place, Marsh Green, Edenbridge, Kent. Tel: 073 286 4476.

Why Osborne claimed not to have Pamela's home address is a mystery unexplained in the surviving letters. The 'short passage' comprised his reminiscences of their meeting and marriage in *A Better Class of Person*, the typescript of which Osborne had delivered to his publishers. However, postal delays, Pamela's negligence and her spending Christmas in York resulted in her not replying until the end of December. By that time, she had shrugged off Mother Peter in *Once A Catholic* and, having equipped herself with a housecoat and a vacuum cleaner, assumed the more satisfying character of the feisty Mrs Bird, the housekeeper to the Brown family who adopt a marmalade sandwich-eating bear from Peru. At the same time, she was rehearsing Michael Meacham's production of *Happy Days*.

PL to JO ms letter Texas

Haymarket Theatre

Leicester

29 December [1980]

My dear J—

Your letter arrived just before I went away for Christmas, forgetting to take your address—sorry for the delay—I'm here until March 21ˢᵗ, so please have the material sent here. I'm only in London at weekends. Thought I'd sent you that address last year, I must have left it out—it's 23a Priory Road NW6. Tel: 328-0352.

Forgive haste—I'm literally up to my neck in 'Happy Days' rehearsals, while doing matinees of 'Paddington Bear'—Imagine! But will clear your thing as soon as I can.

See you in the spring, perhaps? It's been a long time. Take care.

Love

P.

In *Happy Days*, Pamela was required to appear for the first act buried up the waist and in the second up to the neck in a mound of scorched earth beneath which the only other character, Winnie's husband Willie, is largely hidden and silent. Winnie methodically follows a precise daily routine of rooting through the threadbare contents of her handbag and dreaming that one day she might 'simply float up into the blue… some day the earth will yield and let me go, the pull is so great, yes, crack all round me and let me out.'[13] Pamela signed the formal agreement approving Osborne's recollections of their meeting and marriage in his memoirs. A suggestion for lunch or dinner followed:

JO to PL ms letter Garrick Club BL

5 January 1981

My dear, I don't know whether or not you got my note in Leicester. It just occurred to me how it wd be to have a longish lunch together. Any time that suits?

Happy New Year

Love

John

JO to PL ms pc Christmas Place BL

Jan 9th 1981

By all means ring me—I shall be in all day on the 14th. If it's all a bit prob-
lematical for you, as you're so busy, I could always come up to Leicester, see
the play, and perhaps we could have supper? There must be pretty reasonable hotel? Do you remember 'My Wife's Family'? Not as sexy as you.

Love ever

John

Osborne's suggestion that he travel to Leicester to see Pamela in *Happy Days* would
entail his first visit to the city since 1949, when he had briefly appeared in repertory
with the Saxon Players at the Theatre Royal, an elegant building since demolished
to make way for a depressingly commonplace office block. *My Wife's Family* by
Fred Duprez was the first play in which he and Pamela had appeared together in
Bridgwater, thirty years previously. By reminding her of it, Osborne seems to be
testing the water to see what Pamela's reaction to their resuming their friendship
might be. As no written response to his card seems to exist, Pamela may have
replied by telephone. The momentum, however, continued.

JO to PL ms pc BL

19 Jan 81

Hope Winnie went well and the sand's not in your eyes. Was thinking Feb
14th to be a good day for me to come up, see the play etc

Love

John

If Osborne had thought *Happy Days* had already opened, he was mistaken. Pamela was still rehearsing for the opening on 27 January. Her performance in the Studio Theatre won 'national acclaim,' declared the *Leicester Mercury*, 'with special note being made of her amazing range of facial expressions.'[14] As Pamela's performance seems to have escaped the more prominent dailies, the 'national acclaim' probably refers to Peter Tatlow's enthusiastic review in *The Stage*. Tatlow was particularly struck by 'her eyes, slightly bulbous and glazed, and twisting clown's mouth [that] soon alert us to the pain and fear barely beneath the surface.'[15]

In the month since he had suggested he travel to Leicester, Osborne had become sufficiently confident to herald his imminent arrival with a Valentine's Day card, one that once again evokes their first meeting and furthermore resurrects their old nicknames of 'Bears' (or Bear) and 'Squirrel.'

JO to PL ms Valentine's card of a grey squirrel BL

St Valentine's Day 1981

To darling Squirrel from everloving Bear—thirty years on!

[unsigned]

When *Happy Days* closed on 21 February, Pamela was already rehearsing the part of Claire in Edward Albee's 1966 play, *A Delicate Balance*, also directed by Michael Meacham. Less well-known than the earlier *Who's Afraid of Virginia Woolf?*, but often considered a finer play, *A Delicate Balance* centres upon Agnes and Tobias, a successful East Coast couple whose composed and seemingly secure world of accomplishment, wealth and social ease is threatened by the arrival of Claire, Agnes's alcoholic sister, Julia, their recently divorced daughter and their friends Harry and Edna. The production won admiring local reviews and immediately after the run ended on 21 March, Pamela returned to Kingston and the Overground to play Delia in Angie Langfield's production of Ayckbourn's *Bedroom Farce*, a 1975 play dealing with the tangled relationships of four married couples, and from where a disappointed Peter Tatlow reported that the 'sum total of laughs was below par.'[16] Osborne approved of Albee but Ayckbourn, both popular and impressively prolific, was just one of many of his contemporaries whom he was privately beginning to resent. Not only Ayckbourn, but Peter Nichols, Tom Stoppard, almost everyone he could think of seemed to be able to secure productions with an ease that had been snatched from his own grasp. Moreover, he found most new plays intensely disappointing, even infuriatingly so. When he saw Ayckbourn's *Absurd Person Singular* a few days after its opening at the Criterion Theatre in the summer of 1973, he confided to a notebook that he thought it a 'low-lying feeble comedy with pretensions.'[17] He probably avoided going to see *Bedroom Farce*, therefore, but sent a chirpy card instead.

JO to PL postcard m/s BL

Christmas Place
Thursday 21 May [1981]

Take care, dear Squirrel. Love you always. In haste,

B.

Your knickers—advertised appropriately in <u>HONEY</u> colour—are a triumph! Afraid you're stuck with them now.

On the frail evidence of their surviving correspondence, this is the second occasion— the first being an offhand remark in a note on 21 June 1965—that Osborne introduces the subject of Pamela's underwear, something that would quickly become a feature both of their letters and their later encounters at Priory Road. These were probably some he had bought for her as a gift. The appropriateness of the 'honey colour' is a reminder of the closing lines of *Look Back in Anger*, spoken by Jimmy: 'We'll be together in our bear's cave, and our squirrel's drey, and live on honey, and nuts...'[18]

JO to PL ms pc n/a BL

23 Jun 81

So sorry you're blue. Can you have lunch—long—July 2nd? Or <u>any</u> other day more or less. Try if you can. Saw tantalizingly little of you in Leicester—sand up to the neck!

Take care love always

J

Pamela was back at the Haymarket, appearing in a revival of Michael Meacham's production of *Happy Days*. Her anxiety, referred to above and in her letter below, was a result of her being once again, and this time horrendously, in debt.

PL to JO ms letter Texas

Haymarket Theatre
Leicester
12th August 1981

Darling—

Many thanks for your new telephone number, and for your last dirty pc! I'm in Leicester till the 22nd but should love to slip down and see you for a day or two if you're going to be at home in September—the rest and air would be good after this stint. Can I ask if you would do something for me? You've offered on occasion, I know, and I've usually been OK, but now I'm appallingly in debt for nearly £900 [equivalent to £3200 in 2018]—it's happened over the last year when I haven't been doing enough profitable work. I hate asking, as you know, but I'm so anxious about all this I can't think what else to do. So—anything you decide you can manage by way of gift or loan (or a combination) would stop me going quite mad. I'm doing a play in Northampton in October/November and possibly a Christmas show after that, but this won't wait.

Just say if you'd rather not and I'll find another way—will love you just the same!

Ever

Squirrel

Although Osborne's telephone number at Christmas Place was ex-directory, he still changed it occasionally, causing considerable exasperation among his friends and others who often discovered they were unable to contact him quickly. Osborne's 'dirty pc' was possibly one that he had adorned with a salacious message made by using words and phrases clipped from newspapers. This was an occasional practice of his in postcards to Pamela—

always discreetly concealed in envelopes—during the early 1980s. The letter above implies that Pamela was answering another invitation to stay with the Osbornes in Kent. However, she did not 'slip down' in September and wife number one would not meet wife number five until the end of the following year.

More significantly, though, this appears to be first time since 1968—an interlude of thirteen years—that Pamela, who had begun to sign herself 'Squirrel' and was clearly at ease in their resumed affection, had appealed to Osborne for money.

During the previous few years, Pamela had had several long stretches without any stage work, and although she filled in with market researching, her financial position was as fraught as ever. Her fears were compounded by Britain being thrown into an economic recession and each day bringing woeful news of business closures and unemployment levels rising to a level not seen for fifty years. Regional theatres were as budget-conscious as everyone else and although the acting profession was not one that gripped the headlines, actors in regional theatres were not highly paid at the best of times. As a leading actress, Pamela could expect to earn a basic rate of about £60 a week (equivalent to £211 a week in 2018). Several theatres, such as Leicester Haymarket and Nottingham Playhouse, where she appeared in 1981, added a subsistence contribution towards the cost of living away from home. Yet this was still short of the national average of about £115 a week (equivalent to £400 in 2018). While Hazel Coppen was alive, the rent at Priory Road had been shared between them. But now that she lived alone, Pamela was paying the full amount in an area where the average for similar properties would have claimed most of her wages, and considering that food had to be bought and household bills paid, the unpredictability of income meant that she was constantly negotiating a fine line between survival and calamity. Unemployment benefit at £20 a week was hardly a viable alternative for long, and therefore when she was not rehearsing or appearing on stage, she depended wholly upon the availability of casual work.

So far, her plight was similar to that of many actors. Yet she also had an additional lifeline, which many did not, in her case a former husband who to the outside world at least, appeared very well-off. But much of Osborne's energy these days was going into maintaining the appearances of a lifestyle he felt he deserved, and Pamela was probably entirely unaware that he was in such parlous financial difficulties himself.

He could ill-afford a request for £900, but he quickly dispatched it nevertheless, his renewed support proving crucial in ensuring Pamela did not face further difficulties with her bank, or even a court appearance for non-payment of debt, a dread that more than once crept into a corner of her mind. At the same time, he suggested they meet, not at Christmas Place, but over lunch in London:

JO to PL ms pc n/a n/d BL

[late July/ early August 1981]

My darling

<u>So</u> sorry things are rough. But v <u>good</u> you told me. Could you come up for lunch on the 25th? My love may not be as perfect as in Corinthians but it endureth may even casteth [sic] out fear.

As always

J

Osborne awkwardly juxtaposes phrases from *Corinthians* Chapter 13, verse 7, and *First Epistle of John* Chapter 4, verse 17, hence Pamela's acknowledgement of mixed attributions below.

PL to JO ms postcard Texas

[Haymarket Theatre, Leicester]
Monday morning
17th August [1981]

Oh darling—I've just picked up your parcel and the letter. Oh! you really are stunning. I can't believe the torment's over, so suddenly and delightfully (God loveth a <u>cheerful</u> giver, and surely forgiveth mixed attributions in the cause of warmth and wit!) I'll see you for lunch on the 25th then, (now it's safe to return to London!) Let me know when and where?

Love my badge!

Deepest thanks and love,

Squirrel

What the parcel contained, or what the badge was, is unknown. Perhaps the package contained underwear. The badge may possibly have been an illustration of a squirrel. On the morning of 25 August, Osborne had an appointment for an acupuncture session, in the hope of alleviating his recurring migraines and periodic general lassitude. The treatment, which he soon abandoned as a failure, was administered by Dr Felix Mann, a prominent acupuncturist, at his consulting rooms in Devonshire Place. The following postcard confirming their lunch arrangement—the key components of which he spelled out in capital letters—is similar to many that Pamela and Osborne exchanged during these years:

JO to PL ms music hall postcard n/a n/d BL

So glad you got my note OK. Could you meet me in the PUB on the corner of BAKER STREET AND MARYLEBONE HIGH STREET OPPOSITE BAKER STREET STATION ON TUESDAY (25th) AT TWELVE NOON? IF YOU MISS ME GO ON TO ODIN'S RESTAURANT IN DEVONSHIRE STREET. Longing to see you. As ever, J

Let me know if it's OK?

Odin's Restaurant, now closed, was owned by the then fashionable restaurateur Peter Langan, 'the sort of alcoholic,' recalled a *Spectator* journalist, 'who is mistaken for a raconteur.'[19] It was expensive, and known as a showcase for Langan's collection of vibrant modern art as much as for its traditional French cuisine served at tables furnished with crisp white linen. Among the pictures to admire on the walls was David Hockney's pastel drawing of the interior, while the covers of the menus the waiters wafted in front of you were designed by Patrick Proctor. It was that sort of place.

JO to PL ms pc n/a n/d BL

Darling—

So sorry about the bill! <u>What</u> a smashing time! See you <u>v</u> soon. Take care

Love always, J.

Why did Osborne apologize for the bill? Had he discovered, at the crucial moment, that he had left his wallet at the acupuncturist's? Or had Pamela rashly insisted upon paying? In October, she was back at the Thorndike Theatre, Leatherhead, appearing among the beleaguered background peasantry—not at all her usual place—in Leon Rubin's production of Chekhov's *Three Sisters*. This turned out to be an interpretation emphasizing 'all the gloom, despair and weariness' that could be wrung out of the play and Pamela's income from the fortnight's run, presumably as depressing as the production, would hardly have enabled her to buy many lunches at Odin's.[20] The following month, she went not to Northampton for a Christmas show as she had mistakenly thought, but to Nottingham Playhouse to play a 'flatterable, jealous and vain' Queen Elizabeth in a major revival of Schiller's *Mary Stuart* directed by her friend Richard Digby Day, who had become the theatre's artistic director the previous year.[21] 'It was the best performance she gave during the time we worked together,' remembered Digby Day, 'and one greatly helped by her physical presence. Her height, her extraordinary red hair, which she would sometimes have cut in rather peculiar ways, and those wonderful blue eyes, all contributed to her being a commanding figure on the stage.'[22]

Yet despite her being so highly regarded by influential directors such as Digby Day, Frank Hauser, who had left Oxford and was now directing in London and Chichester, and Michael Meacham in Leicester, Pamela's prospects remained as uncertain as ever. At Christmas Place, however, there seemed to be hope on the horizon. At the end of the year, the publication of *A Better Class of Person* resulted in the best reviews Osborne had received for many years and went a long way to restoring him to literary prominence. A copy of the book and a large bouquet was dispatched to Pamela with optimistic New Year's card:

JO to PL florists' card n/a n/d BL

[December 1981/January 1982]

Happy New Year to a Better Class of Squirrel

All love

John

In March 1982, Pamela was at Wimbledon, in one of the several revivals that year of Ira Levin's *Deathtrap*, this one slightly ahead of the film version starring Michael Caine that was released a couple of months later. The Wimbledon production, directed by Kim Grant, another former actor turned director, boasted Richard Johnson, a Shakespearian actor returning to the stage after an absence of several years of devoting himself to film and television. 'Time has etched an intriguingly rakish look on the actor's photogenic features,' approved one reviewer.[23] Johnson had probably been enticed by the popularity of the play as much as the leading role of the Sidney Bruhl, a once successful playwright who discovers himself suddenly bereft of inspiration. Pamela appeared in the supporting part of the loopy psychic Helga Ten Dorp, whose unreliable visions supposedly provide the comedy element designed to offset the suspense hopefully generated by the principals. After Wimbledon, the production set off on five-month national tour lasting until the end of July, providing Pamela with a welcome burst of financial security if not otherwise being particularly rewarding.

While Pamela was touring, Osborne was defying debt by planning his next extravagant gesture, and one dazzlingly emblematic of the country gentleman he was endeavouring to become. The Cranmer's Ball, named in honour of Thomas Cranmer, the sixteenth century Archbishop of Canterbury, an architect of Anglicanism and compiler of the *Book of Common Prayer*, was a bounteous annual garden party at Christmas Place attended by guests both from the world of show business and the surrounding area. Marquees sheltered tables loaded with food and drink and jazz bands entertained while Osborne, decked out in a striped blazer, white flannels and a cravat, would stride benevolently across his lawns, champagne in hand. All thoughts of financial liabilities were banished by food, drink, music and company. That year, he was hoping that Pamela might join his guests, but he was disappointed.

JO to PL ms letter on JO notepaper n/a BL

[Edenbridge]

July 1ˢᵗ 1982

My darling,

Ta ever so for your note. I'm sorry indeed that you couldn't make it. I kept looking for you with the fare in my hot little hand. It was absolutely smashing. Lovely people—nearly 250 this time. We almost ran out of grub. Three marquees, super jazz band + rather grumpy Harold and Lady Pinter!

I have to come up on <u>August 9ᵗʰ</u> Monday (I'm going to Cornwall for two weeks tomorrow for the Regatta and Tall Ships Race.) I have to see the quack in Harley Street. It seems I have a mild form of diabetes (no DRINK, well…) My appointment is for 10 o.c. May I come over afterwards? I don't expect it will take long. We might have a late lunch or something. Anyway, I'll bring a bottle or two of forbidden champagne. If I don't hear from you I'll assume it's ok.

I'll be down here in Edenbridge from August 4ᵗʰ till September 16ᵗʰ working on VOL II. It would be so nice if you could come and spend a few restful days. I know you'd enjoy it. Helen is v keen to meet you.

Take care, I long to see you, which as know [sic] I always do.

My love as ever it was

B

The fare that Osborne was clutching was for a taxi to ferry Pamela from Edenbridge station to Christmas Place. He and Helen had begun to spend several weeks of each year in Cornwall, at a cottage they had bought at 8b The Lugger, Portscatho, a fishing village popular for second homes and holiday lets on the south Cornish coast. The purchase was an impulsive Betjamesque whimsy. While Osborne was married to Jill Bennett, they had visited John Betjeman at Trebetherick, on the north coast of the county, where the poet owned a house. Fired by enthusiasm, Osborne acquired his own. The Regatta and the Tall Ships Race were prominent local events. Although Osborne had little interest in either sailing or ships, he signed up to the local sailing club, attracted by the social opportunities promised by its restaurant and bar.

Back in London, Dr Kenneth Marsh had diagnosed Osborne as suffering from type 2 diabetes, prescribed insulin and advised that he give up alcohol: hence the 'forbidden champagne.' Marsh's strictures went unheeded and Osborne's loyalty to champagne, a drink with a high sugar content and a risky proposition for a diabetic, continued undiminished. His suggestion that he 'come over' with 'a bottle of two' is the first evidence in the letters since 1965 of Osborne visiting Pamela at Priory Road. 'VOL II' was *Almost a Gentleman*, the second volume of his autobiography, which he had recently begun writing. Pamela, who had no work in the offing after the *Deathtrap* tour ended, had turned to a series of part-time jobs.

Meanwhile, the tone of their correspondence and presumably their telephone calls became ever more animated. Each found it important to know where the other was, and what they were doing. Lunches in town and encounters at Priory Road became keenly anticipated events, their intimacy reaching a stage at which Osborne felt confident enough to further explore his interest in the more specialized byways of female underwear. In his note of 21 May 1981, he had complimented her on her 'honey coloured' underwear. He now suggested she begin wearing directoire knickers, a request with which she enthusiastically complied.

A vintage garment, directoires are loose fitting, the legs reaching to elasticated hems just above the knee. Osborne and Pamela considered them jauntily erotic, suggestive of Edwardian raffishness and the breezy vulgarity of the seaside postcards of which Osborne was fond. Twenty years previously, Pamela had thought *Under Plain Cover*, Osborne's play in which a couple enjoy dressing up games and various kinds of underwear are eulogized, 'very sexy.'[24] The tangential association would not have escaped them. Osborne's gifts of money began arriving at Priory Road with urgent instructions that she should acquire more directoires, preferably to be premiered at their next meeting. At the same time, they were discussing his surprising notion that Pamela join Helen and himself for Christmas in Kent, a plan to which Pamela eagerly agreed. It was also arranged that she would bring Angie Langfield as her guest.

JO to PL ms postcard n/a BL

[Cornwall]

[November 1982]

Squirrel darling,

So delighted about Christmas. Will make all arrangements. If you're free December 4th afternoon, will try to pop over with champagne for an hour or two. Will ring. Dying to see you. Take care Bears.

Enclosed: buy yourself some sexy directoires.

Pamela was about to begin rehearsals for *Cinderella*, the Christmas pantomime at the Connaught Theatre in Worthing, directed by Richard Digby Day and starring Bobby Crush, a popular television pianist and light entertainer, as Buttons. On 4 December, however, the day on which Osborne had proposed a champagne meeting, she had already arranged to go to York to visit Joyce Kay and attend one of the local musical events. Whether she met Osborne either in London or Worthing to give a directoire demonstration on an alternative date is unknown, but the Christmas plan went ahead nevertheless. He had written to Pamela from Cornwall, but although he had notified her of his address more than once, she was hardly the most organized of people and had immediately mislaid it.

PL to JO ms n/a Texas

1 December '82

Dearest Bears—

I couldn't answer because I stupidly lost the card with your Cornwall address and equally stupidly hadn't put it in my address book—but <u>thank</u> you, I'll buy the directoires in Brighton or somewhere, it was a lovely surprise—Anyway, you should be back in Edenbridge within a couple of days to get this late thanks. Wretchedly, I'm having to dash to Yorkshire this weekend and not returning till Sunday evening so I'm afraid I'll have to miss seeing you on Saturday—what a bore—but I'm commuting to Worthing next week and will ring you one evening when I get home, after that I'll be staying there, getting a small flat or something—perhaps we could meet there sometime if you've got a free day—I'm unlikely to be rehearsing every day. Oh, I <u>am</u> looking forward to Christmas!—it's a smashing idea. I hope you didn't freeze in Portscatho – longing to see you again!

A lot of love

Squirrel

JO to PL ms postcard n/a n/d BL

[December 1982]

Dearest Squirrel

All fixed for Christmas! Ring here if you're not sure. See you on the Eve. Loved your card

Always

Bears

Pamela travelled from Worthing to Christmas Place after the opening of *Cinderella* on 24 December. The show ran for a month, until 22 January. This was the first time that Pamela and Helen had met, and perhaps the first time that Osborne had met Angie Langfield. Although the arrangement might have seemed to have the potential for a strained Christmas all round, it appears to have passed off remarkably well. But although both Pamela and Osborne would recall it fondly the following year, a Christmas visit was not repeated. Nevertheless, both Pamela and Angie would sometimes be among the guests at Osborne's summer garden parties, occasions at which Langfield would remember him as 'charming… He and Pamela had a warm, affectionate relationship.'[25]

JO to PL ms pc n/a BL

10. 1. 83

Dearest Squirrel

It was so lovely having you here. Thank you for the smashing presents. The Coffee Machine is a <u>great</u> success. I'd like to come and see you but feel you'd rather not? Please ring. Rather low at the moment—what the Greeks call ENDOGENOUS. I miss you. As always. And love you

Bears

The aftermath of Christmas, the short, slothful winter days and the January anniversary of the deaths of Tom Godfrey and George Devine tended to plunge Osborne into seasonal despondency. Why he imagined that Pamela might not welcome him seeing her is not clear. Presumably, he is referring to visiting her at Priory Road. Were they thinking that this might compromise their loyalty to their respective partners? Whatever the reason, his, or their, misgivings quickly evaporated and Osborne began visiting Pamela regularly.

JO to PL ms pc n/a BL

13. 1. 83

Squirrel my darling

I'd been thinking of you almost all day when you rang. But then, as I think you must know by now, you've never been out of my heart. Christmas was such a delight, in spite of general fatigue, and, in my own case, a certain dreariness of spirit. I must see you again soon.

I feel we've regained touch in a strange way. I'll ring you at home next week.

My love as always and always

Bears

Ten days later, on 23 January, Nellie Beatrice, Osborne's apparently greatly disliked mother, a memorably and, some thought, cruelly portrayed principal character in *A Better Class of Person*, died in hospital in London aged eighty-nine. She was the last of Osborne's and Pamela's parents to pass away, having outlived Tom Godfrey, and Elspeth and William Lane. Meanwhile, Pamela was once more visiting friends in York. By the beginning of February, she was still in the north and hemmed in by deep snow:

PL to JO postcard ms n/a Texas

1st February 1983
York

Darling Bears—

Thought about you while I've been here—and about the end of an era of Nellie Beatrice and so forth—as you say, it's a life event of some sort, whatever went on between you, or failed to. Don't know if you're in Cornwall but hope all's well. It's very wild and blizzard up here, wall-to-wall snow and stuff. Take care see you before too long—

love always Squirrel.

love to H[elen]

For some reason, Osborne had suddenly become apprehensive that Pamela was being exploited, either emotionally or financially. Perhaps this was to do with one or more of her friendships, her frequent visits to the north, or perhaps it just reflected his own disquiet. He was also concerned as to whether the money he was now regularly giving her was being used for her household and essential expenses, as he intended and she confirmed, or if some of it was being siphoned off to fund her passionate espousal of the Labour Party and such causes as the Campaign for Nuclear Disarmament.

As an active member of CND, Pamela had several friends in the movement, attended rallies, completed sponsored walks to raise money for the cause and during the early 1980s, spent some time at the Women's Peace Camp outside the perimeter fence of the Royal Air Force base at Greenham Common in Berkshire. The facility was regularly blockaded by women protesters, the first occasion being in May 1982 when thousands arrived to demonstrate against the government's decision to allow American cruise missiles to be sited there.

Osborne and Pamela would chide each other about their contribution to creating a nuclear-free world. Over twenty years earlier, in 1961, he had marched purposefully down Whitehall in the company of Mary Ure to protest against nuclear weapons, while the arms race of the Cold War had been the subject of his notorious *Letter to My Fellow Countryman* published in *Tribune* in August the same year. The following month, Osborne had reluctantly taken part in a huge CND demonstration in Trafalgar Square, when along with over a thousand others he had been arrested and was obliged to spend a night in a police cell. However, Osborne later deprecated his part in anti-nuclear activities as ineffective, distrusted mass protest movements and, indeed, campaigns of any kinds that were not orchestrated by himself. Now, he enjoyed deriding what he called 'the barbed wire theatricals of Greenham Common' and its cast of women in 'woolly hats' beneath which, he predicted, 'beat conforming, mousy hearts.'[26] However, he perhaps begrudgingly admired Pamela's dedication. If she was interested in such things early in their relationship, it is not inconceivable that he transferred something of her passion to Jean, Archie Rice's socially-conscious daughter in *The Entertainer*.

Osborne's general unease prompted a cautiously enquiring letter:

JO to PL ms letter BL

8b The Lugger
Portscartho
Cornwall
6. 2. 83

Squirrel darling

The last thing I want to do is compound your difficulties whatever they may or may not be. I am indeed shooting in the dark but, as always, can only rely on my fugitive instinct, which is fallible enough but does hit the shot now and then to my surprise. I have a feeling that you are being <u>exploited</u> in some way and consistently. If there is any truth in this patchy guesswork—and it is concern and not prurience—I [sic] wd be so good if you wd trust me. If you shld want to only a little. I hate the idea that you may or have been <u>USED</u>. It may be so or not. I have no way of knowing. It cd be melodramatic conjecture, which it sounds like as write it. [sic]

Certainly, there is no constraint on you to offer me your confidence. I don't ask for it. I wld like to do more than help you in this primal way. I suspect it is not possible, for many good reasons. In which case, think no more on it. I only put it to you—believe me, tentatively—because I think you do know by now that my care, friendship and love for you is abiding. Turn to me if you have a mind to. Later if not now. It makes no matter for it will always remain the same. This is <u>not</u> pressure for I have no right to exact it. It is hard, possibly irrelevant, to tell you. I do <u>not</u> want to intrude. Reticence is most admirable—up to a point—and no one cherishes it or admires it more than I do. But it can also blaspheme against feeling and loyalty. I don't ask you to respond but to know that I wld like to be of more help than I am. However, only if you wish it. It is presumptuous—esp to your spirit—- even to utter it, or may seem so. It is not presumption that makes me write in this seemingly importunate way. You don't need to reply. Only remember.

Yr loving and concerned B

ALWAYS

His anxieties were allayed, at least for the moment. At the end of February 1983, Pamela returned to the Haymarket Theatre in Leicester, to begin rehearsals for Justin Greene's production of Tennessee Williams' *The Glass Menagerie*, in which she was appearing in the leading role of Amanda Wingfield. It was a part she had previously played in Derby. Both Pamela and Osborne were long-standing admirers of Williams. In 1952, Osborne had played Stanley Kowalski in *A Streetcar Named Desire* at Kidderminster and in 1957, in the wake of *Look Back in Anger*, he had celebrated the publication of a collection of Williams's plays in an article for the *Observer*. They were, he pronounced, 'about sex and failure,' and in so saying he gave a thumbnail guide to his own writing. 'I like my plays writ large,' he added, 'and that is how these are written.'[27] By coincidence, on 25 February, at the same time as Pamela was rehearsing *The Glass Menagerie*, Williams died in New York, the result of accidentally choking on the plastic cap of a nasal spray dispenser. He was seventy-one. Pamela must have spoken about this to Osborne, who sent a card shortly afterwards:

JO to PL ms pc n/d n/a BL

[Christmas Place]
[after 25 February 1983]

Darling: Sad about Tennessee. I knew him slightly and was very fond of him—esp his malicious giggle. Hope you're alright up there in the chill midlands. Am here until March 10th then back to Cornwall till Easter. Longing to see you. Get yourself some KNUTS and KNICKERS.

All love

B

The card above arrived with a cheque: hence the instruction to 'get yourself some KNUTS and KNICKERS.' The reference to 'KNUTS' is a convoluted play on words. A 'knut' (pronounced 'nut') was Edwardian slang meaning a privileged, amiable but intellectually negligible young man about town. The type had been popularized in a song sung by the actor Basil Hallam, a star of *The Passing Show*, a revue composed by Arthur Wimperis, and staged in London in 1914. The chorus of *Gilbert the Filbert*, which Osborne knew well, runs: 'I'm Gilbert the Filbert the Knut with a K/ The pride of Piccadilly, the blasé roué....' The character of the knut—although not the appellation—reappears in many of P. G. Wodehouse's stories. The visual play on words suggests an alliteration with 'knickers,' while the pronunciation is another reference to the final passage *Look Back in Anger*, in which nuts, consumed by both bears and squirrels in the wild, signify the sustaining good things in life.

JO to PL ms pc BL

Portscartho
Cornwall
12. 3. 83

Darling,

Am here till the end of the month. Will be around from April 5th to 18th. If there's <u>any</u> chance of dropping in on you (when you're not rehearsing?) let me know. It wd be good to see you before you go on tour.

As ever

B

Pamela was still in Leicester, and Osborne had addressed his postcard to the theatre. *The Glass Menagerie* had been well-reviewed locally but again overlooked nationally. In April, she was due to return to London to begin rehearsals for a national tour of *Habeas Corpus*, Alan Bennett's 1973 farce of thwarted libidos, in which she was playing Lady Rumpers. Meanwhile, another bouquet was dispatched to Leicester in time for Easter.

PL to JO ms postcard Texas

Leicester 5 April 1983

Dearest Bears—the Easter flowers are wondrous and transform my dressing room—thank you. I finish here this week and am then in London till the 24th rehearsing the tour: shd have a day off, it's not a big part. I think you're around till the 18th—is that right? I'm vaguer than usual because my bag was nicked in the market here a couple of weeks ago and diary and address book were in it—this also means I've lost your Cornish address and can't remember it offhand. Please let me have it again before you return—shall see you before that in any case. Could you ring me, do you think, Mon or Tues evening? Do hope so—

All love Squirrel.

Habeus Corpus opened at the Devonshire Park Theatre, Eastbourne, on 25 April before setting out on tour. Starring two familiar components of the *Carry On* film series, Jack Douglas as Arthur Wicksteed, a philandering General Practitioner, and Patsy Rowlands as his wife, the 'hilarious atmosphere' of Kim Grant's production was 'well-sustained all through,' thought Clifford Russell of *The Stage* when the play landed at Dartford for a week in July. Lady Rumpers, a fearsome aristocrat concerned for the purity of Felicity, her daughter, whom Wicksteed vigorously pursues, was, he noted, 'superciliously played by Pamela Lane.'[28] After several months at Leicester playing leading roles, a supporting part in a tour, however good the play, was not something to which Pamela particularly aspired, but it kept the money coming in, as did the 'numerous television productions' over the years that she listed in her biographical notes in theatre programmes. These were largely uncredited appearances, probably day jobs, in such popular series as *The Troubleshooters*, about the fortunes and misfortunes of an oil company; *Dr Who*, the perennial science fiction saga and a Saturday tea-time fixture, and *Angels*, a soap-opera dealing with the lives of student nurses. Nevertheless, as she trundled about the country, Pamela became increasingly dejected. Osborne attempted to cheer her up with a fresh batch of directoires and suggested they meet when the tour arrived at Richmond.

JO to PL ms pc n/a BL

29. 4. 83

My darling—Thank you for your note. I guessed you were glum. Glad the directoires arrived safely. Enclosed details of my whereabouts. Let me know yours. Esp RICHMOND: we could spend a while together... I think of you and love you.

As indeed always

B

Habeas Corpus toured to Richmond in May. Osborne was visiting Chichester to watch the rehearsals of a revival of *A Patriot for Me*, directed by Ronald Eyre and starring Alan Bates as Redl and Sheila Gish as the Countess. As a result of Robin Dalton, Osborne's agent, choosing to devote her energies to film production, he had acquired a new agent in Kenneth Ewing, who had immediately begun supervising an upturn his new client's fortunes. *A Patriot for Me* opened at Chichester Festival Theatre on 12 May. Osborne very much admired the production and its reception, including Michael Billington's assertion in *The Guardian* that this 'great, neglected play... confirms Osborne's stature as our finest creator of isolated, self-discovering heroes,' boosted his confidence and his wellbeing enormously.[29]

Looking through Pamela's tour itinerary, he noticed that she would be appearing in Cardiff in early June, reminding him of his first job as an assistant stage manager and understudy in *No Room at the Inn* thirty-five years previously, in 1948:

JO to PL ms postcard n/a BL

May 31st [1983]

My darling,

The New Theatre Cardiff was the first provincial date I ever played. For some reason we started at 6.30. I had digs in Plantagenet Street (probably no longer there!) Don't forget to ring me when you've the notion. Long to see you! Keep a doughnut for me.

As ever

My love

B

Plantagenet Street, a street of terraced houses, is near the city centre and noted among variety aficionados, of which Osborne was one, as the birthplace of Tessie O'Shea. A banjulele-playing entertainer, especially popular during the war and once billed as 'The Wonder of Wales,' she was subsequently known as 'Two-ton Tessie,' both the title of her signature song and an allusion to her expansive presence.

PL to JO ms n/a postcard Texas

Cardiff 7 August [1983]

Darling,

Plantagenet Street is still here, went past it today on the way to coffee and doughnuts! We struck a spate of pre-election bombings in Belfast last week—glad to be out of it. I'll ring this or next week.

Love ever

Squirrel

On 24 May, the IRA had planted a 1000-pound bomb outside the Royal Ulster Constabulary station in Andersonstown in west Belfast, causing an estimated £1-million of damage. Two days later, two people were killed in separate incidents. The general election on 9 June returned Prime Minister Margaret Thatcher's Conservative government to power with an increased majority.

On 8 August, while Pamela was in Cardiff, *A Patriot for Me* transferred from Chichester to the Haymarket Theatre in London and plans were finalized for the production to go on to Los Angeles the following year. When the *Habeas Corpus* tour finished at the end of July, Pamela saw *A Patriot for Me* before taking the train up to Leicester to rehearse Angie Langfield's production of Athol Fugard's *A Lesson from Aloes*.

She and Osborne had now known each other for thirty-two eventful years. Apart from their immediate families, it was the longest time either of them had ever known anyone. This, their newfound intimacy and Osborne's excavation of the past in order to write his memoirs, had prompted him to a further bout of sentimental reflection.

JO to PL ms pc n/a BL

23. 8. 83

Darling one,

I've just been re-reading some of yr letters to me. They are most touching (one esp about trying to redeem your zircon ring from the pawnbrokers (Horns!) in Hammersmith Road), and, most of all, so reassuring. What a triumph it's been for us to be so close and in such memorable contact.

You must be getting low in directoires: hence enclosed.

Darling Squirrel, in haste, as always,

your most loving B.

One of the letters Osborne had been rereading was that of 7 January 1954, in which Pamela asked him to reclaim a ring she had pawned.

It may have been during this exchange—it was certainly during this summer—that Pamela presented Osborne with the surprise gift of a pair of silver cufflinks.

PL to JO ms lettercard Texas

Haymarket Theatre
Leicester
26.8.83

I'd just written this card when I heard from you today—so eloquent, and it made me very happy. You must know how deeply I share your pleasure in (and amazement at?) our renewal of old but never neglected or forgotten feelings, but it can't be said too often.

I was glad you'd kept a few of the old letters—as I have some of yours—they seem to have survived burglaries fires and floods as well as the ravages of time and transport—as much moved as moving! Well, they are, oddly, the latter, don't you think? Had forgotten the pawnbroker episode but it all came back in a trice. I hope we did something nice with the pledge money, a blow-out at Lyons, maybe.

Darling, thank you for ensuring a bottomless (?) supply of directoires. I wouldn't be seen dead in anything else now—you were quite right. I <u>was</u> getting through them rather disgracefully—bless you, Bears.

So relieved you found your ring, but knew you would. I left my tweed jacket on the train, but nothing in the pockets, so it didn't matter.

Into the third rehearsal week of the Fugard now and getting slightly giggly at being deranged in a South Efrican [sic] accent! The two other AKTORS [sic] are fun, luckily. <u>Must</u> do a bit of work—

Love ever

Squirrel

'He would write wonderful letters,' Pamela told her friend, Julia Lockwood.[30] However, none of the surviving letters Osborne wrote at this time would seem to merit Pamela's description of being 'so eloquent.' She was evidently referring to one that arrived on 26 August and now disappointingly lost, or even a telephone conversation that took place that day.

Pamela's expanding collection of letters had indeed survived at least one burglary—that in which she lost her china collection in 1979—and a flood: not literally, but water leaking from a burst pipe in a flat above had once caused considerable damage to her own property. As there is no record of Pamela's possessions surviving a fire, she might have been referring to the small electrical fire at Woodfall Street in 1961 while Osborne and Mary Ure were living there. Or perhaps she was just indulging in a bit of poetic decoration.

Athol Fugard's *A Lesson from Aloes*, first produced in 1978, is a three-hander set in Port Elizabeth in 1963, in which Piet, an Afrikaner, and Gladys, his wife, entertain Steve, a South African bricklayer recently released from prison, to dinner. There were several productions of Fugard's work in Britain during the eighties, when the apartheid system of racial segregation in South Africa, introduced in 1948, once again became a focus of worldwide protest. The system ended in 1994. Gladys, a South African of English descent, is recovering from a nervous breakdown, hence Pamela claiming to be 'deranged in a South African accent.' The other actors in the cast were David Weston and Saul Reichlin. Although she joked about adopting a South African accent, Pamela was intensely serious about the production, which opened in early September. 'We worked in great detail both on the political background and the emotional interplay of the characters,' she told a correspondent who had seen the production and sent her a grateful letter. According to Reichlin, Pamela was 'utterly believable, deeply feeling, and eerily genuine in her portrayal of a woman in the stages of breakdown that can so easily descend into melodrama.'[31]

JO to PL ms pc n/a BL

31. 8. 83

Squirrel darling,

Thanks so much for your note. Off to Venice on Tuesday. Back on the 22nd. Hope you are serious about DIRECTOIRES? Will make INSPECTION next time I see you! Let me know when you get back to London and can spend some time together. Will think of you. Take care. Till later.

Yr loving B

JO to PL ms pc n/a BL

27. 9. 83

Dearest Squirrel,

Back from Venice. Quite wonderful. Didn't notice how tired I was. Restored but feeling very low indeed. It will pass of course. How are you? Yr card was delightful. When can I see you? It is odd surely, to be in love for thirty years?

B

In the event, he saw her almost immediately, travelling up to Leicester to see one of the final performances of *A Lesson from Aloes*, which closed on 1 October. 'Pamela said he had enjoyed it,' remembered David Weston.[32] It's a measure of her reticence, however, her constant desire for privacy, that Saul Reichlin was entirely unaware of Osborne's visit. 'If the great man [Osborne] came to the show, it was kept quiet,' he recalled. 'I don't know who else knew, but I was certainly kept in the dark.'[33] While both Weston and Reichlin had concluded that Pamela and Angie Langfield 'were obviously partners,' and that 'Pamela appeared very close' to Angie, nothing was said.[34] In Pamela's view, nothing need be said unless it needed to be said. Weston also knew of Pamela's marriage and recalled that she 'spoke about John a couple of times, and was obviously fond of him.'[35] Reichlin, however, was unaware until Weston told him that Pamela and Osborne had once been married or that she even knew him. 'I can only assume she must have sworn everyone who knew to secrecy,' he concluded many years later, 'no doubt to avoid the tiresome questioning that would otherwise follow her about. Pamela never breathed a word of either status [her relationships with Osborne and Langfield].'[36]

Pamela returned, exhausted, to London and unemployment. She and Osborne met for an afternoon at Priory Road on Monday, 10 October. In the evening, he saw Tom Stoppard's new play, *The Real Thing*, at the Strand Theatre and next day left with Helen for Portscartho. Pamela wrote to him the following day, Wednesday:

PL to JO ms letter n/a Texas

12 October 1983

Did you ring last night? Sorry—I quite forgot I'd be out for evening and didn't get back till about one. I'm so <u>very</u> glad you could make it on Monday, despite tiredness—the bore of all those people swarming about in the morning!

I'm beginning to feel more lively at last. Can just about face my unanswered letters, drumming up work and the whole damn thing. Hope you had a good trip down, and can soon begin catching up on those 80 thou[sand] words. Ring or write when you can, and feel like it—think I'll be home till Christmas now.

My love as always, Squirrel.

PS How was the Stoppard?

The '80 thou' words' was a portion of what would become *Almost a Gentleman*, which, in fits and starts, would take him almost ten years to complete. In *The Real Thing*, Henry, a successful dramatist, embarks upon an affair with Annie, an actress and the wife of the leading actor in one of his plays, who champions a political activist whose well-meaning but appallingly written play Annie demands Henry knock into shape. With Roger Rees and Felicity Kendall in the leading roles, the play had opened the previous year to excellent reviews. It was 'that rare thing in the West End (or anywhere else for that matter,') pronounced Michael Billington, 'an intelligent pay about love.'[32] Osborne saw the second cast, the leading actors being Paul Shelley and Susan Penhaligon. He did not enjoy his evening, but these days, he lacked patience with most plays written by his contemporaries.

There were times, though, when he inexplicably rejected the opportunities that others had worked hard on his behalf to create. Having produced no new play since *Watch It Come Down* in 1976, Osborne was continuing to rely both for his income and reputation on his earlier work and desperately needed the money and the exposure a prestigious revival might bring. Kenneth Ewing and Osborne's friends were astonished, therefore, when that summer he refused to sanction a production of *The Entertainer* starring Alan Bates and Joan Plowright at the National Theatre, and already advertised as forthcoming in the company's brochure. Osborne never explained his reason for this, although it appears that Laurence Olivier, Plowright's husband and who had originally played Archie Rice, retained a considerable affection for the play and objected to its being produced at the South Bank with his wife in the cast now that Peter Hall was the National's artistic director. Neither Olivier nor Osborne had much affection for Hall. As the National's director at the Old Vic, Olivier very much wanted to lead the company into the South Bank building in 1973, but when Hall was appointed in his place the same year, Olivier cast him in the role of usurper. Osborne had nursed a considerable antipathy against Hall for closing *Watch It Come Down*, claiming falling ticket sales, a decision Osborne vociferously disputed. Old grudges were still chafing away. 'Olivier called upon John to make an enormous sacrifice,' suggested Gordon Dickerson, Osborne's literary agent in succession to Kenneth Ewing, long after the event.[38] Although it would mean a financial and professional loss, refusing to permit a National Theatre revival of *The Entertainer* presented Osborne with an opportunity both to proclaim allegiance to Olivier and tweak Hall's nose.

■ ■ ■

Looking out from his window at The Lugger upon a grey October sea, Osborne's mood of maudlin introspection and self-pity returned. The following—probably drunken—letter, handwritten on pages from an A5 notebook in the early hours after a night wrecked by insomnia, is repetitive, disjointed, at times opaque and incomplete. Yet it is heartfelt and reproduced as it survives.

JO to PL ms letter n/a BL

[Cornwall]
18.10.83

Oh dear, oh dear, it _is_ late

My darling,

It's about 3am.

I've had the most intractable headache all day and did very little. It's so still here and the faint sound of the sea outside.

Dear, beautiful bushy tail [sic] squirrel, goodness, I do love you. I don't know and don't ask what you feel for me. I know you do love me. I feel such a—and what a misused word it is—tenderness when I am with you. From you.

I fell in love with you thirty-two years ago. My feelings—_no_, passion, always passion—are unchanged.

My desire, my curiosity—oh, my dear girl, you always

What I am trying to say, quite inadequately, is that you are, always have been and will be at the centre of my heart. It _has_ been painful in the past, now, during the last year or two, I am so struck by my _good fortune_. My fortune to have loved someone for a lifetime, someone who always stuns and enlivens me—and yes, as you know, baffles and exasperates me.

But what reassurance it gives me. I longed for you in those early morning scuffles. Oh, and I don't have to tell you, quite unfailing _lust_. In 1951 I simply didn't have the _nerve_ to coax you into directoires—afraid, alas, of ridicule. Wrongly, I think.

Always, as in the very first, your most smitten

Bears.

What I am trying to say unsuccessfully—it is now 3.20am—is that I feel so exhilarated and changed and <u>vindicated</u> by my love for you. It hasn't changed, it hasn't been disrupted by events or distorted in the memory. So many things have been, as you know, and the bitterness is hard to abate at times. Nolan is just one example [...].

I had always wanted daughters—not sons. How I wish you and I had had them, four or five loving, hearty girls! Funnily enough, quite a few—well, say, half a dozen teenage or twentyish girls are like a sick dog. When I was twenty-one, my heart still stops—indeed literally—when I see you. Your spirit remains as mysterious as it ever was but your body is no less than eternal homecoming.* You are as voluptuous and erotic as when I first saw that beautiful red head of hair and fell in love forever.

I hope you don't mind getting a 32-year-old love letter. You are stable, even if fleeting, but always inescapably stable.

Well—that old play of mine was, as you must know, a pretty anguished love letter! Put together with some skill, I hope.

*Must try harder

presumptuous in ever approaching you. And yet I find it so hard not to.

I often wonder whether—if indeed you do—you should want to see me at all—especially with the constraints we both have.

<u>Any</u> road, as those Northern writers will say, I love to be able to write to you even if you find it preferable to not to see me.

Always your devoted B.

PS I almost sent this.

food to me. Write me letters, cards, remember my birthday. It sounds very cloying when I write it down, but I'm sure it isn't.

I suppose I should go to bed. I find it hard to sleep at the moment.

Dearest Squirrel. Goodnight. Thirty-two years of my love for you

'That old play of mine' is *Look Back in Anger*. The 'constraints we both have' refers to Helen and Angie Langfield. Nolan is Osborne's daughter by Penelope Gilliatt, whom he disowned in 1982. Although Osborne declares above that he 'almost sent this' letter, implying that even as he was writing he was having reservations about posting it, and in his letter of 3 November below, writes that the sentiments in it 'might be best spoken at another time,' the letter nevertheless came into Pamela's possession. No direct reply appears to survive.

PL to JO postcard ms n/a Texas

1.11.83

Just to say am thinking of you down there [in Cornwall] scribblin' – I hope you're catching up. Not much of news and views from this end but I'm doing the usual round—CND rallies (!) a few galleries and going to the pics, reducing the mail mountain etc.

Love always, Squirrel.

PS Love to Helen.

The following card from Osborne, although dated only two days after that from Pamela above, is not a response to it, but to another card, now lost, in which Pamela appears to have written that she had been 'thinking,' presumably about their relationship. Judging from Osborne's card, so had he.

JO to PL ms letter n/a BL

[Cornwall]
3. 11. 83

Squirrel darling—

Lovely to get your card—and to know that you're thinking too. Wrote you a very long small hours letter last week but thought it might be best spoken at another time. Am progressing slowly but fairly regularly 1200-1500 words a day. Doesn't sound much but it adds up if you keep at it. Bought a bicycle in Truro the other day but have not yet ventured out on it. Longing to spend time with you again—in a couple of weeks or a bit later, depending on progress. Will let you know. Maybe 16th or early December.

JO to PL ms pc n/a BL

15. 12. 83

Dearest Squirrel,

Thank you for your card—most timely come upon the hour. Have tried to ring you but you are clearly working during the daytime. I hope this gets to you before you're off to the Yorkshire Connection. Edward is being very dreary and is hinting at suicide in darkest Derbyshire. So: I think we'll just have Robin (the Aussie agent mother-in-law) and Bill at Christmas. Let me know when you're back at Priory Road. It seems senseless to <u>send</u> a present. I shall miss you

Ever yr

B

With no stage work since *A Lesson from Aloes* closed in October, Pamela had taken a temporary job before going to York to join Joyce Kay and the musical circle for Christmas. This was enormously disappointing for Osborne, who was hoping for, perhaps even assuming, a repeat of the previous year's visit. 'Edward,' who appears so despondent, is a formalization of 'Bears.' and appears here as an alter-ego of Osborne's, a version of the onstage teddy bear from *Look Back in Anger* who reappears more prominently—but equally silently—in *Déjàvu*, Osborne's final play, produced in 1992. Robin and Bill were the formidable Robin Dalton, an Australian, Osborne's former literary agent and her husband, the writer Bill Fairchild. Although he had thought it 'senseless' to send Pamela a present, he nevertheless dispatched a card and a gift to Kilburn.

PL to JO ms letter n/a Texas

[London]
17 December 83

Dearest Bears—

Joyous thanks for your lovely present and card today! I won't bore you with the details of the transformation effected by the former (a dramatic rescue from bleakery [sic] not to say squeakery [sic]!) merely include it in my delight at receiving the latter. I was afraid I might have been missing a call during daytime, never got round to an answering machine. Finished my 'orrible temporary job yesterday and starting on a telly on Monday (a sitcom I think, no script has arrived!) recording in Nottingham on 5th January—after that I'm back here. Three days off for Christmas, so I shall honour my Yorkshire commitment if trains allow. Oh dear, I wish it was last Christmas, it was such a smashing one, but Robin and Bill will be perfect company for you both, and we'll all have a jolly good time.

Shaky writing, just back from bomb alerts in the West End, it was all quite weird. I shall have to get your present in the New Year! Meanwhile a card is on its way. Happy Christmas, darling—

Ever yours, Squirrel

PS: What's up with melancholy Edward? Lovesick?

Pamela's anticipated recording at Central Television's studios in Nottingham was for an episode of *Shine on Harvey Moon*, a popular series that ran for several seasons. Set in the East End of London immediately after the war, it starred Kenneth Cranham as Moon, a demobbed working-class RAF serviceman who joins the Labour Party and the trades union movement. Rather than being a sitcom, it was a light-hearted drama. *Sisters and Brothers*, the episode in which Pamela played Mrs Humphries, was transmitted on 15 June 1984.

The 'bomb alerts' to which she refers occurred on the afternoon of 17 December, when the Provisional IRA warned that a bomb had been placed near Harrods department store. Half an hour later, a bomb exploded in a car parked in Hans Crescent, close to one of the store's side entrances. The blast killed three police officers and three civilians, injured 90 people, and caused huge damage. In a separate incident, part of Oxford Street was evacuated after it was thought a bomb had been placed near the C&A department store.

Even at this stage, Osborne continued to hope that Pamela might have second thoughts and cancel her 'Yorkshire commitment' in favour of spending Christmas in Kent. A reproachful postcard greeted Pamela on her return.

JO to PL ms postcard Christmas Place BL

Epiphany [6 January 1984]

No I don't imagine Edward was 'lovesick'. He's too selfish for that. I think, like yourself, he had a better offer—you might have had difficulty there. [sic] Friends seem to abound but so does treachery. I still make the mistake of thinking people <u>change</u>. That's the lesson from this already unpromising year. Rather disappointing but not so surprising.

B

PL to JO ms letter Texas

23a Priory Road, NW6
10th January 1984

Just back from a numbing little TV in Nottingham to find your terse card in the usual crop of disastrous New Year letters. Whoopee. I can't imagine Edward had a 'better offer' than to spend Christmas with you and Helen. At all events, I hope he fared better than I did—one of the most boring sacrificial exercises on record. Why this talk of treachery? Why so dispirited? What's up?

The next couple of months look familiarly blank, so I'm doing market research till things move again. Are you going to be in Edenbridge for a bit? Or even in London for a day? People change so much you never can tell.

S

Evidently still unhappily mooning about Christmas Place, Osborne replied by return of post.

JO to PL ms letter Christmas Place BL

11. 1 84

Dearest Squirrel—as ever

Forgive my 'terse' card. Not much of a New Year welcome no doubt. A lot of puny but consistent treacheries seemed to reveal themselves and did indeed dispirit me. Absurd, but when sad things come it is a case of 'not single spies but in battalions'.

And your pre-Christmas note seemed chilling and dismissive. Due to all sorts of things I daresay but still painful to read.

I really must stop mourning the past and what didn't happen between us. Grief must be accommodated but things like your note do arouse it—anyway, me.

I also realise you have been under what's known as 'all kinds of strains' which I know nothing about and never will.

Work is not going well but may not matter anyway. I am more than fortunate to be here and have amazing friends. Do you really think that people change?

I shall come up to London next week. Will you be at home? Please let me know.

As ever, your fond, fondest B.

Although Osborne was generally disgruntled, the specific nature of the 'puny but consistent treacheries' is unknown. It seems, though, that he felt that Pamela was showing insufficient attention and commitment to him. The 'pre-Christmas note' that caused his 'grief' clearly does not refer to Pamela's letter of 17 December, which could hardly, even by Osborne's forensic standards, be considered 'chilling and dismissive' and must therefore denote a card now lost. The meaning of 'all kinds of strains,' perhaps a quotation from one of Pamela's letters, is unclear, although in addition to her usual financial anxieties, Pamela had not been well, suffering from an attack of shingles, which causes weariness, sometimes dizziness, and produces a troubling skin rash. The 'work' to which Osborne refers may be either *Almost a Gentleman,* or *God Rot Tunbridge Wells,* the screenplay he was writing for a Channel 4 Television film to mark the tercentenary in 1985 of the birth of Handel. It would be directed by Tony Palmer.

PL to JO ms letter Texas

23a Priory Road

London NW6

31st January 1984

How are you? I must have been out when you said you might ring a couple of weeks ago, doing my market research thing, I expect—or perhaps you didn't anyway. I haven't rung since because I got the idea it was better if you did it (and because I've been somewhat selfishly busy staving off battalions up here). I've just re-read your last letter, though, and realize that I know nothing about the treacheries and troubles which were bringing you down when you wrote—perhaps happily reversed by now—but you said that work was not going well and 'may not matter anyway'. I don't know what this means but it sounds very disturbing. I wish I'd been able to meet you last Tuesday, but it was a long-promised outing to the Venice Exhibition for my Yorkshire 'aunt' and she'd made special arrangements to travel down for it and stay a couple of days.

I'm not at the flat much at the moment—staying with friends off and on while I mend my torn tail and re-fur-bish [sic]—but I call in for letters and spend some evenings here, so please write or ring, 'specially if you're coming to London—and don't put me down as a deserter! I'm not—'all kinds of strain' sounds dreary enough but is appropriate.

Ever

S

PS Will let you have my address if I move—there's a possibility but I don't know just yet. S

Pamela's Yorkshire 'aunt' was Joyce Kay and the exhibition was *The Genius of Venice 1500-1600* at the Royal Academy. Pamela did not move but remained at her Priory Road address. By February, Osborne had become more conciliatory:

JO to PL ms ps n/a BL

1 Feb 1984

Thank you for note re Yorkshire auntie. I shall be in London on Feb 6th in the forenoon—i.e. about 10.45. Will you be chez Squirrel? If I don't hear from you I'll assume that you will be.

My love

B

At the same time as proposing an assignation with Pamela, he fired off a hectoring letter to Oscar Beuselinck. Osborne's bank statements were still an alarmingly lengthening river of red, and the letters from the Inland Revenue awkwardly intimidating. Desperately, he demanded that Beuselinck investigate the financial accounts of Woodfall Films, the company that had produced *Look Back in Anger*, *The Entertainer*, *Tom Jones* and *The Charge of the Light Brigade* among others, in the far-fetched hope that he, Osborne, might be owed money. On 6 February, Pamela had evidently been 'chez Squirrel.'

PL to JO ms postcard n/a Texas

9 February 84

Darling Bears—Wonderful to see you and feel close to you once again (not just in bed). I feared the Christmas business might have distanced you in some stupid way—foolish of me. Oh—you've just rung. I could have said all this on the phone! Glad Oscar took your strictures well, probably too exhausted by his women and his Garrickphobia to do otherwise! I've just been upstairs to check on post and there indeed was your lettercard and glorious selections from your Golden Notebook!—and the money <u>too</u> which, I expect you know, was a mercy beyond expectation, thank you for realizing and thinking of it. In haste to the dentist—but let's see each other again v soon.

Your S

Although he made three successive attempts, Beuselinck was a man, as his obituarist put it, who 'found being a husband difficult,' and was susceptible to being diverted by other liaisons.[39] Hence Pamela's jibe about his 'women.' Enormously proud of his working-class origins, Beuselinck enjoyed deriding what he believed to be the cultural pomposity enshrined in such places as the Garrick, a long-established club in Covent Garden of which Osborne and many writers, actors and politicians were members. It is unclear what the 'glorious selections from your Golden Notebook' might be. Perhaps Osborne had sent her some work-in-progress extracts from the second volume of his memoirs. If so, Pamela might have been referring to *The Golden Notebook*, a novel by Doris Lessing—a friend of Osborne's—originally published in 1962, in which the writer Anna Wulf records aspects of her life in four notebooks and attempts to summarise them in a fifth, gold-coloured book.

Most notable in the letter above, however, is Pamela's reference to their sexual relationship. During these years, Pamela refers to this only twice, once, as above, and secondly and indirectly in a letter of 1 June 1984 when she expresses her delight at 'your [Osborne's] lightest embrace whether of affection or passion.' Their physical intimacy had been dormant since the mid-1960s and it is unclear when it resumed, but likely dates are in 1981, when they began to call each other 'Bears' and Squirrel' again, or perhaps in 1982 and the introduction of the directoire knickers factor, or in the summer of 1983 when they celebrated what Osborne called the 'triumph it's been for us to be so close and in such memorable contact.'

However, their relationship was essentially that of a deep and trusting alliance, and one that had been sustained, arguably against the odds, for over thirty years, and by the early 1980s, each had reached a greater understanding—or acceptance—of the other. Perhaps this was a result of the contentment each had with their respective partners and a maturing outlook on life in general and a feeling that they each could afford to be more charitable. Yet while there is a palpable element of nostalgia in their correspondence, there is also an atmosphere of a renewed and thrilling sexual rediscovery. Osborne's long-standing, hitherto secret obsession with directoire underwear, which Pamela accommodated, contributed a frivolous dimension to an intimacy that might be rationalised as being less the furtive passion of an extra-marital affair than something altogether more incidental, based upon a deep and long-standing affection and posing no threat to their relationships with their respective partners.

There was also, of course, the question of the money. An 'enclosed' in the form of a cheque accompanied many of Osborne's letters and he also gave her money when they met at Priory Road, unobtrusively leaving an envelope on the dresser. To an outsider, there is something unsettling about this, but their financial arrangements, they agreed, had nothing to do with what Pamela had described as 'our renewal of old but never neglected or forgotten feelings,' and with any sexual involvement between them. Perhaps Pamela had even emphasized this in a letter or card now lost. This undated card from Osborne appears to indicate his agreement:

JO to PL ms pc n/a n/d BL

Darling—Of course I understand—quite separate. The enclosed will help in the meantime. See you Monday week 9th

All love

B

If this card was indeed written in 1984, the 9th fell that year on a Monday in January, April and July.

JO to PL ms pc n/a BL

13. 2. 84

<u>Smashing</u> to talk to you. You must tell me about the Bush evening—more feminist idiocy? So unlike our own lives. Till soon, my love, dearest Squirrel.

B

The 'feminist idiocy' was *Unsuitable for Adults* by Terry Johnson, a play set in a room above a run-down pub in which a strident activist comic rehearses her act. Pamela had seen Mike Bradwell's production of the play at the Bush Theatre in Shepherd's Bush.

Another Valentine's Day card arrived at Priory Road that year, this one a Donald McGill postcard in which a pop-eyed man discovering a voluptuous young woman exploring a woodland exclaims: 'I can show you more things than the birds and the bees ever dreamed of!'

JO to PL ms pc n/a n/d BL

14 February 1984

My Valentine—Always.

PS: Yes, SOON AGAIN!

PL to JO ms postcard n/a Texas

23 February [1984]

Thanks for the merry V Day card. I larfed a lot as Harold Hobson would say. The feminist idiocy at the Bush turned out to be a lot better than I thought (for a bloke!) You'd have hated it! I'm back with Fugard again till March 17th. Darling, hope you're well and ok.

S

Pamela was playing in a revival of Angie Langfield's Leicester Haymarket production of *A Lesson from Aloes* at the Thorndike Theatre, Leatherhead.

PL to JO ms postcard n/a Texas

[Leatherhead]
1.3.84

Darling—ever so many thanks for yr card <u>and</u> attachment (I don't mean the 33-year-old variety, though indeed heartfelt thanks would hardly be out of place for that). The home fires burn again. Yes—I'll be at home on the 9th—let me know if you're coming up. Glad to hear you've improved dorsally if not mentally! Forgive hasty card, rehearsing 'appy Athol all day today.

Love ever S xx

The 'attachment' was a cheque. Osborne appears to have had an accident—possibly a riding accident— and hurt an arm: hence his improving 'dorsally.'

JO to PL ms pc n/a BL

Dearest Squirrel,

Happy birthday

Yr loving

Bear

Easter Sunday that year fell on 22 April. Pamela's birthday was a week later. She was fifty-four. Coincidentally, the first week of May saw both Osborne—again—and Pamela involved in alarming accidents. In Kent, while he was out riding, Osborne's dogs frightened his horse, which threw him to the ground. Having been notified of this, Pamela relayed her own troubles:

PL to JO ms n/a Texas

10th May 1984

Dearest B—I do hope you're healing nicely and very much better—or at least that the first agonies have subsided.

This seems to be the accident time—I had my first spill on the bike on Friday evening—SPLAT! on to the very hard surface of Edgeware [sic] Road. Riding with a friend, we swerved to dodge a manic car, locked our handlebars in a freakish way and were both promptly knocked out cold! It must have created a bit of a stir because we came round on the pavement to find an ambulance had been summoned and we were whisked off to hospital. She was allowed home but I've been languishing in the Royal Free with a fractured skull. I was freed yesterday (sort of on parole unless any of a half-dozen unattractive symptoms manifest themselves over the next week) and am staying with friends next door to be supervised and generally spoilt.

All this just to explain why I am not now in Yorkshire as planned and may not be in my own place if you do give a ring next week (I'm fit enough to toddle down there and collect post, though.) Apart from a thumping headache and a black eye I don't feel too bad—except fairly furious that I can't

Dearest Squirrel **194** The 1980s

go to interviews for two or three weeks. (This, of course, is the very time I shall be offered something luscious!)

Darling, I'll give you a ring when this apology for a migraine diminishes and hope to see you fairly soon after that.

Take great care,

My love as always and always—S

PS Hope Oscar's sorting out Woodfall for you.

The Royal Free Hospital is a large teaching hospital in Hampstead, north London. In the event, Beuselinck's investigations into the financial accounts of Woodfall Films revealed a history of profligacy that had frittered away most of the money the company had earned. It emerged that, among other extravagances, Woodfall had apparently once owned five Rolls Royces, although it was unknown who, if anybody, drove them. To his intense annoyance, Osborne gained nothing from the exercise for which he was obliged to pay Beuselinck's fee.

JO to PL ms letter n/a BL

11. 5. 84

Squirrel my darling

Oh dear!

I knew you'd get your lovely tail fouled up on a <u>bike</u> of all things and in Edgeware [sic] Road on a Friday evening. Very Squirrel-like carrying on, I'd say. Do hope you're feeling better soon. These things really one [sic] quite a shock—even my small argument with dogs and horses left me reeling somewhat for a few days. Went to Brighton for fish and chips, magnificent Chinese food (must take you.) Spent an inordinate amount of money, bought <u>two</u> very flash suits to impress the yokels in L.A. and saw ¾ an hour of two indifferent films—Educating Rita (witless and condescending—so much for your working-class writers) and Greystoke—unimaginative and only tolerable for glimpses of Ralphie.

Let me know when you're ready for more rewarding (?) athletic pursuits. I'll be here until about June 7th.

I don't have to tell you that you are loved and missed. Till I come and let down your tyres.

Ever your B

Osborne was preparing to go to the United States to see the Chichester production of *A Patriot for Me* when it transferred to Los Angeles, hence the purchase of 'very flash' suits. *Educating Rita,* a 1980 play by Willy Russell, was made into a film starring Michael Caine and Julie Walters and released in 1983. The story deals with the relationship between Frank, an embittered, alcoholic Open University lecturer, and Rita, a young hairdresser intent on improving herself and taking a course in English Literature. The play, and to a lesser extent the film, were enormously popular. *Greystoke: The Legend of Tarzan, Lord of the Apes,* is a 1984 adventure film based on Edgar Rice Burroughs' 1914 novel, *Tarzan of the Apes.* Ralph Richardson, in his final film appearance, played the 6th Earl of Greystoke and as a result earned an Academy Award nomination as Best Supporting Actor.

JO to PL ms postcard nd BL

Wed[nesday, May 1984]

So relieved you're OK and more or less bushy-tailed again. See you soon.

Love always B

It appears that there was no electricity supply to Pamela's flat for a few days. This may have been because she had omitted to pay a bill or a reminder while in hospital, and as a result the supply had been cut off until such time as the account was settled.

PL to JO ms letter Texas

23a Priory Road
London NW6
18th May 1984

Dearest b—

I settled down to the drey this morning to find your letter and rodent relief—oh, darling, thank you so very much it's even more than I asked for and guarantees a nutty May into the bargain—whew.

God bless our—to me—astonishing reunion—despite our respective constraints it feels more than ever firm and enduring: this is, I think, more than the pious and somewhat fragile hope that attends your average reconciliation—<u>which</u>, since it's taken some thirty years, is as it should be. I hope my fortunes improve soon—the decline has coincided very objectionably with our renewal—it only strikes me in weaker, desperate moments, as on Wednesday, when I'm forced to push out the begging bowl again, and I'm suddenly frightened (<u>quite</u> unjustifiably, I know) that you'll think I regard you as more approachable for help when I'm in need—forgive me. It hardly needs saying that the reverse is truer. Anyway, I'll stop being so graceless and generally embarrassing immediately. I think I must be taking too many codeine. The head and eye are improving daily (the tail's not doing too badly either!) and I rejoice that you'll be able to come up soon.

I'm being taken off to the South Bank tonight for an evening of Jewish-American pain, a preview of 'Golden Boy'—well, there's nowt on the telly, and it'll give my darling neighbours a night's break from my company. Power should be restored to my flat early next week and I can go back there to sleep.

Here's another card to tickle your fancy—

Love ever S

Pamela uses the term 'drey,' meaning the nest of a squirrel and another echo of *Look Back in Anger*, where the image occurs in Jimmy's final speech, both to denote her desk, where she kept personal and professional papers, and, more generally, her home. *Golden Boy*, a 1937 play by Clifford Odets, had opened for previews at the National Theatre in a production directed by Bill Bryden, a few days earlier. The play deals with the dilemma of Joe Bonaparte, who dreams of becoming a violinist but is presented with the chance of making money and winning fame as a prizefighter, with the attendant risk of damaging his hands. Odets was the son of Jewish Russian and Rumanian immigrants to the United States, and his plays are regarded as important in the history not only of American, but of Jewish-American theatre. The card 'to tickle your fancy'—now seemingly lost—was probably a reproduction of a picture of an actress or female music hall artist, or a seaside cartoon. Meanwhile, Pamela was also feeling nostalgic.

PL to JO ms letter Texas

23a Priory Road

NW6

1ˢᵗ June 1984

Darling B,

Thanks for returning the package of letters etc, one or two Labour Party addresses I needed, but the rest were due to be thrown out, I'm afraid, so sorry you had the trouble. I must get the wilderness of my 'desk' under control now I'm back. At least your letters (of 30 years or more) are neatly stacked away in a more <u>secret</u> part of the drey, in a very large envelope marked, lugubriously, 'For immediate destruction in the event of my Death!'—well, you never know when an endangered species will be extinguished by London traffic or something and it appears that a) discretion and b) ultra-clean knickers are of the essence in this naughty world.

I do love you, my savage, benign bear wherever we are in our separate necks of the forest, and to re-encounter you suddenly, briefly, is as literally breathtaking as ever, so I never seem to verbalise (a trendy word for an <u>old</u> complaint of mine, I know but one which I seem to have overcome largely with other intimates over the years—what a pity I didn't meet you later!) – to continue: never tell you that your lightest embrace whether of affection or passion revives the oldest memory I wish to keep—of deep familiarity, excitement, reassurance and of a trust now greater than before. (Bless me, this is near atavism—perhaps I'm feeling unduly ancient today)—but its survival is at once totally amazing and utterly natural.

I'm going to York for a week next Thursday—no, that's wrong, I'm coming back earlier, on Tuesday night—anyway, I expect you'll be in Cornwall—do let me know for how long so I could drop a line. I'm out this weekend but back on Monday and Tuesday if you feel like ringing—Somewhat in haste, but ever your

S

PS Just read this through—whatever else, you do <u>nothing</u> for my prose style!

Why Osborne was in possession of letters written to Pamela is unknown. The 'very large envelope' at Priory Road contained not only Osborne's letters and postcards but also Pamela's copies of the programmes for the original productions of *Look Back in Anger* and *Inadmissible Evidence*, and a dozen enthusiastic press reviews of the latter play. She also kept the formal announcement of her wedding to Osborne that appeared in the *Bridgwater Mercury*. If the Lanes had authorized its publication, then it was a case of social decorum masking private anguish. Perhaps Pamela had inserted it herself. She also kept the letter that Osborne had written to her father on 1 July 1951, promising that 'she will be looked after and cared for always.'

JO to PL ms letter BL

Cornwall
July 5 1984

Darling S

So delighted you're coming to Cranmer's Ball. Shall I get Robin to bring you down or will you be bringing someone? Do try to make it this time. Also August 19/20th. Will let you know which. Most likely the 19th. It seems ages since the last.

Like the South of France here, without the horrible Frogs. Working in the garden all day, gazing at the sea. Came up for Betjeman Memorial. Quite spiffing. Sat in the choir five places from the Prince of Wales. What would they have once said in Derby—or Bridgwater, come to that! Miss Hunter-Dunn was there as well! I don't have a London address for [John] Dexter. I have his NY apartment number… or the Met.

He's so elusive—always says he'll ring and doesn't. Otherwise you could try him c/o Triumph Apollo. Or what about the National? With a cast of 80, that's where he should be doing it.

Enclosed for endangered species (research for breeding?)

See you soon

My love always

B

John Betjeman had died on 19 May. His memorial service was held in Westminster Abbey on 29 June, when to his delight, Osborne found himself prominently seated not only near the Prince of Wales but also Lord Renfrew of Kainsthorn, one of Betjeman's close friends. A leading archaeologist and palaeontologist, Colin Renfrew was an expert on the prehistory of languages and Professor of Archaeology at Cambridge University. Joan Hunter Dunn is the tennis-playing object of the narrator's adoration in Betjeman's 1941 poem, *A Subaltern's Love Song*. A real-life figure, she had been married to a civil servant for seven years when Betjeman met her, fell in love and composed the poem in her honour, using her maiden name instead of her married name of Jackson. She was now sixty-nine and a widow.

John Dexter had been at the Metropolitan Opera, New York, since 1974, first as Director of Productions and then as Production Advisor. He also worked extensively in London, often for Triumph Apollo, a theatrical production company. Pamela had appeared in Dexter's production of *Last Day in Dreamland* by Willis Hall at the Lyric, Hammersmith, in 1959, and had heard that he was about to direct Jean-Paul Sartre's *The Devil and The Good Lord*, also at the Lyric. As the play has eighty characters, Pamela, who had not appeared on stage for over three months and was anxious to work with Dexter again, was hoping, not unreasonably, that there might be a part for her.

The aspect of Osborne and Pamela's relationship in which directoire knickers continued to feature, now branched out into nomenclature, their shared interest being celebrated by their adding the word 'Droitwich' to the address line of their letters and cards. This was not an allusion to the Warwickshire spa town but an acronym invented by Osborne reminiscent of the contractions used by corresponding lovers during World War 11. According to a note in his handwriting in his archives, it stood for 'Directoires Right On In Time When I Come Home'. 'Right on' might be interpreted literally, but the phrase was also a rabble-rousing slang expression common at the time, loosely meaning 'yes! Let's do it!' or 'in complete agreement.'

PL to JO ms letter Texas

The Drey
Droitwich
8th July 84

B. dearest——

Think I've done my bit for peace for a while—eleven-mile sponsored walk along the Grand Union Canal towpath for CND today! I went with two amusing people and a delicious dog, which ate most of our picnic in Victoria Park.

Thank you, my darling, for <u>more</u> than securing the safety of the drey again and the continuation of the species—I'll depute younger members to attend to the delightful matter of breeding and report in due course.

You've been marvellously helpful about Dexter—elusive he may be but I'm sure I can track him down with all this information. Vastly encouraged, I'll make a start tomorrow—come to think of it, it was at the Lyric Hammersmith that I last worked with him, the old one, that is, some years ago in Willis Hall's play with Adolf (whose series is at last about to hit our screens, I see.) Well, if there's something I can do in it, it will fill a gap in my working life which is beginning to make its icy grip felt.

Monday the 9th. Had an idea there might be something in the post from you this morning, so I left this unsealed. So glad you've won a victory for Evensong—well done! Series Two sounds like a computer course for the Open University. Was reading this when the wireless announced that York Minster had been struck by lightning, some say as a direct result of the enthronement of the Bishop of Durham.

About the 19th—was keeping both this and the 20th free as I said—but also in my post this morning is a letter calling me into hospital on Monday the 16th—a pretty minor operation on my ear to remove a piece of shrapnel of sorts left over from my accident—it will probably be done the following day, but I can't be certain that I'll be home before Thursday afternoon. Is there any chance of you switching to Friday the 20th? Do hope so, but realize you may have already arranged other things in London for the 19th. Anyway, if you want to let me know at the last minute my address from next Monday will be:

McLaggan Ward

Royal Free Hospital

Pond Street

Hampstead

London NW3

If you <u>can't</u> make the 20th instead, I'll see you at Cranmer's Ball—I haven't arranged to bring anyone, by the way, so I'd be glad to come with Robin if she has a spare seat: the trains are a bit unpredictable on Sundays. Perhaps I could ring her when I get back from hospital? If she's full, I'll bring a friend with a car.

So glad Betjeman's memorial went off so well—and you so agreeably positioned close to Renfrew in the choir! This would have made banner headlines in the Bridgwater Mercury. Darling, must to post, or you'll never get this.

Till soon, whenever, the 20th or 22nd.

Ever your

S

The Grand Union Canal, stretching for 137 miles between London and Birmingham, is Britain's longest manmade waterway. Victoria Park is in east London and the nearby Regent's Canal provides a link to the Grand Union. Dexter's production of *The Devil and The Good Lord*, with a cast of twenty that in the event did not include Pamela, opened on 26 September. 'Adolf' was Osborne's nickname for Jill Bennett. The television series was *Poor Little Rich Girls*, a lighthearted drama series written by Charles Laurence based on an idea by Jill Bennett and the actress Maria Aitken, who played the leading roles of cousins from wealthy backgrounds obliged to live on slender means.

In Kent, Osborne had hurled himself into a crusade for the retention by the Anglican Church of the 1662 *Book of Common Prayer*, which he feared was being superseded by the more contemporary form of liturgy that many in the clergy were then advocating. *Series Two* was one of three experiments with a modernized liturgical form that had culminated in the introduction of the *Alternative Service*

Book in 1980, a publication Osborne took every opportunity to disparage. Its language, he maintained, was a desecration of that of the *Book of Common Prayer*, which he regarded as the bedrock of Anglican worship. Pamela very much enjoyed following his campaign from the sidelines and retained a clipping from a local Kent newspaper, which Osborne had sent her as evidence of his success. This was a report of the decision of the Edenbridge Parish Church Council to abandon *Series Two* and revert to the traditional *Book of Common Prayer* for Evensong. The contemporary liturgy 'had not been readily accepted' by everyone in the parish, confessed the vicar, 'the most notable opposition coming from actor and playwright John Osborne. The back of his car sported a *Save the Prayerbook* sticker.'

The Church bristled with controversy that year. Over 12,000 people signed a petition against the consecration of the Rev. David Jenkins as Bishop of Durham on 6 July, due to the widely-held but misinformed conviction that he held heterodox beliefs, particularly on the resurrection. Jenkins was the epitome of a progressive and liberal church, and his views were largely misrepresented. Three days after his consecration in York Minster, the building was struck by lightning, resulting in a disastrous fire that some of his detractors suggested might be usefully interpreted as a sign of divine wrath.

Pamela attended that year's Cramner's Ball, and this may have been the occasion at which Helen took a surely unusual snapshot that survives in one of Osborne's voluminous photograph albums. Osborne is sitting at a table set on the lawn at Christmas Place, grinning broadly, flanked on one side by Pamela, former wife and current lover, and on the other by Jocelyn Rickards, a former lover, who is taking a photograph of Helen, current wife, who in her turn is taking the photograph. The relationship between Osborne and Jocelyn, however, was altogether different than that between himself and Pamela. Their sexual relationship had ceased when Osborne married Penelope Gilliatt, and as a successful costume designer, Jocelyn had been financially independent longer than he had known her. They remained good friends. Following Osborne's marriage to Penelope Gilliatt, Jocelyn had married the artist Leonard Rosoman. After their divorce, she married the director Clive Donner who accompanied her to Osborne's garden parties.

Pamela was still in possession of a 'notebook,' probably the 'Golden Notebook' referred to on 9 February. Her having recently been in hospital had made

Osborne anxious to retrieve it. She duly dispatched it to him, although why she did not merely hand it to him when they met is a mystery. However, he quickly acknowledged both its receipt and a strenuous afternoon:

JO to PL ms letter n/a

August 1st [1984]
DROITWICH

Darling S

Thanks so much for sending off the notebook so promptly—also <u>discreetly</u> typed from St John's Wood. Helpful.

Yesterday was marvellous.. I nearly fell asleep over lunch after all that mid-morning directoire thrashing. I'll ring you about Lingfield to see if you're free... Didn't leave anything on top of the dresser so enclosed is for re-enforced gussets and fresh elastic. My love always,

Your B

Osborne was planning a day out at Lingfield Park, a racecourse in Surrey. Did Pamela accompany him? Or was this the occasion for which she had invested in the hat celebrated below?

JO to PL ms pc Christmas Place BL

DROITWICH
August 31 [1984]

Darling Squirrel,

Longing to see you looking so squirrelsome and spiffing in your hat. Try wearing it with your directoires. Am struggling to write GFH all next week, but will be up on Wednesday 12th. Try to be in during the FORENOON if you can. Will ring/write to confirm.

My love hastily

B

Osborne's use of the word 'spiffing'—and Pamela's in her letter written in late September—was a recent, and as it turned out, temporary affectation. It first crops up in Osborne's letter of 14 September 1979. Perhaps as a not altogether idle amusement, he was experimenting with vocabulary such as 'spiffing' that he thought befitting the character of an English country gentleman. He also introduced into his letters terms generally considered anachronistic, such as 'forenoon', and 'Epiphany,' hoping for a similar effect. John Betjeman had done much the same. Although Pamela cautiously tried a 'spiffing' or two and in her letter of 8 July above wrote of the 'wireless' instead of the more contemporary 'radio', a usage Osborne probably noted and approved, she generally steered clear of archaic, sticking to 'morning' over 'forenoon'.

'GFH´' is George Fredric Handel, the leading character of *God Rot Tunbridge Wells*.

The following postcards from Osborne to Pamela are undated, but appear narratively appropriate here.

JO to PL ms postcard n/a n/d BL

Thursday
DROITWICH

Darling—

I forgot to tell you about my accountant. He's going to dream something up in the next week or two: 'Script Consultant' I think!

See you Thursday

My love B

Instead of sending Pamela frequent, if irregular cheques, Osborne was planning to make consistent monthly payments into her bank through his accountant at Temple Gothard. These payments would be signalled by the designation of 'script consultant.'

JO to PL ms postcard n/a n/d BL

My darling—

Spoke to Oscar [Beuselinck]. It can be done—so don't worry. I do wish I cd have stayed—sorry I was a bit tired. Better next time. Please don't be scornful about the directoires. They were a triumph. So were you.

My love always

B

The 'script consultant' plan had been submitted to Oscar Beuselinck for legal scrutiny.

The following note from Pamela in reply to a letter from Osborne in which he enclosed another cheque, is also undated and the accompanying envelope is lost. However, it was probably written at about this time, or another time during these years when Pamela was so concerned about debt that she feared a court summons for non-payment.

PL to JO ms letter n/a n/d BL

Tuesday

Darling Bears—

Thank you—my next appearance will not now have to be in court—and for your extraordinarily moving letter which I'll try to answer over the weekend—I am working the odd few days this week or would do it sooner. I'm alright, though, and not under pressure.

Love you v much

Squirrel

PL to JO ms letter n/d Texas

Priory Road
NW6
Friday
[September 1984]

Dearest—

<u>Very</u> sorry not to have seen you before I get stuck into Colchester, and you go to L.A.

I'm staying with my neighbour who's just going to post, hence the jagged scribble—have just about stopped being supine after a couple of near-equine injections and shall take the air tomorrow!

I thought I'd dropped you a card to say I'd heard from Temple Gothard, and all was well. I'm sorry, what a wretched girl you must have thought me—am getting dreadfully absent-minded, probably because I haven't been working and studying lately—or so I hope.

I don't know when you're off, but in case we don't speak or anything before you go—very good luck, my darling, have a success and a spiffing time and enjoy yourselves—and please send me a picture pc—and also please get in touch when you come back!

Oh dear, no more time.

More than much love

Ever

S

Shortly after she posted this, Pamela began rehearsals at the Mercury Theatre in Colchester. It was her first stage work in six months. With a capacity of 500, the concrete and glass building had opened in 1972, and 'follows the new National and Barbican Theatres for progress, flexibility, style and comfort,' announced the local paper.[40] Michael Winter, whom Pamela had known since working with him at Bournemouth in 1968, had become the artistic director in 1984. She was due to appear in Edward Albee's *Who's Afraid of Virginia Woolf?* and Raymond Briggs's

When the Wind Blows, a stage adaptation of his graphic novel about an elderly couple whose lives are devastated by a nuclear strike.

Osborne, meanwhile, was packing the 'flash' suits he had bought earlier in the year in readiness for travelling to Los Angeles to see the Chichester revival of *A Patriot for Me*. As both Osbornes detested flying, they were to sail on the QE 2, a luxurious transatlantic liner. An arrangement had been made with Cunard, the ship's owners, that Osborne give a 'talk' on board after a screening of *Tom Jones*, presumably in return for their waiving, or considerably reducing, the Osbornes' fares. From New York, they travelled by train to Los Angeles, a three-day journey during which Osborne bought copious supplies of champagne. The play opened at the Ahmanson Theater on 5 October, and according to the *Los Angeles Times* the following day, 'will never get a better production on these shores. Indeed, it may not have had a better one in England.' While in Los Angeles, the Osbornes stayed with Tony Richardson, who had been resident in the city for several years, and when the former collaborators took the opportunity to resolve the animosity between them since their falling out over *The Charge of the Light Brigade* sixteen years earlier.

Back in England, Pamela was preparing for the opening of *Who's Afraid of Virginia Woolf?* on 11 October, playing Martha opposite Leon Tanner's George. Tanner was an Australian and a keen Anglophile, having made his home in Stratford-upon-Avon. *Virginia Woolf* was, and still is, a play that defines Edward Albee in much the same way that *Look Back in Anger* defines John Osborne, and indeed the two plays have often been compared. Both are furious accounts of a disintegrating but mutually dependant marriage, the former set in American academe, the latter in rented rooms in the English midlands. The marital battleground over which the middle-aged George, a member of the history department at a New England university, and Martha, his wife and the daughter of the university President, is, however, drunkenly violent, and the fallout upon their guests Nick and his wife, Honey, drawn reluctantly into Martha's world of manipulation and vengeance, more decisive.

'Pamela Lane was a wonderful actress,' remembered the director, Jeremy Howe. 'She was sharp and fast – both on the uptake and in her acting. She was fun to work with but I think over the years, I knew less about Pamela and her hinterland than pretty well any leading actor I have ever worked with. She had absolutely no small talk. At any read-through she would be at the back, almost invisible. She never complained about anything – the late calls, the fatuous notes I might have given her, the dowdy costumes. She would be as reliable as clockwork and give great performances, which I sometimes thought had little to do with the rehearsals or any input I had had in the process. She was wonderfully self-contained. There was an element of the trooper about Pamela, but what we never did at Colchester was offer her bit parts, always the hardest to cast in rep: she was way too good to have her anywhere other than centre stage.'[41]

She may have been centre stage, but for *Who's Afraid of Virginia Woolf?* she was obliged to negotiate an immensely cluttered set. The furniture in George and Martha's living room was arranged before diaphanous burgundy drapes behind which showroom dummies stared blankly at the audience, while empty gin and whisky bottles protruded from beneath the sofa and the chairs and lay in wait for the unwary. 'It was very much in the vein of the theatre of the absurd,' explained Howe, 'about living in the moment and making a two-and-three-quarter hour journey in front of the audience. Is the end cruel or redemptive? I wanted Pamela and Leon to make up their minds as they were playing as to how they would do the ending. Pamela was brilliant. She was not afraid of letting rip emotionally. She and Leon Tanner tore shreds out of each other every night and seemed to really enjoy themselves.'[42] Yet as with *The Glass Menagerie* and *A Delicate Balance* at Leicester, the production was enthusiastically reviewed locally but ignored nationally, even by *The Stage*.

On his return from the United States, Osborne sent Pamela a postcard chosen not from his stock of seaside cartoons with their mildly vulgar innuendo, but something altogether more restful, even fragrant, to divert her, revive her, perhaps, from the exhaustion of Martha's emotional tyranny. His choice was an art reproduction, usually Pamela's territory, an illustration of Renoir's 1811 painting, *On the Terrace*, which shows a young woman in a blue dress and a girl, perhaps nine or ten years old, in a white sailor dress, on the terrace of a Parisian house, the Seine in the background. The girl is wearing an elaborate floral hat.

JO to PL ms pc n/a n/d BL

Thursday
[8 November 1984]

Darling S

I literally pressed my nose against the little girl's hat. What revelation! How about next WEDNESDAY—14th—sometime? If I don't hear, will assume it's ok. Longing to see you. So glad VW went well for you.

Until then—DROITWICH

Yr B

By now, Pamela was coming to the end of the run of *When the Wind Blows*, in which she played Hilda Bloggs opposite Berwick Kaler as Jim, and which closed on 17 November. Politically, she was instinctively sympathetic towards the play. However, Jeremy Howe discovered that 'she wasn't a fan of it because she felt the author hadn't developed the characters beyond their cartoon stereotypical origins. Besides, she could smell a duff line from 400 yards.'[43] Nevertheless, according to Richard Digby Day, who saw the production, her performance was 'profoundly moving.'[44] Osborne also travelled to Colchester to see it, presumably from devotion to Pamela as it is not a play he would have found enlivening, but he appears to have left no impression of it.

JO to PL ms pc n/a BL

Friday
[16 November 1984]

Is it possible to put our liaison as above forward to Friday 23rd? I may have an actor call. Thursday may still be ok. Will be at Royal Norfolk Hotel, Bognor, Tuesday evening and Wed. You could leave a message if I'm not in. Longing to see you. Bath was nice. Trevor Howard splendid as G.F.H.

[unsigned]

Osborne was following the filming at Bath and Bognor Regis of *God Rot Tunbridge Wells*. At one stage, it was proposed that he play a small part in it, but the idea was abandoned. Trevor Howard gave a bravura performance as the aging composer.

JO to Pl ms pc n/a BL

DROITWICH
23. 11. 84

Dearest darling Squirrel,

How wonderful to see you again after so long. And looking so good and lively. I'm off to Cornwall on Tuesday... <u>Do</u> come to my birthday dinner if you can. I'd love you to be there. Also, see what you can manage over the Christmas holiday. I do love you so much. It never ever fails.

In haste

Ever your most loving B

The absence of national reviews of her performances at Leicester, Nottingham and Colchester was particularly aggravating for Pamela. She had played a succession of leading roles in plays recognised as modern classics, and yet she found it impossible to capitalize on her achievements. She now had no further stage work scheduled for four months, and the following year, 1985, she told Osborne later, became one in which she would be 'more cowed and conditioned by money/debt/insecurity than I've ever been in my life.'[45] Osborne, on the other hand, defiantly lived beyond his means, continuing his consumption of champagne but occasionally overlooking his insulin injections, the result being that sometimes his days were rather haphazard. But if his wine merchants' bills were hefty, then so were all the others. Writing the first volume of his memoirs had failed to staunch the outward flow of cash that he did not have in the first place and by the mid eighties, he owed the Inland Revenue almost £99,000 (equivalent to £283,000 in 2018), and his bank overdraft stood at £100,000 (£286,000). Yet despite this, he continued to assist Pamela financially, picking up the bill after their lunches and ferrying money to her through his accountants.

On 29 December, he belatedly celebrated his fifty-fifth birthday with a dinner party at Christmas Place. Although invited, Pamela did not attend. There was a misunderstanding; either Pamela had not made it clear, or Osborne had not fully registered, that for the second year in succession she would be spending much of December and then Christmas and New Year in York. Again Osborne bridled, inferring that her friends in the north took precedence over him, and it prompted a pained new year letter:

JO to PL ms n/a Texas

January 1985

Alas, how poverty begets poverty. It seemed, on the face of it, unlikely that you would appear on the 29th but I had not realized that the telecommunications system had not yet penetrated Yorkshire. Are there still not carrier pigeons winging down from the dales to the rest of the world? Several others told me, well in advance, of their change of plans. Rooms need preparing, beds made, food laid in but these are doubtless the Greenham bourgeois obsessions. Still, there is some common currency of good manners and thoughtfulness prevails in certain isolated pockets of the country.

However, it still seems bizarre that you should feel so beholden or intimidated by others that you cannot confess that you have already firmly accepted an invitation from someone who has known you for longer, which makes no difference, but who might even have contributed a continuing footrail at least to your life [sic]. Not so, it seems.

It is especially irksome to be put in the false position of seeming demanding and, above all, aggrieved. You owe me nothing but good manners are <u>always</u> welcome. In this respect, I <u>do</u> have some reason for complaint. At the least, your behaviour is churlish and, at the worst, unkind. Gratuitously so.

But there it is and, no doubt, ever will be. Are you a squirrel or merely a mouse? Happy New Year

J

The incident was resolved, but not forgotten. The following month, the customary Valentine's card arrived at Priory Road. On the reverse, Osborne had attached two newspaper clippings, one a Valentine's greeting: 'Squirrel: I'll be nuts about you, no matter who you hibernate with, George'; the other an advertisement for directoire knickers.

JO to Pl ms picture postcard of Brighton Royal Pavilion BL

Bears, Directoires, why am I always ahead of my time!

Love

B

■ ■ ■

In March, Pamela was at the Playhouse in Leeds, rehearsing *Golden Girls* by Louise Page, a widely-admired dramatist whose work had been produced by the Royal Court and the Royal Shakespeare Company. A play about the rivalries of five women athletes training for the European Games in Athens, *Golden Girls* highlighted several issues swirling about international sports at the time: the increasingly rigorous competitiveness, the use of performance-enhancing drugs and the demands made by sponsors. The Royal Shakespeare Company had first produced the play the previous year, but Page had extensively re-written it for its northern premiere. Pamela sent a breathless postcard:

PL to JO ms postcard Texas

Leeds Playhouse
28.3.85

Thank you for the new tel[ephone] n[umber] for Christmas Place. Did you get my Leeds address card, or were the dogs forced back to base camp? Anyway, I'm here till May 11th at the moment in track suit and trainers. Puff, puff; too old for this.

Love to you and Helen

S

Golden Girls opened in April, with Pamela playing 'Laces' MacKenzie, a trainer: hence the track suit and trainers and, considering that she was a smoker and prone to asthma, the 'puff, puff.' Yet she 'excels' wrote R. L. Reyner in *The Stage*, in Cordelia Monsey's 'brilliantly directed' production.[46] On 6 April, *God Rot*

Tunbridge Wells, Osborne's 'comical tragical' meditation on the life of Handel was broadcast on Channel 4 Television. The following day, having glanced at the largely dismissive Sunday newspaper reviews, he 'had a few more glasses of champagne and fell into a prolonged coma.'[47] An ambulance sped him to an intensive care bed in hospital, ironically at nearby Tunbridge Wells. He was dangerously ill and at one point his condition was critical, yet he revived and, once sufficiently able to reach for a telephone, he arranged for a hamper from Fortnum and Mason, the long-established Piccadilly store famous for delicatessen and 'quality' foods, to be delivered to Pamela in Leeds.

JO to PL Fortnum and Mason complements slip n/d BL

[April 1985]

Squirrel

Happy Easter if it's not too late.

My love

B

Easter Sunday that year was 17 April, but in the event, the hamper did not arrive until after the holiday. Once *Golden Girls* closed in early May, Pamela returned to London and Priory Road. Osborne remained in hospital until the end of the month. His illness was diagnosed as the result of his drinking and his mismanaging his insulin injections, although tests also showed that he had ingested rat urine, probably from polluted water in his swimming pool, rats having been seen in the nearby stables. This was the interpretation that Osborne preferred. He wrote to Pamela a month after he returned home.

JO to PL ms pc n/a BL

29. 5. 85

Glad you got the hamper alright. I was about to ask for my money back at Fortnum's. Have been rather bad company and the weather's been foul so just as well you stayed up with London's intellectual life. But <u>do</u> come and look at the lake for a few days. That wld be so nice. Give me a ring.

The quacks are giving me dozens of blood tests. They couldn't understand the sudden lethal nature of it. They now think it may have come from rats (RATS! Yes, not lethal) pee visiting the pool from the stables block. The DOGS are INOCULATED! NOT ME!

See you soon.

'London's intellectual life,' was a phrase frequently and enthusiastically used by Penelope, and one that had induced in Osborne, acutely conscious of the disparity in their social backgrounds and academic credentials, a spasm of dread.

Pamela had no stage work between the ending of *Golden Girls* on 11 May and beginning rehearsals for *The Adventures of Paddington Bear* in Watford on 18 November—a long six-month break. Instead, she worked for Filofax, the manufacturers of 'personal organisers,' loose-leaf binders containing a diary, address pages and various 'planning' and 'time management' accessories that were extremely fashionable at the time. More rewardingly, for her dignity, she also began participating in an academic programme overseen by her friend Richard Digby Day, in which she gave seminars to groups of visiting American drama students, escorted them to the theatre and afterwards led discussions on the productions they had seen.

Yet the following few months were dominated by a crisis in her relationship with Osborne. Suddenly, the flow of correspondence judders to a halt and a five-month gap, coinciding with Pamela's Filofax and seminar stint, occurs between the letter above, written in May, and that below, dated in October. It may be that letters written during this period have been lost or destroyed, but something happened during the autumn that significantly altered the delicate balance of their friendship. Pamela's letter below indicates that once again she had appealed to Osborne for money—evidently a large amount—in apparent addition to the 'monthly allowance' she was still receiving. For the first time, Osborne's response had been noticeably reluctant, perhaps even begrudging, hence her reference to the 'elegant and bleak' compliments slip accompanying his cheque and her promise of repayment. He had been suspicious before about how his money was being spent, and this appeal had prompted his misgivings again. He was also probably more than usually financially sensitive as he and Helen had just returned from another expensive holiday in Venice, which they had awarded themselves as convalescence after his illness. Yet Pamela detected both the change in his tone, and an accompanying emotional withdrawal.

PL to JO ms letter Texas

23a Priory Road
London NW6 4NN
28th October [1985]

Dear Bears,

I got the cheque this morning—thank you and God (if that's the right order.) I think it must have come on Saturday from the postmark, but I was somewhat melodramatically padlocked out that day till I could contact my landlord this morning, get a change of knickers and conduct a drama seminar with the bright-eyed young Yanks—hence the delay.

Jean is reassuring about prospects for next year, even so, it may mean that I'll have to repay you in bits as it comes in. Paddington Bear at Watford will obviously scarcely keep me in marmalade sandwiches, so I can't promise to start yet.

I'm doing a fair bit of theatre going—courtesy of the Americans, and exhibitions, and a part-time job for Filofax. I've marched, lain down and stood up for CND and been to one or two good parties.

Your compliments slip was elegant and bleak—I have to believe this denoted haste of dispatch, and not condemnation: of my importunity, or of my not being, say, at the Ag[ricultural] Show or Cranmer's this summer. Or perhaps things have taken a turn and you've gone off me or in another direction—I don't know. Still, all in all, in a year of financial adversity that would be, as ever, the worst reversal of all.

Glad that your holiday was a success and I hope your strength grows as thick as your fur.

Why Pamela was 'melodramatically padlocked out' of 23a Priory Road for the weekend at least, is not clear. If she had fallen into arrears with the rent, it seems a heavy-handed response. Perhaps a fault in the energy supplies had made the flat uninhabitable while it was being rectified. Her letter to Osborne was written on Monday. 'Jean' was Jean Diamond, Pamela's agent at London Management. Pamela was about to begin rehearsals for *The Adventures of Paddington Bear* at the Palace Theatre, Watford, in which she would be playing Mrs Bird, the housekeeper, for the second time.

Osborne's asperity continued, and he angrily but meticulously clipped away Pamela's valediction at the end of the letter above. Either she had mis-written, or he had misread it as being signed from 'yours, Squirrel,' as opposed to her customary and more intimate 'your Squirrel.' This had been sufficient for him to unleash a furious (and possibly drunken?) response in a letter now apparently lost, but to which Pamela refers as a 'scourge' in the letters below. He questioned her love, accused her of using him for his money and, in a year in which he had narrowly dodged the dark wings of death, of neglect. Its invective was such that it shocked and confused even Pamela, who, if nothing else, had in over thirty years such an unrivalled experience of her former husband's vicissitudes as to be immune to much of the vituperation he might have flung in her direction. On a train to York, she composed a reply that is at once contrite, robust and assertive, and suggesting that the basis of their relationship with one another must be reassessed. In doing so, she reverted to a more formal manner of address. While the following two letters represent only her side of the exchange, one can imagine his while reading them. There is something of the atmosphere of Jimmy and Alison Porter projected into late-middle age:

PL to JO ms letter Texas

Train to York
7.11.85

My dear John,

I'm getting out of the gulag for a few days—this journey is my first chance at a second attempt to answer your letter. The first was in parts as unjusti-fied in its counter-attack as were parts of the attack which led up to it <u>and</u> as disloyal and unloving, so I scrapped it. Will try to do better this time; but the first response was to be so angered and cast down by it (yours) I couldn't even begin to understand what had prompted it. (Incidentally, I had meant my customary 'your' at signing my last letter, it has never occurred to me to sign myself 'yours' to you. I'm deeply sorry, but a) you won't believe me, b) it hardly matters in any case because even 'your' would have been greeted as a coy dissimulation and I would have been charged with that instead of coldness.) I am mortified that you could see my last letter in the way you did, and the 'friendly chat' (at worst, whimsical) surrounding my thanks as DISSEMBLANCE, FEIGNED AFFECTION rooted in self-interest. Should letters be entirely about love or money? I might have done better just to send a receipt. (No, sorry, wipe that.)

You are right to charge me with two particular things, offences, hurts. 1) I was dreadfully wrong not to trust your benevolence and not to treat the whole matter in the 'old style' as what it is—and totally separate from anything else to do with us. (God, this train is really hitting my prose style.) You just have to understand that in 1985 I've become more cowed and conditioned by money/debt/insecurity than I've ever been in my life and this bled through to you: perhaps childishly, I told myself: 'You have been given regular pocket money, you haven't managed and there is NO health in you!' I imagined all the other ways you could have used such a sum, till—finally—it took all my nerve to pick up the phone and ask for it. When it arrived, I was deeply relieved as you can imagine, and my sense of indebtedness took over as I replied. 2) My neglect and carelessness towards you this year is of course undeniable, particularly after what you've been through. I've not selected targets for neglect and made you one of them— no, my neglect has been more or less total, I think, not least of myself (except for a persistent urge to survive the whole damned mess of this year, not to go under completely or to sign absolutely anything).

We're nearly in York. I'm going to have to hurry this. Where you have reduced me utterly is in suggesting that this pattern of indifference stretches to include the preceding years. Now I can trust nothing. Was that very memorable letter you wrote me, which I still keep close to my heart and secret, just a late night boozy prank or wank, a fantasy? Or what it seemed to be, a genuine outpouring, a revelation of a letter, such as I'd never ever had from you? If the former, I'll destroy it, if the latter I'll keep it forever.

Besides this, I think of your visits to me in London and particularly of my share in your celebrations, coming to stay with you and Helen (which I've loved), your lovely flowers and funny cards, your friendship and at times such a great closeness even within a short (Brief??) encounter. I'd thought that my pleasure and excitement in your presence was evident, but you tell me not.

Now lately not much news of you. You too can be reticent, it seems. Since my last visit (which was a short but wonderful respite)—and I <u>do</u> know that you've been resting, getting strong, going away or messing about at home, working—your life is there and I make small claim on your time, I think, more out of regard for your privacy than by inclination.[sic] We shall have to define what parts we play in each other's life, that's clear. In essence, in every way, you are for me what you always were at the beginning and again, more markedly, in these last three years. I <u>am</u> in love with you still, (if you'll <u>allow</u> me to say so), that seems as inescapable as does your continuing jurisdiction and my long-standing trial. I'm <u>always</u> answering charges, that will never change, I know. As for your affection and friendship and not in your other hat, as benefactor, I think you know how I prize them.

We're approaching [our] destination. I should finish and post this at the station in case I don't have time to finish it tonight and add more, as I'd like to, in another letter as soon as I can.

To be continued!

My love as ever, Pamela.

In using the rather strange phrase 'there is no health in you,' Pamela is possibly referring to Psalm 38, verse 3: 'Because of your wrath, there is no health in my body/there is no soundness in my bones.' If so, she was using the New International Version and not the King James, where the phrase does not appear, and, considering Osborne's advocacy of the latter, surely in the circumstances a tactical misjudgement. The 'very memorable letter' to which Pamela refers above may be the 'extraordinarily moving' letter from Osborne she mentions in her undated 'Tuesday' note written perhaps the previous summer. That letter seems lost.

She took up the theme of love and life again once she returned to London.

PL to JO ms letter n/a Texas

[London]

17 November 1985

My dear John,

I've walked several miles of Yorkshire moors since I last tried to write to you on that rocky train: enjoyed the trip more than I could have imagined, and it seems to have released me from the grip of gloom that London occasionally—or even frequently—exerts. Jean is encouraging about prospects in the New Year, so I'm more optimistic, I hope not foolishly.

I've re-read your scourge—it's dreadfully formal: have I mistaken the tone? Is it the formality of <u>rebuke</u> or of <u>something else</u>? Is it possible that you want to cut our connection altogether, and I have simply been too naïve/stupid/arrogant to detect it? Burdened with some of your emotional optimism, I still can't believe it is so, or that you wouldn't have said it more directly if it were—I'm accustomed to trust you, and in particular for that kind of honesty, but it would clearly be absurd to take your continuing affection for granted if it no longer exists, so please reassure me (or otherwise, if you have to). I think I've already told you that you have mine—and my abiding passion—for as long as you want: only advancing age prevents me from promising another 34 years.

Jean has suggested me to Alan Jay Lerner as standby for Beryl Reid in 'Gigi' should her legs or memory fail her, which they sometimes do—a mixed blessing as an assignment, and I doubt if London's ready to receive my rendering of 'Ah, yes, Ah remember eet [sic] well', so will hope for tellies instead. Tomorrow I start rehearsing the Christmas show at Watford.

Towards your peace of mind—if not universal peace—none of your money has gone to CND!—or indeed anywhere except the settlement of my own, household debts—and in none of my alliances have I been exploited financially (though sometimes emotionally). You have supported none but me, in case you were curious (as you have every right to be) about such a possibility. I really don't want to get into this money thing again, it seems inadvertently to have confused the main issue wildly enough already—except to say that it would be very helpful if my monthly allowance could be amended to read as 'gift' rather than 'script reading fee'—if this is possible and not prejudicial to you. I'm in trouble with the DHSS (via the Inland

Revenue) for not declaring these 'earnings' and must repay sums of benefit: I can manage this, but it rather negates your philanthropy if we can't make an alteration through the accountants for the future—perhaps, if you agree, I can ring them to see what can be done.

No particular news of plays etc over the last couple of weeks as I've been away—saw an awful new Olwyn Wymark about D. H. Lawrence while I was in York and an even worse Gorky adaptation ('Vassa') at Greenwich. Am steeping the American students in 'Troilus and Cressida' at Stratford next Saturday, bless their hearts, and I'm hoping for enough time off next week to see a few films (Colonel Redl among them).

I hope you're not away from home—I want to hear from you soon.

My love

P

Gigi, a musical by Alan Jay Lerner and Frederick Loewe, had opened in John Dexter's production at the Lyric Theatre on 17 September and ran for seven months. The title role was played by Amanda Waring, while Beryl Reid, who was then sixty-six, played Mamite. In the event her legs and memory held out, and Pamela did not understudy anyway.

The DHSS, or Department of Health and Social Security, was at that time the government department dealing with National Insurance and sickness benefit matters. The Inland Revenue dealt with income tax matters. The alteration in the designation of Pamela's 'monthly allowance' was duly made. York Theatre Royal produced the world premiere of *Lessons and Lovers: D. H. Lawrence in New Mexico* by the prolific Olwyn Wymark on 6 November. *Vassa* by Maxim Gorky, adapted and directed by Helena Kaut-Howson, and starring Janet Suzman, opened at the Greenwich Theatre on 7 November. The Royal Shakespeare Company production of *Troilus and Cressida* was directed by Howard Davies and starred Anton Lesser and Juliet Stephenson. *Colonel Redl*, a Hungarian/Austrian film based upon *A Patriot for Me*, directed by István Szabó and starring Klaus Maria Brandauer, opened in London on 4 October. Osborne received a screen credit and of more immediate importance, a £25,000 courtesy fee, despite not a word from the play being used. The film was nominated for an Academy Award for Best Foreign Film, won the Jury Prize at the Cannes Film Festival, and Best Foreign Language Film at the 1986 BAFTA Awards.

Pamela spent Christmas in London while Osborne remained in Kent. Yet the autumn difficulties between them remained unresolved. The passion of the previous three years quickly cooled, and there appear to be no more long lunches and Priory Road encounters. 'Droitwich' is consigned to the past. A distance had opened between them. Exactly what the nature of the crisis was, and how it was resolved, is a matter of conjecture, but with one exception, there appears to be no surviving written communication between them for over a year, from Pamela's letter above, written on 17 November 1985, until 5 December 1986, when Osborne sent her a brief note informing her of his change of address.

Their estrangement may have been caused by a combination of Pamela's persistent inability to manage money, Osborne's acute financial vulnerability, his emotional volatility, and their defining again 'what parts we play in each other's life.' Perhaps Osborne had concluded that he could no longer afford to help support his former wife. She had always more or less managed to stay afloat, but Osborne, to put it bluntly, was now broke. He owed over £233,000 (equivalent to over £665,000 in 2018) to the Inland Revenue, his bank and his accountants. Christmas Place was still mortgaged. Then there were his and Helen's living expenses, which were not exactly frugal. In addition, there were additional costs, including the wine merchants, those jaunts to Venice and their love of ocean cruises, against which their occasional journalism— Osborne was paid £125 (£356) for a weekly *Diary* column in *The Spectator*, while Helen also wrote articles and various reviews—did not make much of an impression. On the credit side, there was money in Osborne's production company account, while the worldwide royalties from his plays usually generated between £50,000 (equivalent to £143,000 in 2018) and £100,000 (£285,000) a year, although the current year, 1986 proved a disaster, bringing in only about £25,000 (£72,000). The prospects looked bleak. With no new play for a decade and unperformed work lying reproachfully in his desk drawer, drastic and immediate action could no longer be avoided. The Cornwall cottage, that wildly rash purchase, was sold, and the Cranmer's Balls, those recklessly generous, unthinkingly expensive summer celebrations, abandoned.

Possibly, at the end of 1985, Pamela also felt the cold axe blow of Osborne's cash-cutting and the 'monthly allowance' also came to an abrupt end, so precipitating the break between them. There is no evidence in the remaining correspondence of his support continuing, which is not quite the same thing. Yet a break of some kind occurred that winter. An alternative explanation is revealed in a tantalisingly enigmatic passage in *Almost a Gentleman,* the second volume of his memoirs, which was published six years later in 1991. Osborne recalls a rendezvous in Venice with Penelope Gilliatt thirty years earlier, and writes: 'What others would nail as her [Penelope's] greeting gush felt to me on that September morning more like the embrace of a voluptuous goddess. It is tempting to deride and disown what may have been howling fits of delusion. But the abandonment of sense and judgement cannot honestly repudiate it, just as my passion for Pamela had been a folly and, most demonstrably, a delusion. That one took more than thirty years before she stamped on it finally with her own authority.'[48] He then turns to other matters.

Quite what Osborne meant by this allusion to Pamela is not explained in the book. But his realisation after thirty years that 'my passion had been a folly and, most demonstrably, a delusion' would place the incident exactly at this time. Had Pamela concluded that their life of letters, hurried postcards, lingering lunches and brief encounters with their attendant frippery of champagne, underwear and cash on the dresser, could no longer be fairly sustained? There were, after all, their respective loyalties and 'constraints' to consider. Perhaps Pamela, as she had done when she declared an intermission in their relationship in Derby in 1954, pronounced the verdict, 'finally with her own authority.'

As with her earlier decision, she did not allow the present watershed to affect her work, which was in any case too hard to come by to be entered into anything other than wholeheartedly. In February 1986, she returned to the Mercury Theatre, Colchester, where she played Mrs Danvers, the resentful, manipulative housekeeper in Daphne du Maurier's *Rebecca*, directed by Richard Digby Day. The play was one of those repertory warhorses actors and audiences alike found almost impossible to avoid, and both Osborne and Pamela knew it well, he having appeared as Maxim de Winter, in Kidderminster in 1952 and she as Mrs de Winter in Derby two years later. At Colchester, Digby Day thought her 'terrific.'[49]

The single postcard breaking what seems to be almost six months of postal silence arrived at Christmas Place on the thirtieth anniversary of *Look Back in Anger*.

PL to JO ms pc Texas

8th May 1986

My dear B—

Happy anniversary today, thirty years on. Thinking of you.

Much love

S

A few weeks later, on 5 June, a revival of *The Entertainer* opened, not at the National Theatre but at the Shaftesbury in the West End. Directed by Robin Lefèvre, the production had originated at the Leicester Haymarket. Peter Bowles played Archie Rice, the first actor to do so in the West End since Olivier in 1957. Frank Middlemass, the former member of the Roc Players who had been Osborne's best man at his wedding to Pamela, played Billy, Archie's father, while Sylvia Sims appeared as Phoebe. Yet much of the West End suffered from falling ticket sales that summer and *The Entertainer* was no exception, the production closing after nine weeks on 27 July. The same month, and reunited with John Dexter at last, Pamela returned to the West End for the first time since 1965, when she had appeared in *A Heritage and its History*. She was at the same theatre, the Phoenix, in Dexter's revival of Eliot's *The Cocktail Party*, which had transferred from Bath. This was a starry production, including Alec McCowan, Sheila Gish and Rachel Kempson, actors with whom Dexter had often worked. Pamela played Miss Barraway, secretary to McCowan's Sir Henry Harcourt-Reilly, a psychologist. But most critics wondered whether the play was really worth such a glossily-mounted revival. Its elegant Art Deco sets and an impressive performance as Celia by Sheila Gish, who had played the Countess in the Chichester production of *A Patriot for Me,* could not disguise Eliot's 'quite remarkable lack of skill as a dramatist,' according to Gerard Werson in *The Stage*.[50] Pamela escaped notice.

On 6 October, she appeared in a radio play, *Expeditions* by Lee Gallaher, set in Dublin and starring Robert Stephens, who almost thirty years earlier had played the title role in *Epitaph for George Dillon* and in 1966, had appeared in *A Bond Honoured*. Stephens played Mulqueen, an author 'trapped in a novel he cannot write,' explained the synopsis in *Radio Times*.[51] The play was directed by Jeremy Howe, whom Pamela had known since they had worked together two years previously at Colchester, and who would go on to become Head of Drama at BBC Radio. The recording was made during the summer and Howe's recollection confirms that despite whatever had happened the previous winter and the postal silence between them, the friendship between Osborne and Pamela had endured. 'Only once in my time working with her did she really talk about John Osborne, whom she called "My former husband,"' Howe remembered, 'and that was when we were working on *Expeditions*. I'm sure that Robert Stephens knew, as did I, that she had seen Osborne the previous weekend and he seemed to want to provoke her about it. She blanked him immediately, which was quite a difficult and determined thing to do. Later on, she said to me: '"that bloody Robert Stephens. If he thinks I am going to dish the dirt on my former husband he doesn't know who I am." And it was then that I realised that she and John were still very good friends – which surprised me.'[52]

■ ■ ■

A month later, on 27 November 1986, Christmas Place was sold and the Osbornes left Kent for a new home in Shropshire. The Hurst was a grey stone house of twenty rooms, built in 1812 and secluded in its own grounds a few minutes' drive from the village of Clun and deep within Housman's 'blue, remembered hills.' It was the first time Osborne had made his home north of London, the furthest he had lived from the capital, and the most isolated. Travelling to or from London by car was a long haul and even by train it was an awkward journey, requiring both planning and application. The nearest station, Craven Arms, is eight miles away and the nearest towns, Shrewsbury and Ludlow, a little further afield. It was not a place from which spontaneous expeditions might be made.

The reasons for the move were partly environmental, but mostly financial. Increasing noise and traffic fumes polluted the relatively clean Kentish air. Convinced that pilots flying into Gatwick Airport were using the lake in the grounds of Christmas place as a marker, Osborne had taken to obsessively monitoring the frequency of aircraft and the sound levels. On the ground, as the recession receded, sterling boomed and the City of London turned into a stockbrokers' Las Vegas, young professionals flush with quick winnings descended upon the once-peaceful roads and lanes of Kent and Sussex, searching for the rural life and good schools for the children. Their high-performance cars shook the leaves in the hedgerows, while lorries thundered dustily past Osborne's gate *en route* for Channel ports, ignoring the notice he stuck into the grass verge instructing them to shove off. A property boom was underway, the prices of houses and converted oasthouses were higher than for many years and there was a steady supply of willing buyers. It was a good time to sell.

Leaving Kent would also have brought an additional benefit for Helen, in that it vastly increased the distance between her husband and his former wife. On the face of it, the two women had a cordial friendship. Pamela had visited Christmas Place and frequently rang the house, while her letters and cards—always in envelopes— addressed in her distinctive handwriting, slithered regularly through the letter box. Helen was a shrewd and sharp-eyed woman, yet how much she knew at that time of the deeper emotional, sexual and financial aspects of the relationship between her husband and his first wife, or how much she suspected or tolerated, is unknown. Osborne did admit to Helen that he and Pamela had had a sexual liaison, but that was after the Osbornes had lived in Shropshire for some years. How did he explain during the early 1980s his so often taking the train to London for the day, when part of the reason for their living at Christmas Place was precisely that it was a refuge from London? Were those excursions satisfactorily covered by his meeting his agent, his accountant or his lawyer, lunching at the Garrick or conferring with various doctors? How did he justify the journeys further afield, to Leicester and Colchester? Perhaps there was no need for dissembling or concealment. But whatever the circumstances, a move from Kent to Shropshire would have presented a resolution for a compromised but loyal wife. And perhaps Pamela, having signalled an ending 'finally with her own authority,' did not entirely regret it either.

■ ■ ■

Yet although their alliance had changed, it was still intact. The letter below, written in response to a postcard from Pamela that is now lost, is dated 1987, but surely Osborne had mistaken the date and it was actually written in 1986. He and Pamela had continued to see each other and had presumably corresponded since their winter crisis at the end of 1985, yet no letters or cards, apart from Pamela's marking the thirtieth anniversary of *Look Back in Anger*, seem to survive until Osborne's letter below, written the following December. Were there other letters that were destroyed? Enclosed with Osborne's card was not a cheque this time, but a printed compliments slip bearing his new address: THE HURST, CLUNTON, CRAVEN ARMS, SALOP. There is no telephone number. The letter itself is without an invitation and although he still made forays by train to London, there is no suggestion of a meeting. Rather, its tone is detached, almost valedictory. It appears to be the penultimate surviving letter he wrote to Pamela.

JO to PL ms letter BL

5. 12. 87

Thank you for your card. I swear I saw you from a cab last Friday, sauntering in Grosvenor Square.

Looking very chipper and most unGreenham like. Was it you? Dexter rang to wish me a Happy New Year of all things! The move has been six weeks of utter slog. Haven't worked so hard since one night stands in Wales. No finger nails left, not much of a loss. It's amazing up here. I can't believe my good fortune. A chunk of ancient England and the Welsh at good arm's length. Monumental. This is the last resting place.

In some weary haste but nevertheless

Love

B

It was indeed in many ways an idyllic life. The views from The Hurst, from almost every window and from the arched front door, reached by six wide stone steps, were spectacular. Rhododendrons bloomed and apple trees provided fruit in the grounds. Beyond them, receding banks of trees rose from countryside rolling as far as the hills on the horizon. Just watching the sunset and the colours changing with the seasons would be evocatively theatrical experiences. But once the Osbornes turned away from admiring the view, it was immediately evident that the house, which they had bought impulsively without having asked for a structural survey, required such extensive renovation that any immediate financial advantage created by the move would be quickly wiped out. In fact, living at The Hurst initially cost them much more than it would have done if they had stayed put at Christmas Place.

They had successfully escaped traffic congestion and aircraft noise, but the debts and the bills merely moved with them. Yet the house had an undeniable grandeur and the Osbornes decided to live up to it, employing gardeners and a housekeeper and opening accounts with local butchers, grocers, the garage, the purveyors of dog food, and with Tanner's of Shrewsbury, specialists in champagne and fine wines who quickly discovered that in the Osbornes they had very dedicated customers indeed. Visitors to The Hurst, like those to Christmas Place, both marvelled at and were perturbed by the champagne that was available at all hours.

At the same time, efforts were made to regularise Osborne's finances, or at least gauge the precise extent of his liabilities. Until now, his attitude had been to blame his lawyer and his various accountants for allowing his debts to reach so catastrophic a level. He employed them, he reasoned, and therefore it was surely their responsibility to shield him from calamity. In this misconceived assessment, he was not entirely alone. Helen colluded with her husband's view that life was to be enjoyed. Although she very much wanted them to claw their way back into solvency, she was also a heavy smoker, certainly not averse to alcohol and had a pronounced liking for travel, which she insisted was both necessary and, considering her husband's health, restorative. She also championed the notion that writers of Osborne's standing should be regarded as a national asset and largely or even wholly exempt from taxation, as she imagined the situation to be in France. Although politically hostile to the European Union, this was a perspective that Osborne enthusiastically endorsed. At the same time and with his agreement, she suggested they ditch the expensive London accountants and instead engage Peter Forrester, a Shrewsbury accountant and the husband of one of her new friends in Clun, to conduct a thorough review of his financial affairs. This at least was a rational strategy. It may have been in private conversation, therefore, that the extent of Osborne's financial assistance to Pamela over the years came to light.

In May the following year, Pamela was in Bath, working once again with John Dexter. *Portraits* was a new play about the artist Augustus John written by the venerable and apparently indefatigable William Douglas Home, in whose plays

Pamela had appeared in Bridgwater and Derby. 'An aura of blimpishness always surrounds William Douglas Home,' mused Michael Billington in *The Guardian*, adding, charitably, 'somewhat unfairly.'[53] Yet *Portraits* was one of those plays written by a veteran dramatist that might arguably be thought more worthy than worthwhile. It pivots on John's relationships with three of his most eminent subjects: the painter Matthew Smith, the photographer Cecil Beaton and Field Marshall Montgomery, the latter kept furiously alert during his sitting by Bernard Shaw, cheerfully claiming that Allied war crimes were comparable to those committed by the Nazis. The play, noted Billington, 'is really about despair at the prospect of nuclear annihilation,' although the idea was 'insufficiently explored.'[54]

That John is required to paint during the performance clearly made the case for casting Keith Michell, a proficient artist himself, in the leading role, while Pamela appeared as Dorelia, John's mistress and a woman once seen as an exemplar of Bohemianism. As Dexter's original plan was for Osborne to play Bernard Shaw, this might also have been the first time he and Pamela had appeared on stage together since 1954, but Osborne's health was far too uncertain—and his drinking perhaps too ingrained—for him to countenance the rigours of a theatrical run. In another curious twist of coincidence, the role was taken instead by Richard Wordsworth, with whom Pamela had appeared in *Peter Pan*—and with whom she had had an affair—seventeen years earlier. Wordsworth, noted Dexter, was 'uncanny.'[55] On 11 August, the production transferred to the Savoy Theatre in the Strand, where it achieved a 'pugnacious liveliness' reported an otherwise disappointed Michael Billington. Pamela's 'dogsbody mistress' he noted, was 'a deft thumbnail sketch.'[56]

It had been wise of Osborne to stay where he was. In June, he had been admitted to the private Nuffield Hospital in Shrewsbury to undergo an operation for a twisted hernia. Afterwards, he convalesced expensively with Helen in Venice at the sumptuous Hotel Danieli, overlooking the lagoon, 'steps away from the Bridge of Sighs' announced the brochure, 'and the famous monuments of Piazza San Marco.' Back at the Savoy Theatre, playing the 'little woman of infinite earthly wisdom,' Pamela Lane, as so often over the past thirty-five years, could only imagine such opulence.[57] Certainly she had never experienced it herself. And perhaps, like many others, she wondered, when Osborne was professing how broke he was, quite how he managed to live as he did.

■ ■ ■

From bohemianism in the West End, Pamela moved to grim reflection on the fringe, joining the Monstrous Regiment company to give a 'delightfully understated performance' as Joyce in Carol Bunyan's *Waving*, one of three 'post-menopausal women' who, having spent years as increasingly reluctant appendages to their husbands, reminisce and reflect on life and calculate the measure of failure.[58] Pamela was working once again with Angie Langfield, and the production opened in Sheffield on 4 February 1988 before launching itself on a national tour. It was probably the closest Pamela ever got to the Costa del Sol, where the play is set and where the women, sitting in the sun, contemplate their husbands swimming far out to sea. In May, the tour reached Leicester, from where Pamela sent a card to Osborne wishing him well on yet another holiday in Venice. During the intervening months, Osborne had revealed his telephone number at The Hurst, invited Pamela to ring, and had dispatched either a gift of underwear or some money towards a fresh supply.

PL to JO: ms pc BL

Leicester
Monday 5/88

Darling B,

Rang you last night but no-one there—so a quick card to wish you a good time in Venice—and <u>thank</u> you for yours last week and the bumper directoire contribution. In haste but with v much love—see you in October—

Ever your Squirrel

Much love to Helen

In October, Osborne travelled to London not only to see Pamela but to look in at the rehearsals for Strindberg's *The Father*, directed by David Leveaux at the National Theatre and for which he had provided the English language adaptation. Fevered, volatile, awkward, Strindberg was a playwright whom Osborne admired immensely. One of his earlier theatre-going experiences had been at the Arts Theatre in 1953, when Wilfred Lawson, who possessed, according to the actor Christopher Lee, a 'divine madness,' had played the Captain.[59] 'Both John and Helen told me how much Lawson's performance had impressed itself upon John's psyche and sense of what the theatre was about,' recalled Gordon Dickerson.[60] And a play dealing with marital discord and a father and daughter at loggerheads was one with which Osborne felt an instinctive affinity. His intervention at rehearsals, though, was not a success and, disowning the production, he fled back to Shropshire. He had the consolation, though, when the play opened on 26 October, of it being well-reviewed.

■ ■ ■

At the beginning of the decade, Pamela had been sitting on a beach, pondering generally on life. Now, in November 1988, she scrambled 'impatiently out of her coffin' at her own funeral service, observed Pat Ashworth in *The Guardian*, a 'flamboyant, witty and irreverent spirit as ever walked the earth.'[61] She was appearing, first at the Birmingham Repertory Theatre and then on another tour, in Gay Sweatshop's production of *Twice Over*, a play by Jackie Kay, directed by Nona Shepphard. Cora's mission in resurrecting herself is to urge Evaki, her adolescent grand-daughter, to make public at last the relationship Cora had with another woman and which during her lifetime she had confided only to her diary.

Although Pamela kept a diary in which she recorded professional appointments, there is no evidence that she maintained one as a record of her thoughts and reflections. She was not organized enough, and probably too restrained. While she was highly professional and ordered in her work, the same did not apply to her private papers. She was candid with herself, but reticence would probably have prevented her committing that candour to a diary. Besides, keeping a journal requires time, discipline, and a certain propensity to reflect upon life and philosophize a little, but Pamela was not one to meditate too much on life and what might have been. According to Richard Digby Day, she was 'a fatalist. She never complained. Just got on with it.'[62] And at the end of the eighties, as her sixtieth birthday bore down upon her, getting on with it entailed a return to Colchester followed by the security guaranteed by Agatha Christie.

The 1990s

■ ■ ■

■ ■ ■

'One and a half hours before the first and only interval', cautioned Liz Mullen, a critic for *The Stage*, reviewing Michael Winter's production of *The Rivals* at the Mercury Theatre, Colchester. 'Another one and a half hours after that.' Despite her initial apprehension, however, she discovered that the time passed 'in painless pleasure.'[1] The production had opened at Redgrave Theatre in Farnham in late August 1990 and transferred to Colchester a month later, where it ran for another four weeks. Thirty-seven years earlier at Derby, Pamela had bewildered local critics by playing an alarmingly 'original' Lydia Languish. But the years had had a moderating effect. Having graduated to the role of Mrs Malaprop, Lydia's guardian, Pamela's 'unforced and innocent mutilation of the English language,' thought Mullen, 'proved much more endearing' than the comic overplaying often associated with the role.[2] She was 'very restrained,' remembered Richard Digby Day, 'and restraint is unusual but important in that part.'[3]

Earlier that year, on 24 March, John Dexter, Osborne and Pamela's friend since Derby, had died of heart failure in London. At about the same time, Pamela made the momentous decision to give up smoking. She had also made what turned out to be her final television appearance. Evidently a fixture on the list for any series requiring the fleeting intervention of the nursing profession, she appeared on 11 January as a ward sister with a couple of lines of dialogue in *The Big Sleep*. This was an episode of *One Foot in the Grave*, a hugely popular comedy series starring Richard Wilson as Victor Meldrew, a full-time curmudgeon coping with enforced retirement. If this reminded her of her previous one-day jobs for *Dixon of Dock Green* and *Emergency Ward 10*, then her next venture recalled even earlier memories of weekly repertory.

Agatha Christie's *The Mousetrap*, in which seven people find themselves snowbound in a remote guesthouse to be informed by a police sergeant arriving on skis that a murderer may be lurking nearby, had first opened in 1952. That year, Pamela was twenty-two and newly married, living with Osborne at Hammersmith. The Coronation was broadcast live on the magical new medium of television, the wartime rationing of tea ended and in winter the Great Smog chokingly enveloped London. Thirty-eight years later, when the nation was anticipating the technological age and thirty-two percent of households were working out how to use their new computer, *The Mousetrap* was showing no signs of calling it a day. Garlanded in the *Guinness Book of Records* as the world's longest continuous theatrical run, it was given annual life support by a change of cast and director. In November 1990, this was administered by Richard Digby Day, who signed up Pamela to play the cantankerous Mrs Boyle, dead by the interval.

Like Madame Tussauds, with which the occasional disgruntled London critic frequently compared it, *The Mousetrap* was largely sustained by overseas tourists and coach parties. Sitting scornfully in the stalls for *The Guardian* one evening during 1991, Nicholas de Jongh derided 'the actors talking in the loud, slow diction the English reserve for conversations with foreigners or those who have forfeited a marble or two.' Beyond the guesthouse windows, he observed sourly, 'it is snowing and the snow looks so unreal that you imagine the flakes have been recycled for decades'.[4]

This latter point was true enough. The travellers had arrived supposedly through a blizzard, and yet, mysteriously, there was not a trace of snow on their coats. This anomaly had stumped the props department, who had not yet discovered an artificial snow that authentically melted when exposed to indoor temperatures. Not that the audience minded. *The Mousetrap* had become a curiosity as much as a play, suspended in a time of its own between past and present, its longevity provocative to critics but reassuring to many others. It was as if the world of weekly rep had been carefully embalmed and placed on permanent exhibition in the West End. For years it had been an anachronism, but no matter what mockery might be hurled in its direction, the scoreboard in the theatre foyer remorselessly continued to clock up each passing performance. Osborne and Helen, down on the train from Shropshire, joined the tourists and the Christie devotees to see the production one evening, and 'loved the whole thing.'[5]

Osborne made occasional sorties to London, either alone or accompanied by Helen. If alone, he would have lunch either with Pamela or at the Garrick, where he would join a contingent of the 1400 Club, members who gathered at the bar and mooched into lunch at two o'clock. If staying overnight, he would book a room at the lavish five-star Cadogan Hotel, where the rates were not for the faint-hearted and, one would have thought, not for Osborne's bank balance either. But he chose it partly because it was near Sloane Square, partly because it had been the scene of Oscar Wilde's arrest in 1895, but mostly because he felt that it was what he deserved.

On 3 November, as Pamela was nearing the end of her year in *The Mousetrap*, Osborne was once again thrust into the public gaze, or at least that part of the public that watched *The South Bank Show* television arts programme, when he appeared as the subject of an hour-long profile occasioned by the publication of *Almost a Gentleman*, the second volume of his memoirs. Three days later, he was at the Cadogan, from where he sent Pamela a plaintive, even elegiac note. This appears to be his last surviving letter to her.

JO to PL ms letter BL

The Cadogan Hotel
6.11.91

I don't think anyone has declared their love so repeatedly, so insistently, or for so long as I have.

I shall be at the above for 24 hrs <u>December 5th–6th</u>. On my own, for what it's worth.

My godson, Ben, is playing Dorian Gray at Watford.

Ah well...

[unsigned]

'My godson, Ben' is Ben Walden, an actor and the son of Brian Walden, a former Labour Party MP and a journalist who during the 1980s established himself as a formidable political interviewer on television, and his former wife, the journalist Jane McKerron, a long-standing friend of Helen's. Now twenty-three, Ben Walden played the leading role in Osborne's adaptation of *The Picture of Dorian Gray*, directed by Lou Stein, at the Watford Palace Theatre from 11—20 November.

Whether Pamela replied to Osborne's appeal or whether they met as he hoped that frosty evening in December is unknown.

Meanwhile, *Almost a Gentleman*, in which Osborne covered the decade following *Look Back in Anger*, was creating quite a stir in the review columns and newspaper features pages. In a 'fast forward' passage inserted shortly before the book went to press, he wrote angrily about the suicide on 4 October 1990 of Jill Bennett, his fourth wife, a tirade that infuriated his critics and appalled many of his friends and hers. Earlier in the book, he wrote of his separation from Pamela and of his mixed feelings over their divorce, but nothing of their subsequent association, apart from two stray clues unnoticed at the time. He included his diary entry of 3 February 1965, recording their meeting at Priory Road and their 'easy slide between sheets,' and elsewhere that his 'passion for Pamela' had subsequently been proved 'a folly and… a delusion,' but he did not elaborate on either. As Osborne had sought Pamela's consent for the passages concerning her in *A Better Class of Person*, it is likely he had followed the same procedure this time and if so, she accepted what he had written. But as *Almost a Gentleman* was typed, edited and proofread by Helen, she must also have approved the manuscript.

A few years after Osborne's death in 1994, Helen confided to a small group of women friends living nearby and who met regularly for lunch, that sometime after she and Osborne had arrived in Clun and while he was writing the book, he had told her that during the early 1980s he and Pamela had resumed a sexual relationship. Helen's response, according to her friends, was one of stoic acceptance. But precisely under what circumstances the admission came about, or how much Osborne told her and therefore exactly what Helen was stoic about, is unclear. So many thoughts and feelings are known only to those involved and pass with them. But it appears that as throughout the years of their association Pamela bore Osborne no acrimony, Helen in her turn held none against Pamela. Those same friends noticed that Pamela was the only one of Osborne's former wives against whom Helen, a woman who spoke her mind with relish and seldom missed an opportunity to do so, expressed no hostility. As a former drama critic, suggested Susan Dowell, one of the occasional lunchers, perhaps Helen chose to consider her husband's relationship with his first wife as a narrative lacking a conclusion and therefore acknowledged that 'there was unfinished business between them.'[6]

■ ■ ■

At The Hurst, debts, failing health and a fading theatrical reputation resulted in Osborne in his early sixties feeling both embattled and isolated. Although he loved the house, in the fastness of the Shropshire hills he lived remote from the theatrical world with which he was most familiar but from which he felt cast out. Many of his *Spectator* diary paragraphs reflected his restlessness, alternating between reports of the superior quality of the local game butchers to reminiscences upon times past, the days of George Devine, the Royal Court and his old friendships. His dependence upon his wife, both domestically and professionally, was also becoming more marked. Helen's guardianship extended from typing his scripts to writing and signing letters on his behalf, negotiating with his publishers and even writing a review of Ingmar Bergman's autobiography, *The Magic Lantern*, under his name for the *New York Review of Books*. Close friends saw physical frailty beginning to erode him. Behind the stone walls of The Hurst, the relationship between Helen and Osborne, who did not take easily to being managed, was not without its difficulties. Meanwhile, the alcohol still flowed, and Peter Forrester continued to hack a path through the cluttered labyrinth of Osborne's accounts.

While finishing *Almost a Gentleman*, Osborne had also been '*struggling*' to complete a new stage play.[7] His past in the form of his two volumes of autobiography had twice come up trumps, and perhaps, he reasoned, it might do so a third time. Over thirty years after *Look Back in Anger*, therefore, he had decided to revisit Jimmy Porter. *Déjàvu* might go some way towards paying off his debts, he hoped, and it might even, when added to the royalties from productions of his earlier plays, secure some sort of pension. In any case, the two plays would provide a neat symmetry to a career of almost forty years.

In the earlier play, Osborne had ransacked his relationship with Pamela as base metal for the creation of Jimmy and Alison Porter. In contemplating a play that 'might be regarded as *Look Back II*,' he might have thought of doing much the same thing, continuing Jimmy and Alison's story during the years into middle age and beyond and exploring once again some of the themes that had preoccupied him throughout his career: male vulnerability and failure, the nature of love, emotional fragility, resilience, and England itself.[8] But if he ever considered the idea, he rejected it.

'It isn't easy to explain,' says Alison in *Look Back in Anger*, attempting to clarify to a mystified Helena what Jimmy expects of love and friendship. 'It's what he would call a question of allegiances and he expects you to be pretty literal about them.'[9] It's a remark that might have been made by Pamela herself and possibly was, or indeed by many who knew Osborne over the years. Allegiance was one of the qualities Osborne valued most and, as he interpreted it, the commitment of others was either absolute or it was nothing. 'Friends seem to abound but so does treachery,' he had reminded Pamela as recently as 1984.[10] A sentiment expressed many times, no doubt. Perhaps writing another 'anguished love letter' and a true sequel to *Look Back in Anger*, which could have stood a good chance of a much-needed commercial success, would have been a betrayal of the allegiance of both Pamela and Helen, the two women closest to him and to whom he owed most.[11]

Instead, he wrote something else, a play standing at a tangent to *Look Back in Anger* and that attempts at the end a grand flourish of resilience. Jimmy Porter, once seen as the anti-hero of the 1950s, becomes JP, a hero for the 1990s, solitary, bruised but still determinedly defiant. Audiences at *Déjàvu*—not that there were many—discovered JP living alone in a converted farmhouse in the country, roaming a spacious kitchen equipped, as was Osborne's at The Hurst, with an imposing Aga. The beached survivor of two marriages and divorces, JP has been sustained at least in part by a legacy bequeathed upon him by Colonel Redfern, his first father-in-law and a man towards Jimmy felt some sympathy, as did Osborne towards William Lane. Alison survives only in that it is the name of JP's daughter by his second marriage, discovered standing at the ironing board. Cliff, visiting for a few days and slumped in an armchair, turns out to have become a middling figure at the BBC. Of the bear and the squirrel that feature in *Look Back in Anger*, only the bear remains, a mute pin cushion stabbed by JP's thrusting needles of contempt against bureaucrats of European federalism, the lower-middle classes, feminists, reformist clergy, social workers and do-gooders generally, in JP's eyes dull conformists all, and obsessions familiar to the readers of Osborne's weekly bulletins in *The Spectator*.

Starring Peter Egan and directed by Tony Palmer, *Déjàvu* opened on 8 May 1992, the thirty-sixth anniversary of the opening of *Look Back in Anger*, at the Thorndike Theatre, Leatherhead, where Pamela had appeared several times, and transferred to the Comedy Theatre on 10 June. The play was unwieldy and disjointed, and the critics mystified, cautious, disappointed. Following quickly diminishing ticket sales prompted partly by an unexpected heatwave, *Déjàvu* closed seven weeks later. In Shropshire, Osborne accepted that the play had been a failure, at least financially. 'Now I'll have to write another one,' he muttered bitterly to Peter Egan.[12] But he never would. If Pamela was quick enough to see the play, she gave no verdict on it. 'She never mentioned it to me,' said Richard Digby Day.[13] Nor to Angie Langfield.[14]

■ ■ ■

In October, Pamela returned to Colchester for two plays, appearing first as a gossiping neighbour in an adaptation of Catherine Cookson's *Fifteen Streets*, a romantic novel set in the north of England in 1900, in which a dock labourer falls in love with his daughter's teacher. In November, and more substantially, she appeared as Mrs Pasmore in Geoff Bullen's 'superbly played' production of David Storey's 1989 play, *Jubilee*, a melancholic portrait of the despair of a former miner and his wife in the furiously materialistic decade that anticipated the closure of the coal industry. In their retirement bungalow in north Yorkshire, conversation between the Pasmores, observed Liz Mullen of *The Stage*, 'has long been replaced by mild squabbling, with only dregs of affection and a strong sense of duty holding them together on their sixtieth wedding anniversary.'[15]

On 9 May 1993, Penelope Gilliatt, Osborne's third former wife, died of alcoholism in London. Osborne had avoided the funerals of Mary Ure and Jill Bennett, and he did not attend Penelope's either. Six months later, in November, as Pamela began another year of playing Mrs Boyle in *The Mousetrap*, he began planning *England, My England*, a television screenplay commemorating the tercentenary of the death of Henry Purcell, to be directed by Tony Palmer. Yet Osborne's health was now deteriorating rapidly and in the event, he was unable to write much more than an outline. His friend Charles Wood stepped in to continue the project, the resulting film being broadcast on Channel 4 on Christmas Day 1995.

While retreating from Purcell, Osborne received astounding news that knocked him back even further. Initially, the 'season' of his earlier plays broadcast in the first few weeks of 1994 on BBC radio had been a cause for optimism, not least because the writers' fees might hinder the advance of some of his more clamorous creditors. The season included *Look Back in Anger, The Entertainer* and *Epitaph for George Dillon*, the play he had written with Anthony Creighton in 1955. Glyn Dearman's production was aired on 23 January on Radio 3. Not having heard of his old collaborator since they had last met—and fallen out—thirty years previously, Osborne had managed to convince himself that Creighton was dead. This supposition he passed on as information to Gordon Dickerson, his agent, petitioning him to send him not only his—Osborne's—share of the *George Dillon* fee, but Creighton's as well. Dickerson demurred, advising the impecunious and ailing playwright that even if Creighton were dead, a beneficiary might emerge and therefore Creighton's share must be set aside. It was just as well: the broadcast suddenly, astonishingly, produced the man, Creighton materialising from years of obscurity by telephoning Dickerson and enquiring about his fee. Having forwarded Creighton his due share, Dickerson rang his client with the news. 'I don't think I've ever heard such terror in anyone's voice as when I told Osborne what had happened,' Dickerson remembered. 'I don't think it was only that he realised he would not get the money he was hoping for, but that he remembered the manner in which he had written about Creighton in his memoirs.'[16]

Osborne had indeed written dismissively about Creighton in several passages of *Almost a Gentleman*. But as he had not sent the typescript pages to him for approval as he had those concerning her to Pamela, he presumably feared that in addition to all his other troubles, his former friend might now bring an action against him. Yet Creighton had told Dickerson that he did not wish to resume contact with Osborne, and neither did he. Content with his share of the *George Dillon* fee, he withdrew.

During the intervening years since he and Osborne last met, however, Creighton had made something of a quiet resurgence. Having triumphed in his battle against alcohol, he had puttered along in the twilight world of London's evening institutes, teaching drama and tutoring aspiring playwrights. He presided 'as a kind of *eminence grise* on matters dramatic,' recalled a former student, the dramatist James MacDonald, who attended some of his classes during the 1970s and noted that if the subject of Creighton's collaboration with Osborne arose, he appeared to accept the disparity between their subsequent careers 'with grace,' and never said 'a bitter word about his more successful colleague.'[17]

Pamela and Creighton had not met since the late 1950s. Yet, at the time that he telephoned Gordon Dickerson, Creighton was living alone, as he had done for many years, in a small rented flat in Belsize Park, just over a couple of miles away from where Pamela lived in Kilburn. It was forty-two years since she and Osborne had rented a room in Creighton's Hammersmith flat. She might easily have passed him on the street; they might have bumped into each other in a supermarket or stepped on to the same bus, yet they did not and remained entirely unaware of each other's proximity.

■ ■ ■

Six weeks later, on 12 March, Pamela joined the rest of *The Mousetrap* cast at a lunch at The Savoy, not something she was accustomed to, the producers pushing out the boat in honour of Nancy Seabrooke, who, at seventy-nine and after fifteen years of understudying Mrs Boyle had both earned herself a place in the *Mousetrap* column in the *Guinness Book of Records* and had decided to retire. That night, Nancy took a solo bow on stage. She was one of those actors who seemed to have toured everywhere and had worked in the shadows of the great actors of the past, yet remained entirely unknown outside the world of regional repertory. She had spent much of her time with *The Mousetrap* in her dressing room next to the wardrobe department, engaged on her needlework, packing up each night after Mrs Boyle's death to walk the few minutes to her home in Covent Garden. Of the 6240 performances for which she had been on standby duty, she had played seventy-two. If nothing else, *The Mousetrap* was a show of extraordinary numbers.

Pamela was nearing the end of her second year's tenure as Mrs Boyle when, in October 1994, John Rees, the actor who had lived below Pamela and Osborne in Derby and the inspiration for Cliff in *Look Back in Anger*, died while on a riding holiday in Spain, aged sixty-seven. Since leaving Derby in the fifties, he had appeared in several films, including playing a sergeant in Steven Spielberg's *Indiana*

Jones and the Raiders of the Lost Ark in 1981, while devoting a lot of his time to studying German, becoming something of an authority on the works of Goethe and appearing in several East German films.

A few weeks later, on 24 December, John Osborne died at the Nuffield Hospital, Shrewsbury, a few days after his sixty-fifth birthday, his life cut short by a furious consumption of tobacco and alcohol. Among his personal effects Helen took home from the hospital was a copy of *Holy Living and Holy Dying* by the seventeenth century cleric, Jeremy Taylor. While Osborne had occasionally attended an Anglican church, particularly for Evensong, for several years, the modernisation, and in his eyes, the diminution of the Church of England liturgy, had recently increased his sympathy with the traditions of the Roman Catholic faith. This was sincerely felt, but it also had about it the comfort of a former, idealised England, one that held true to the old faith. While Osborne refrained from a deathbed conversion, Helen later admitted to friends that she regretted that she had not asked a priest to administer the last rites.[18]

His funeral took place in a whirling snowstorm at the Anglican St George's Church, a name Osborne considered satisfyingly English, in Clun on the final day of the year. The service was taken by the Reverend Graham Dowell, who, after his retiral had moved to the village with Susan, his wife, shortly after the Osbornes had taken up residence at The Hurst. The new arrivals had become friends. Coincidentally, Dowell had served as a curate at Derby Cathedral while Osborne and Pamela were at the Playhouse, 'although he never spoke of seeing them,' recalled his widow. 'But after we came to Clun, he did tell Osborne that when *Look Back in Anger* opened, he recognised "those bloody bells"' as being those of St Peter's Church, within hearing distance of Pamela's flat in Green Lane, 'and he and Osborne would joke about it.'[19] A liberal in theological matters, Dowell had left Derby to become vicar of the eighteenth-century St John's Church in Hampstead, where he had 'rattled' several members of a congregation composed 'mainly of the well-heeled,' wrote his obituarist, by transforming the church into 'a centre for disarmament activity and campaigns on poverty, feminist and green issues.'[20] These were passions the Dowells brought with them to Clun, where their progressive views encountered Osborne's traditional convictions when their conversations turned to theological issues. 'Although we were not always in agreement,' recalled

Susan Dowell, 'for example, on the ordination of women' (the Dowells passionately pro, Osborne vehemently anti) 'there was always humour and mutual respect.'[21]

The Order of Service for Osborne's funeral comprised his own requests: Psalm 39, a prayer for wisdom and forgiveness: 'And now, Lord, what wait I for? My hope is in thee,' and two hymns: *Oh God, Our Help in Ages Past* and, in acknowledgment of the season: *Hark the Herald Angels Sing*. The church was crowded with actors and colleagues up from London and with friends who lived locally. According to Helen, the congregation numbered almost two hundred, although afterwards this was disputed as being on the high side, pockets of opinion, particularly among the bell ringers, suspecting her of distorting the figure for the sake of local appearances. Pamela was unnoticed among the mourners, but then, it was very unlikely she would have been recognised, except by Helen, who was not scrutinising the pews. Her presence, if that is indeed what it was, was nonetheless a triumph of anonymity by the woman whom Osborne had told was 'at the centre of my heart,' but would probably have considered the day a success if she had avoided attention entirely.[22]

She did not go to The Hurst for the reception afterwards, but instead made her own way to Craven Arms station and a train back to a London throwing itself into welcoming in the New Year. In his will, made on 3 October 1989, Osborne left everything he owned to Helen, including heart-sinking debts of over £337,000 (equivalent to over £615,000 in 2018). These were eventually paid through the posthumous sale of his archive to the Harry Ransom Humanities Research Center at the University of Texas at Austin, and an arrangement that The Arvon Foundation acquire The Hurst as a centre for literary courses.

A Memorial Service for Osborne was held at St Giles in the Fields Church in London on 2 June 1995, yet Pamela was too ill to attend and asked Julia Lockwood to take her place. In November, Pamela returned to 'the pay of Agatha Christie,' appearing for the third time as Mrs Boyle in *The Mousetrap*, a part on which she could rely as much as she had once relied on Mrs Darling and Mrs Bird.[23] She was sixty-five, and it turned out to be her final stage appearance, arguably a muted end to a career that had begun so auspiciously almost forty-five years earlier.

Elsewhere, the theatres that Pamela knew best were either disappearing or falling dark and silent. The Scala Theatre, once the home of *Peter Pan*, had long since been demolished. The old Derby Playhouse had been crushed by bulldozers.

The Thorndike Theatre in Leatherhead, overwhelmed by financial troubles, closed in 1997, although it re-opened as a part-time theatre four years later. At the cash-strapped Leicester Haymarket, production was abruptly halted in 2007, the building abandoned, the doors padlocked, the theatre left to its ghost of the small boy, wandering the corridors searching for rehearsals to watch but now finding none. It was as if Pamela was kicking over her traces.

On 12 January 2004, Helen Osborne died of cancer aged sixty-four, followed on 22 March 2005, by Anthony Creighton. He was eighty-two. Pamela remained living in Kilburn, 'an intensely private woman' who had never spoken publicly about either her former husband or *Look Back in Anger* and the experience of seeing a version of her own marriage on the stage.[24] But a few years after Osborne's death, just after the turn of the century, she agreed to Richard Digby Day's request that she talk about the play in the comparative privacy of the seminar room to an audience of American theatre students visiting London. It was then that she was asked the inevitable question of what she felt when she saw *Look Back in Anger* at the Royal Court all those years ago. 'I felt as though I had been raped,' she replied.[25]

26 October 2010

■ ■ ■

On 26 October 2010, almost sixteen years after Osborne's death, Julia Lockwood accompanied Angie Langfield to visit Pamela at the Royal Free Hospital in London. She had been unwell for some time, suffering from emphysema and relying on oxygen treatment, but that day in hospital she was unconscious and sinking towards death. Later that night, Julia arrived back at her home in the West Country. 'I was walking up the garden path,' she remembered, 'when I looked up and saw a shooting star. I thought: "There goes Pam." Almost immediately after I got into the house, the telephone rang. It was Angie to tell me that Pam had died at 10.15.'[1]

She was eighty. The first of John Osborne's wives had outlived not only Osborne himself and his four subsequent wives but also many of the friends and acquaintances whom they had known in their early days together. During her final years in Kilburn, unable to work, she had subsisted largely on a disability allowance and had been obliged to live as frugally as possible, her welfare monitored by Angie Langfield and close friends. Occasionally, she ventured out to concerts, the last being in February 2009, when she and Richard Digby Day had heard the violist Maxim Rysanov at the London Symphony Orchestra's hall at St Luke's, an eighteenth-century Hawksmoor church in Old Street. 'I don't know how she got there,' Digby Day reflected. 'She looked so ill.'[2]

A cremation service attended by friends was held at Golders Green Crematorium on 11 November, when Karen Archer, who had appeared with Pamela in *Seascape*, read a poem, and Richard Digby Day gave an address, commemorating Pamela as 'a fully paid-up member of the unfashionable theatre.'[3] It was a tribute to an actress many thought outstanding, and who might have won greater recognition had her achievements been more widely noticed.

Thirty-three years earlier, on 19 December 1977, Pamela had made a will at a solicitors' office in St John's Wood. It was a brief, succinct document, leaving her estate, the net value of which, according to the deed of probate, did 'not exceed £38,000,' to Angie Langfield.[4] Yet it also reveals that she made what would be a final gesture towards the man she called a 'savage, benign bear' who had briefly been her husband and who in 1983 had confirmed that: 'I fell in love with you thirty-two years ago. My feelings—no, passion, always passion—are unchanged.'[5]

Her will is in the name of Pamela Elizabeth Osborne, 'also known as Pamela Lane,' and signed, decisively in a firm hand, with her married name.[6]

Notes

■ ■ ■

I have used the following abbreviations:

JO: John Osborne

PL: Pamela Lane

AC: Anthony Creighton

BCP: John Osborne: *A Better Class of Person*, Faber 1981.

AAG: John Osborne: *Almost a Gentleman*, Faber 1991.

CP1: John Osborne: *Collected Plays 1* Faber 1996, includes both *Look Back in Anger* and *Déjávu*. *Look Back in Anger* is also published in a single edition by Faber.

DYE: John Osborne: *Damn You England*, Faber 1994.

■ ■ ■

Introduction

1. JO: Introduction to *Look Back in Anger*, CP1 p; viii, DYE p 45.

2. Richard Digby Day to author.

3. PL to JO: 11 May 1984.

4. JO to PL: 27 September 1983.

5. JO to PL: 18 October 1983.

6. PL to JO: 7 November 1985, 17 November 1983.

7. JO to PL: 6 November 1991

8. JO: BCP p 239.

9. JO: Introduction to *Look Back in Anger* CP1 p xii   DYE p 47.

10. Peter Whitebrook: *John Osborne: 'Anger is not about...'* Oberon London 2015, p 56.

11. Pamela Lane obituary, *The Guardian* 21 November 2010.

12. JO: *Look Back in Anger* Collected Plays 1 p 42.

13. JO: journal 1970 Texas.

14. JO to AC: n/d 1951 Texas.

15. JO: *Look Back in Anger* CP1 p 43,

16. PL to JO: 6 May 1963.

17. JO to PL: December 1983.

18. PL to JO: 28 October 1985.

19. JO to PL: 11 October 1983.

20. PL to JO: 1 June 1984.

21. JO: *Tennant Looks Back at Osborne*: Archive on 4 BBC Radio 4 30 April 2016.

22. Jeremy Howe to author.

23. Peter Whitebrook: *John Osborne: Anger is not about...*' p 324.

24. Julia Lockwood to author.

25. JO: AAG p 3

26. Programme note, York Repertory Theatre 10 September 1856.

27. PL to JO: undated card.

28. PL to JO: 2 January 1954.

29. JO: *Spectator* 1 May 1983, DYE p 249.

30. PL to JO: 17 December 1983.

31. JO to PL: several postcards cheerily arranging meetings survive from the early 1980s.

32. *Bath Chronicle and Weekly Gazette* 4 August 1923.

33. *Taunton Courier* 28 April 1947.

34. *Taunton Courier* 6 May 1946.

35. JO *Face to Face* BBC Television 21 January 1962.

36. *The Stage:* 8 June 1950.

37. *Taunton Courier* 1 April 1950.

38. *Taunton Courier* 15 April 1950.

39. *Taunton Courier* 9 September 1950.

■ ■ ■

The 1950s

1. UK press advertisements for *My Wife's Family* from 1930 onwards.

2. JO to PL: BCP p 239.

3. *The Stage* 26 July 1951.

4.   Lynne Reid Banks to author.

5.   JO: BCP p 243.

6.   JO to AC: June 1951 Texas.

7.   JO: BCP p 254.

8.   JO: Ibid pgs 244-5.

9.   Barry Morse: *Pulling Faces, Making Noises* Universe Publishing, London 2004, p 66.

10. JO: BCP p 245.

11. Ibid p 246

12. Ibid p 240.

13. *The Stage* 30 July 1953.

14. *Derbyshire Life* 3 April 2016.

15. *The Stage* 4 November 1954.

16. *Derby Evening Telegraph* cuttings: September 1953.

17. Ibid.

18. Ibid.

19. Lady Mills obituary: *Daily Telegraph* 3 December 2005.

20. *Derby Evening Telegraph* cuttings: November 1953.

21. Richard Digby Day to author.

22. *Derby Evening Telegraph* cuttings: November 1953.

23. JO: BCP p 252.

24. *Derby Evening Telegraph* cuttings: November 1953.

25. JO: BCP p 112

26. Unidentified Osborne relative to Bessie Grove, JO's aunt: 6 November 1980 Texas

27. JO: BCP p 112

28.   *The Stage* 28 January 1954.

29.   Advertisement for *Life Begins at Fifty*: *The Stage* 24 July 1952.

30.   *Derby Evening Telegraph* cuttings: January 1954.

31.   JO: BCP p 255.

32.   JO to AC Tuesday n/d [1954] Texas

33.   JO: DYE p 52

34.   JO: BCP p 235

35.   JO: *Look Back in Anger* CP1 p 11

36.   JO to AC: n/d [January- June 1954]

37.   JO: *Look Back in Anger* CP1 p 14

38.   John Rees obituary, unidentified newspaper cutting.

39.   JO to AC: various dates February – June 1954 Texas.

40.   *Derby Evening Telegraph* cuttings: March 1954.

41.   Ibid April 1954.

42.   JO: BCP p 255.

43.   JO: *Look Back in Anger* CP1 p 71.

44.   JO: BCP p 262.

45.   *Derby Evening Telegraph* cuttings: September 1954.

46.   Ibid November 1954.

47.   JO: AAG p 1.

48.   Ibid p 5.

49.   Irving Wardle: *The Theatres of George Devine* Jonathan Cape London 1978 p 155.

50.   JO BCP p 265.

51.   *Derby Evening Telegraph* cuttings: April 1955.

52. Peter Whitebrook: *John Osborne: 'Anger is not about...'* p 88.

53. JO: *Tennant Looks Back at Osborne*: Archive on 4 BBC Radio 4 30 April 2016.

54. JO to PL: 10 October 1983.

55. JO: AAG p 1.

56. Ibid p 2.

57. Gaynor Richards to author.

58. JO: diary July-August 1955 Texas.

59. Ibid 1 January 1956.

60. *Derby Evening Telegraph* cuttings: October 1955.

61. Richard Digby Day to author.

62. *The Stage* 22 March 1956.

63. *Derby Evening Telegraph* cuttings: March 1956.

64. *The Guardian* 27 March 1956.

65. Professor Jonathan Powers to author.

66. *The Stage* 8 November 1956.

67. *Clutterbuck* programme York Theatre Royal April 1956.

68. *The Sketch* 4 September 1946.

69. York Theatre Royal programmes 1956 season.

70. *York Evening Press* cuttings York Theatre Royal Collection York St John University.

71. Barry Morse: *Pulling Faces, Making Noises* p 82.

72. *York Evening Press* cuttings York Theatre Royal Collection York St John University.

73. York Theatre Royal programmes 1956 season.

74. Richard Digby Day to author.

75. There are several wayward accounts purporting to be Pamela's response to seeing *Look Back in Anger.* One is that as the curtain rose, she murmured: 'Oh no, not the ironing board:' another, that at an unspecified remark of Alison's, she retorted that: 'I never said that,' while a third story is that when Jimmy Porter attacks Alison for not sending flowers to Mrs Tanner's funeral, Pamela whispered: 'I did send flowers, actually.' This last one only makes sense if you accept that Pamela supposed that Osborne was surreptitiously referring to the death of Anthony Creighton's mother in 1954. A legacy from his mother enabled Creighton to buy the houseboat on which he and Osborne lived for over a year. While mildly entertaining, none of these stories sound very authentic, and neither can they be verified. Pamela's alleged remarks were supposedly made to a companion, yet there is no evidence of Pamela being accompanied to the performance, and if she were, then this mysterious companion has chosen to remain just that: a mystery.

76. PL quoted in Peter Whitebrook: *John Osborne: 'Anger is not about...'* p 105.

77. Ibid.

78. *The Stage* 22 September 1955.

79. George Scott: *An Angry Young Man Falls in Love: Women's Own* 20 February 1960.

80. Mary Ure to JO: 5 June 1958 Texas.

81. *Observer:* 15 July 1956.

82. JO: AAG p 34.

83. *Yorkshire Post and Leeds Intelligencer* 23 February 1949, on the original London production at the Wyndham's Theatre.

84. York Theatre Royal programme 30 September 1956.

85. JO: AAG p 26.

86. Ibid pgs 28, 30.

87. *York Evening Press* cuttings York Theatre Royal Collection York St John University.

88. Ibid.

89. Ibid.

90. Programme York Theatre Royal 19 November 1956.

91. The Theatre Trust website: www.theatretrust.org.uk

92. *The Stage* 7 March 1957.

93. JO: AAG p 43.

94. *The Stage* 11 April 1957.

95. *The Stage* 27 December 1957.

96. *The Stage* 7 March 1957.

97. *The Guardian* 10 May 1956.

98. *The Stage* 17 May 1956.

99. *The Guardian* 10 May 1956.

100. *The Guardian* 2 October 1958.

101. Ibid.

102. George Scott: *An Angry Young Man Falls in Love*. *Woman's Own* 20 February 1960.

103. Lynne Reid Banks to author.

104. *Observer*. 15 November 1959.

105. *The Times*. 11 December 1959.

106. Ibid 19 December 1959.

107. Ibid.

■ ■ ■

The 1960s

1. Julia Lockwood to author.

2. Ibid.

3. Ibid.

4. JO: AAG p 181.

5. *Illustrated London News* 31 December 1960; *The Stage* 6 January 1961.

6. Julia Lockwood to author.

7. Richard Digby Day to author.

8. *The Times* 20 June 1961.

9. Irving Wardle: *Observer* 25 June 1961.

10. Jocelyn Rickards to JO: 30 August 1960 Texas.

11. Penelope Gilliatt to JO: August 1961 Texas.

12. Ibid.

13. *The Times* 9 January 1962.

14. *The Stage* 11 January 1962.

15. Ibid 11 October 1962.

16. Ibid 3 January 1963.

17. *The Times* 27 December 1962.

18. Ibid 5 November 1963.

19. *The Stage* 7 November 1963.

20. Ibid 2 January 1964.

21. Ibid 6 October 1966.

22. Ibid 8 October 1964.

23. JO: AAG p 249.

24. Ibid

25. *The Stage* 20 May 1965, 22 April 1965.

26. Ibid 20 May 1965.

27. *Theatre World* June 1965.

28. *The Times* 19 May 1965.

29. Idid 20 May 1965.

30. *Illustrated London News* 5 June 1965.

31. Penelope Gilliatt: *Observer* 23 May 1965.

32. *Tribune* 17 June 1966, *Daily Mail* 7 June 1966, *The Times* 7 June 1966.

33. *The Stage* 27 May 1965.

34. *The Scotsman* 3 August 1966.

35. *The Stage* 1 September 1966.

36. Penelope Gilliatt to JO n/d 1966 Texas.

37. Jill Bennett to JO: Saturday n/d [1967] Texas.

38. Julia Lockwood to author.

39. *The Stage* 16 November 1967.

40. *Sunday Times* 7 July 1968.

41. *Observer* 26 May 1968; *Plays and Players* September 1968.

42. *Plays and Players* July 1968.

43. *Illustrated London News* 3 August 1968.

44. Richard Digby Day to author.

45. *The Stage* 15 August 1968.

46. Ibid.

47. JO to Jill Bennett: postcard quoted in Peter Charles: Admissible Evidence *Plays and Players* June 1973.

■ ■ ■

The 1970s

1. *The Stage* 3 December 1970.

2. *Observer* 17 October 2010.

3. *Sunday Times* 10 October 1971.

4. JO. *Evening Standard* 30 July 1971.

5. Dr Piggott to JO: 15 April 1970.

6. *The Stage* 22 July 1971.

7. JO: *Hedda Gabler* DYE p 35.

8. *Sunday Times* 2 July 1972.

9. *The Stage* 4 October 1973.

10. Ibid.

11. Pauline Marshall to author.

12. *The Guardian* 16 November 1973.

13. Ibid.

14. *The Guardian* 12 March 1974.

15. Richard Digby Day to author.

16. *The Guardian* 13 September 1978.

17. *Leicester Mercury* 8 September 1979.

18. Ibid.

19. *The Stage* 12 July 1979.

20. Roger Davenport to author.

21. *The Stage* 20 September 1979.

22. Roger Davenport to author.

23. Ibid.

24. *Leicester Mercury* 11 October 1979.

25. Ibid.

26. Malcolm Sinclair to author.

27. *The Stage* 3 January 1980.

■ ■ ■

The 1980s

1. Edward Albee: *Seascape*: quoted Aida Edemariam, *Whistling in the Dark: The Guardian* 10 January 2004, an article also comparing Albee's writing with that of Osborne.

2. Jeremy Howe to author.

3. Paul Venables to author.

4. Richard Digby Day to author.

5. Malcolm Sinclair to author.

6. Jeremy Howe to author.

7. PL to JO: 26 August 1983.

8. JO to PL: 23 August 1983.

9. *The Times* 5 May 1980.

10. Alan Bryce to author.

11. *The Stage* 1 May 1980.

12. Saul Reichlin to author.

13. Samuel Beckett: *Happy Days: Samuel Beckett: The Complete Dramatic Works* Faber 1986 pgs 151-2.

14. *Leicester Mercury* January 1981.

15. *The Stage* 12 February 1981.

16. *The Stage* 14 May 1981.

17. JO: journal 10 July 1973 Texas.

18. JO: *Look Back in Anger* CP1 p 94.

19. Tanya Gold: *The Spectator* 25 January 2014.

20. *The Stage* 29 October 1981.

21. *The Stage* 26 November 1981.

22. Richard Digby Day to author.

23. *The Stage* 18 March 1972.

24. PL to JO: 6 May 1963.

25. Angie Langfield to author.

26. JO. AAG p 146-7.

27. JO: *Observer* 29 January 1957, DYE p 66.

28. *The Stage* 21 July 83.

29. *The Guardian* 13 May 1983.

30. Julia Lockwood to author.

31. Helen Jones to author; Saul Reichlin to author.

32. David Weston to author.

33. Saul Reichlin to author.

34. David Weston to author.

35. Ibid.

36. Saul Reichlin to author.

37. *The Guardian* 12 November 1982.

38. Gordon Dickerson to author.

39. *The Guardian* Oscar Beuselinck obituary 30 July 1997.

40. Opening of the Mercury Theatre, Colchester, unidentified newspaper clipping 1972.

41. Jeremy Howe to author.

42. Ibid.

43. Ibid.

44. Richard Digby Day to author.

45. PL to JO: 7 July 1985.

46. *The Stage* 23 May 1985.

47. JO: AAG p 269.

48. Ibid p 207.

49. Richard Digby Day to author.

50. *The Stage* 7 August 1986.

51. BBC Radio schedules 6 October 1986.

52. Jeremy Howe to author.

53. *The Guardian* 20 May 1987.

54. Ibid 30 May 1987.

55. John Dexter: *The Honourable Beast* Nick Hern Books, London 1993, p 281.

56. *The Guardian* 30 May 1987.

57. Ibid 17 August 1987.

58. *The Stage* 10 March 1988.

59. Christopher Lee in Wilfred Lawson biography: www.imdb.com

60. Gordon Dickerson to author.

61. *The Guardian* 2 November 1988.

62. Richard Digby Day to author.

■ ■ ■

The 1990s

1. *The Stage* 29 November 1990.

2. Ibid.

3. Richard Digby Day to author.

4. Nicholas de Jongh: *The Guardian* 4 August 1991.

5. Gordon Dickerson to author.

6. Susan Dowell to author.

7. JO: journal 20 March 1989. Texas.

8. JO: CP1 p 280.

9. JO: *Look Back in Anger* CP1 p 39.

10. JO to PL: 11 January 1984.

11. JO to PL: 18 October 1983.

12. Peter Egan to author.

13. Richard Digby Day to author.

14. Angie Langfield to author.

15. *The Stage*. 17 December 1992.

16. Gordon Dickerson to author.

17. James MacDonald: Anthony Creighton and John Osborne: *Studies in Theatre and Performance* vol 28 no 3 2008.

18. Susan Dowell to author.

19. Ibid.

20. Graham Dowell obituary: *The Guardian* 4 December 1999.

21. Susan Dowell to author.

22. JO to PL: 18 October 1983.

23. PL to Helen Osborne: 29 July 1996

24. Richard Digby Day to author.

25. Ibid.

■ ■ ■

26 October 2010

1. Julia Lockwood to author.

2. Richard Digby Day to author.

3. Richard Digby Day: Pamela Lane obituary: *The Guardian* 21 November 2010.

4. Pamela Osborne probate papers 22 December 2010.

5. PL to JO: 1 June 1984, JO to PL: 10 October 1983.

6. Pamela Osborne will 19 December 1997.

INDEX

By the same author

John Osborne: Anger is not about…

9781783198771

'Peter Whitebrook's beautifully written and massively insightful book reveals a subject who was a bundle of contradictions… The book leaves one startled by Osborne's profligacy over money and sex, though it's fair to say that he remained unusually loyal to his first wife, Pamela Lane, and his last, Helen Dawson. But the book also moved me by its portrait of a deeply insecure man who turned his lifelong sense of a lost inheritance into some of the most resonant plays of our time. Mr Whitebrook is right to place Osborne alongside Beckett and Pinter as one of the dramatists who redefined contemporary theatre.' Michael Billington

'Whitebrook's account is readable and pacy. He writes with insight and clarity, and is especially good at sketching out the social, cultural and political context of the playwright's life and times. He analyses Osborne's relationship with his father, who died when the boy was only 11, and treats the psychology of his relationship with his mother, Nellie Beatrice, with imaginative sympathy.' Aleks Sierz, *Tribune*

'As Peter Whitebrook's thoroughly researched biography of John Osborne so ably demonstrates, the legacy of one of the most significant writers of the 20th century is simultaneously both invigorating and sad… a readable biography that goes rather further than one might expect, presenting a considerable amount of social history as it analyses the life, work and milieu of perhaps one of the unhappiest playwrights that has lived in modern times.' *British Theatre Guide*

'When he is laying out the background to the establishment of the English Stage Company at the Royal Court… or detailing the censorship deliberations of the Lord Chamberlain's Office, this volume becomes much more than a digest of its many sources. With as clear an eye on his subject's foibles and character flaws as to his talent and achievements, and just as fearlessly judgemental of his many wives and partners as well as his associates in the profession, Whitebrook takes the reader through every peak and trough of a story that has plenty of both… There are also some fine anecdotes that deserve re-telling.' Keith Bruce, *Herald Scotland*

*Nominated for the Sheridan Morley Prize for Biography,
and the Theatre Book Prize 2015.*

WWW.OBERONBOOKS.COM

Follow us on www.twitter.com/@oberonbooks
& www.facebook.com/OberonBooksLondon